SOCIAL POLICY IN EAST AND SOUTHEAST ASIA

Social Policy in East and Southeast Asia provides the first systematic comparison of income maintenance, health, housing, and education in Hong Kong, South Korea, Singapore, and Taiwan. It finds social policies in the four Asian newly industrialized economies to be remarkably developed and comprehensive.

Drawing upon extensive primary research, the author compares the provision, financing, and outcomes of social policies in these Asian countries. The policies of Korea and Taiwan place most importance upon health and income maintenance, while policy in Hong Kong foregrounds health and housing, and in Singapore education and housing. Comparing each country's social policy with traditional ideals of the welfare state, the book concludes that Northeast Asian states, namely Korea and Taiwan, may be best described as "conservative" while those in Hong Kong and Singapore are more "liberal" as their policies focus more on supporting the market than maintaining income.

Locating the importance of Asian social policies in the wake of the recent financial crisis in the region, this work provides a comprehensive analysis of the different types of welfare state in contemporary Asia. It will be of interest to scholars of Asian Studies, Social Welfare, and Public Policy.

M. Ramesh is Senior Fellow in the Public Policy Program at the National University of Singapore and Associate Professor in Government at the University of Sydney.

ROUTLEDGECURZON ADVANCES IN ASIA-PACIFIC STUDIES

1 ENVIRONMENT, EDUCATION AND SOCIETY IN THE ASIA-PACIFIC
Local traditions and global discourses
David Yencken, John Fien and Helen Sykes

2 AGEING IN THE ASIA-PACIFIC REGION
David R. Phillips

3 CARING FOR THE ELDERLY IN JAPAN AND THE US
Practices and policies
Susan Orpett Long

4 HUMAN RIGHTS AND GENDER POLITICS
Asia-Pacific perspectives
Edited by Anne Marie Hilsdon, Martha Macintyre, Vera Mackie and Maila Stivens

5 HUMAN RIGHTS IN JAPAN, SOUTH KOREA AND TAIWAN
Ian Neary

6 CULTURAL POLITICS AND ASIAN VALUES
The tepid war
Michael D. Barr

7 SOCIAL POLICY IN EAST AND SOUTHEAST ASIA
Education, health, housing, and income maintenance
M. Ramesh

SOCIAL POLICY IN EAST AND SOUTHEAST ASIA

Education, health, housing, and income maintenance

M. Ramesh

RoutledgeCurzon
Taylor & Francis Group
LONDON AND NEW YORK

First published 2004
by RoutledgeCurzon
2 Park Square, Milton Park, Abingdon, Oxon, OX14 4RN

Simultaneously published in the USA and Canada
by RoutledgeCurzon
270 Madison Ave, New York NY 10016

RoutledgeCurzon is an imprint of the Taylor & Francis Group

Transferred to Digital Printing 2006

© 2004 M. Ramesh

Typeset in Baskerville by Wearset Ltd, Boldon, Tyne and Wear

All rights reserved. No part of this book may be reprinted or
reproduced or utilized in any form or by any electronic, mechanical,
or other means, now known or hereafter invented, including
photocopying and recording, or in any information storage or
retrieval system, without permission in writing from the publishers.

British Library Cataloguing in Publication Data
A catalogue record for this book is available from the British Library

Library of Congress Cataloging in Publication Data
Ramesh, M., 1960–
Social policy in east and southeast Asia : education, health, housing
and income maintenance / M. Ramesh.
p. cm.
Includes bibliographical references and index.
1. East Asia—Social policy. 2. Asia, Southeastern—Social policy.
3. East Asia—Economic policy. 4. Asia, Southeastern—Economic
policy. I. Title.
HN720.5.A8R36 2003
361.6′1′095—dc22
2003015577

ISBN 0-415-33255-9

CONTENTS

List of illustrations   vii
Acknowledgements   x
List of abbreviations   xii

1 Introduction   1
  Hong Kong 8
  Singapore 10
  Korea 12
  Taiwan 14
  Structure of the book 16

2 Socio-economic background   18
  Economy 18
  Income distribution and poverty 21
  Public finance 23
  International position 28
  Population 31
  Conclusion 34

3 Income maintenance   36
  Policy history 39
  Provision 49
  Financing 62
  Outcomes 71
  Conclusion 82

CONTENTS

4 Health — 84
Policy history 86
Provision 94
Financing 99
Outcomes 107
Conclusion 114

5 Housing — 116
Policy history 118
Provision 129
Financing 136
Outcomes 143
Conclusion 151

6 Education — 153
Policy history 155
Provision 166
Financing 171
Outcomes 178
Conclusion 186

7 Conclusion — 188

Notes — 200
References — 202
Index — 224

ILLUSTRATIONS

Figures

2.1	Public spending's share of GDP, 1975–2000, per cent	25
2.2	Public spending on social policy, share of GDP, 1975–2000, per cent	28
2.3	Current account balance as percentage of GDP, annual average	29
4.1	Health expenditures and infant mortality rate	113
5.1	Schematic view of finance for public housing in Singapore	137

Tables

2.1	Real GDP growth and GDP per capita	19
2.2	Sectoral distribution of GDP by value added, per cent	20
2.3	Share of labour force in agriculture, per cent	21
2.4	Gini coefficient – household income	21
2.5	Overall budget surplus as percentage of GDP	23
2.6	Current revenue and taxes, percentage of GDP	24
2.7	Social policy expenditures' share of GDP, per cent	26
2.8	Social policy expenditures' share of total government expenditure, per cent	27
2.9	Foreign Direct Investment flows, annual average, percentage of GDP	30
2.10	Trade, percentage of GDP	30
2.11	Population growth rate, annual average, per cent	31
2.12	Fertility rate, births per woman	32
2.13	Population, 1965–2025; number and percentage increase	32
2.14	Children's and the aged's share of total population, per cent	33
2.15	Mean household size	34
2.16	Urban population, percentage of total	34
3.1	Social security arrangements in the NIEs	59
3.2	Key qualifying conditions for public assistance	60

3.3	Income maintenance benefits	61
3.4	Funding arrangements of income maintenance programmes	69
3.5	Public expenditure on income maintenance as percentages	70
3.6	Coverage of income maintenance schemes for the aged, per cent	79
3.7	Average income maintenance benefits, percentage of per capita GDP	80
3.8	Share of the aged (65+ years) living with children, per cent	81
3.9	Main income sources of the elderly	81
3.10	Percentage of the elderly population living in poverty, 1996	82
4.1	Physicians and hospital beds, per 1,000 persons	98
4.2	Share of total physicians and hospital beds in the public sector, per cent	98
4.3	Health care financing in the NIEs	105
4.4	Per capita national health expenditures, US$	105
4.5	National health expenditures in the NIEs, per cent	106
4.6	Health care utilization rate, per person per year, late 1990s	112
4.7	Infant mortality rate and life expectancy	112
5.1	Key policy instruments in the housing sector	135
5.2	Public housing stock, percentage of total stock	135
5.3	Ownership and rental housing stock by sector, per cent	136
5.4	Residential housing's share of total gross fixed capital formation, per cent	141
5.5	Public expenditure on housing as percentages	142
5.6	Housing stock as percentage of households	150
5.7	Home ownership, percentage of population	150
5.8	Price and rent-to-income ratio	151
6.1	Enrolment in private educational institutions as percentage of total enrolment, 1996	170
6.2	Enrolment in vocational secondary education, per cent	170
6.3	Pupil–teacher ratio	171
6.4	Public expenditure on education as percentages	175
6.5	Distribution of current public expenditure on education by level, 1996, per cent	176
6.6	Private expenditure as percentage of total expenditure on education	177
6.7	Government education expenditure per student, public institutions, percentage of GNP per capita	177
6.8	Average public primary school teachers' salary as multiple of per capita GDP	178

ILLUSTRATIONS

6.9	Gross enrolment, per cent	183
6.10	Male and female gross enrolment ratios, late 1990s	183
6.11	Average years of school of the population aged 15 and over, 1960 and 1990	184
6.12	Illiteracy rate, percentage of population aged 15 and over	184
6.13	Average mathematics and science achievement of 8th grade students	185
6.14	Social and private returns to investment in education by level, per cent	186

ACKNOWLEDGEMENTS

This book has been so long in writing that I have forgotten the names of some of the people who helped me along the way. My sincere thanks to everyone who helped me, not just those mentioned here.

Much of the research for the book was completed in 2000 for which I am grateful to the University of Sydney for granting me sabbatical leave. I spent the year in Hong Kong, Norway, Singapore and USA and am thankful to all the people who helped me during the period. In Hong Kong, Ian Holliday, Mok Ka Ho, Shaifqul Huque, Linda Wong, and Julia Tao in the Department of Public and Social Administration at the City University of Hong Kong were great colleagues during my short stay. At Harvard University, Amitav Acharya and Dennis Encarnation provided generous hospitality. In Norway, the Department of Comparative Politics at the University of Bergen gave me a writing fellowship and Kenneth Christie, John Fossum, and Stein Kuhnle gave me company and support. In Singapore, the Public Policy Program at the National University of Singapore hosted me for six months – I am particularly grateful to Mukul Asher, Ong Jin Hui, and Scott Fritzen for their support.

I could not have completed the book without very generous support from government officials and academics in Korea and Taiwan who spent a great deal of time explaining the peculiarities of their country's social policies and compiling statistics for me. In Korea, I am grateful to the following for their kindness: Byong-Ho Tchoe (KIHASA), Choon Sik Park (National Federation of Medical Insurance), Hanam Phang (Korea Labor Institute), Huck Ju Kwon (formerly at Sung Kyun Kwan University and now at UNRISD), Hwajong Baek (KIHASA), In Byung-Lo (National Federation of Medical Insurance), Kyungbae Chung (KIHASA), Choon-Sik Park (NHIC), Chang-Bae Chun (NHIC), Sung-Joon Paik (Korean Educational Development Institute), and Yoon Juh Yun and Chul Koh (Korea Research Institute for Human Settlement).

The list of Taiwanese government officials and academics I am thankful to is long and my gratitude to them deep: Jao Chih Chien (Bureau of Statistics), Cheng Wen-Yi (Department of Social Affairs), Ding-Yuan Chen (Public Service Pension Fund), Fu Li-Yeh (National Chengchi University),

ACKNOWLEDGEMENTS

Hou-Sheng Chan (National Taiwan University), Jong-Tsun Huang (National Science Council), Maria Mei-Yang Chang (Manpower Planning, CEPD), Nana Wang (DGBAS), Pern Derg-Ming, (Bureau of Labor Insurance), Shwu-Jiuan Chen (Public Housing Department), Wang Hong-Zen (Tamkang University), Yu-Mei Chao (Bureau of National Health Insurance), Yeunn-Wen Ku (National Chi Nan University), and Sheng-Cheng Hu (Academica Sinica).

The research for this book was partially funded by grant from the Australian Research Council for which I am thankful.

I am also thankful to Michael Howlett of Simon Fraser University for his encouragement and thoughtful comments. Stephanie Rogers and her team at Routledge have been pleasant and very efficient – thank you.

I started writing the book about the same time as Nikisha was conceived. I can hardly wait to read her the chapter on income maintenance for the aged! And, as always, I am thankful to Mandy for simply being my wife. Thanks to my sister and brothers, and their children, for their immense faith in me. My father passed away before this book was completed – I dedicate it to his memory and to my mother who still believes in me despite receiving little in return.

ABBREVIATIONS

BRO	Buy or Rent Option (Hong Kong)
CEPD	Council for Economic Planning and Development (Taiwan)
CPF	Central Provident Fund (Singapore)
CSPRF	Civil Service Pension Reserve Fund (Hong Kong)
CSSA	Comprehensive Social Security Assistance Scheme (Hong Kong)
DB	Defined Benefits
DC	Defined Contribution
DPP	Democratic Progressive Party (Taiwan)
DSS	Direct Subsidy Schools (Hong Kong)
FDI	Foreign Direct Investment
FI	Farmers Insurance (Taiwan)
GDP	Gross Domestic Product
GEI	Government Employees Insurance (Taiwan)
GEP	Government Employees Pension (Korea)
GERCF	Government Employees Retirement and Compensation Fund (Taiwan)
GFCF	Gross Fixed Capital Formation
GNP	Gross National Product
HDB	Housing Development Board (Singapore)
HDI	Human Development Index
HOS	Home Ownership Scheme (Hong Kong)
HPA	Health Protection Account (Hong Kong)
HSLS	Home Starter Loan Scheme (Hong Kong)
HSP	Hospital Security Plan (Hong Kong)
ILO	International Labour Organization
IMF	International Monetary Fund
IRA	Individual Retirement Account
ITASPS	Insurance for Teachers and Staff of Private Schools (Taiwan)
KHB	Korea Housing Bank
KLDC	Korea Land Development Corporation
KMT	Kuomintang (Taiwan)
KNHC	Korea National Housing Corporation

ABBREVIATIONS

KOLAND	Korea Land Corporation
LegCo	Legislative Council (Hong Kong)
LI	Labour Insurance (Taiwan)
LRF	Labour Retirement Fund (Taiwan)
LTHS	Long Term Housing Strategy (Hong Kong)
MI	Military Servicemen's Insurance (Taiwan)
MPF	Mandatory Provident Fund (Hong Kong)
NHF	National Housing Fund (Korea)
NHI	National Health Insurance
NIEs	Newly Industrializing Economies
NPP	National Pension Plan (Taiwan)
NPS	National Pension Scheme (Korea)
OPS	Old Age Pension Scheme (Hong Kong)
ORSO	Occupational Retirement Schemes Ordinance (Hong Kong)
PAP	People's Action Party (Singapore)
PAS	Public Assistance Scheme (Hong Kong)
PF	Provident fund
PPP	Purchasing Power Parity
PRC	People's Republic of China
PSLE	Primary School Leaving Examination (Singapore)
PSPS	Private Sector Participation Scheme (Hong Kong)
ROC	Republic of China, Taiwan
SAVER	Savings and Employee Retirement Plan Scheme (Singapore)
SRS	Supplementary Retirement Scheme (Singapore)
SSAS	Social Security Allowance Scheme (Hong Kong)
TGE	Total Government Expenditure
TPS	Tenant Purchase Scheme (Hong Kong)
UNDP	United Nations Development Programme
WHO	World Health Organization

1
INTRODUCTION

The conventional wisdom in public-policy circles is that East Asia is a region of social-policy laggards. The generalization is not only false, it betrays the vast differences that characterize the region. The different patterns of recent policy changes in different countries has enhanced the differences and made generalization all the more difficult.

The overall level of social development in East Asia is no less remarkable than that of its economic development. But to draw usable policy lessons from East Asia's experience, it is essential to analyse its social policies carefully and compare them systematically. The objective of this book, then, is to analyse a range of vital social policies – income maintenance, health, housing, and education – in the four Asian Newly Industrialized Economies (NIEs) of Hong Kong, South Korea, Singapore, and Taiwan and to identify the patterns of similarities and differences among them. The comparison will indicate the extent to which it is possible to generalize about the region and the lessons that can be learned from its social-policy experience.

The book plans to cast a deliberately wide net and study a broad range of vital social policies affecting social welfare rather than to focus just on social security and/or health, as is usually the case. Social welfare is affected, in addition to overall economic conditions, not just by social-protection programmes but also by education, health, and housing (Gough, 2000: 4). Concentration on social security is particularly inadequate for understanding social welfare in developing countries because they tend to have a young population with a higher need for education and housing than for social security. Moreover, the distinction between social policies intended to promote social welfare directly (for example, social security and health) and those that promote it indirectly (such as education and housing) is non-substantial and is certainly not always obvious to policy-makers (Smeeding *et al.*, 1993).

The NIEs offer a particularly fruitful opportunity for understanding the dynamics and implications of social policies. As some of the fastest-growing economies in the second half of the twentieth century and the start of the twenty-first, they are ideal candidates for shedding light on the link between economic and social policies and, specifically, the extent to which they are complementary or inimical. Deyo (1992) has argued that there is greater compatibility between economic and social policies in East Asia than is usually the case in developing countries. The fact the NIEs have had similar economic growth rates but different social policies, as we shall see in this book, makes their case particularly appropriate for study.

The NIEs share deep similarities and yet are marked by significant differences, which makes them excellent cases for comparison. The best-known similarity among them is their rapid economic growth since the mid 1960s. In all cases, the economy as well as the standard of living grew many folds from which all sectors of the society benefited, albeit in different ways and to different degrees. Without the pressing need for addressing urgent problems of widespread abject poverty and unemployment in recent decades, the NIE governments have enjoyed policy options unavailable to most developing countries. The steady flow of revenues to public exchequer resulting from rapid economic growth allowed governments to devote resources to programmes they deemed worthwhile. Reasons other than a lack of resources thus often lie behind governments' weak or non-existent action in a particular policy sector, especially in the two city-states that enjoyed large budget surpluses for much of the 1980s and 1990s.

The four NIEs also have a lot in common with respect to social development. They are all considered "advanced" in human-development terms: in 2002, Hong Kong and Taiwan[1] ranked 23rd out of 145 nations surveyed, while Singapore came 25th and Korea 27th, with all of them scoring around 0.88 (compared to 0.94 for Norway, which ranked first). At a subjective level, commentators find deep similarities in their social settings, which are believed to be shaped by a common Confucian heritage (Chan, 1996; Kil, 1991; Kim, 1994; Lee, 1990; Nakajima, 1994; Rozman, 1991; Song, 1990; Tu, 1989; Wong and Wong, 1989; for a critique, see Thornton, 1998). Even Singapore, the most diverse among the four, has a majority Chinese population that is claimed to have retained vital elements of traditional Chinese values. The achievement-orientation, elitism, and Familism that are integral to Confucianism are said to have shaped the NIEs' public policies.

Another respect in which the NIEs are similar is that they were ruled by foreign powers until recently – until the end of the Second World War in the case of Korea and Taiwan, 1959 in Singapore, and 1997 in Hong Kong. Their public policies were devised more in response to exigencies of colonial rule than to local conditions, but they continued to shape policies, in the manner of path dependency (Mahoney, 2000), long after the end of colonial rule. The end of colonial rule did not bring about popular participation in policy-making in the region as governments continued to enjoy considerable autonomy from social pressures (Henderson and Appelbaum, 1992; Weiss and Hobson, 1995). Indeed there is broad agreement that the NIE states have enjoyed an unprecedented level of autonomy and capacity, though there is dispute regarding the situation in the 1990s when liberalization and democratization complicated the political conditions.

Yet there are significant variations among the NIEs along economic, social, and political dimensions, which allows us to understand the effects of contextual differences on social policies. Their income levels vary considerably, as does the distribution of income: the two city-states are much richer than the other two economies, but they also have much higher levels of income inequality (see Chapter 2). The NIEs have also had different levels and forms of government intervention in the economy, with Hong Kong usually situated at the least-interventionist end and South Korea at the most-interventionist end (Clark and Roy, 1997; World Bank, 1993). But in social policy sectors, as we shall see throughout this book, Hong Kong is not consistently free-market oriented and nor is Korea consistently statist, reminding us of the perils of generalization and stereotyping.

Their similar standing in the social-development table also conceals the fact that the two city-states perform worse than would be expected for their level of economic development while their Northeast Asian counterparts perform better than expected. Thus, while Hong Kong's per capita income was the ninth highest and Singapore's the twelfth highest in the world, their overall Human Development Index (HDI) ranks were 23 and 25 respectively because of their relatively inferior performance in non-economic areas. The social indicators for Korea and Taiwan, in contrast, were slightly better than their economic indicators, pushing them higher on the social-development ranking.

The colonial experience too varies across the NIEs: the Northeast Asian states were ruled by the Japanese and the two city-states by the British. There were deep differences in the way they governed and the policy legacy they left behind. Later chapters in this book will show how the different colonial legacies continue to lie at the root of social-policy differences across the NIEs. Commentators have also highlighted the NIEs' different political-economic structures and strategies, with Hong Kong characterized as Liberal and the others as Corporatist. We will find these descriptions useful for shedding light on their social policies in the concluding chapter.

The remarkable achievements of the NIEs and the immense opportunities these afford for understanding social policy have not been matched by efforts to understand them. There is to date no systematic study of the complete suite of social policies in East Asia. And among the studies of individual social policies that are available, there is an overwhelming tendency to assume that the region is different from the rest of the world. Commentators highlighting the region's unique social policies typically rest their case largely on low public spending and the closely knit family structure in the region. The region's famously dogged determination to promote economic growth at the expense of other goals only reinforces commentators' conclusions about neglect of social policy. Another common trend in commentaries is to generalize about all social policies, indeed about national and even region-wide political and cultural systems, on the basis of single or limited case studies. Needless to say, such generalizations serve no useful purpose.

Studies on social policy in East Asia typically start with the observation of low public spending on social security and health and high spending on education. This is an incorrect starting point, which inevitably leads to flawed conclusions. The available public-spending data for the region are not always calculated using international statistical standards and often contain inexplicable and inconsistent inclusions and exclusions. But even if accurate comparable data were available, expenditure alone is a misleading indicator because vast sums may be spent on a select group, as is the case in countries where civil servants are recipients of handsome pensions. Another severe problem with public-spending data relates to their consideration without reference to demographic and other contextual data. East Asia still has a young population, which necessarily involves higher expenditure on education and lower on health and social security – it does not necessarily suggest greater policy priority or cultural preference for education. Another contextual factor that is vital but is largely overlooked in the literature is that the high economic growth rate, rising income levels, and low unemployment mitigated the need for state expenditure on social welfare in the region. Spending data also do not say anything about the programmes that are already in place, as in Korea and to a lesser extent Taiwan, but are not yet paying benefits because of eligibility conditions requiring lengthy periods of contribution. Even modest present expenditure on social security will balloon when full benefits begin to be paid. It is likely that public spending on social policy in the two Northeast Asian countries will exceed the levels in the Anglo-Saxon OECD countries within the next few decades. Projections for Korea show that pension expenditures will rise – as a result of the ageing of the population and an increase in eligibility – from 2.1 per cent of GDP in 2000 to the peak of 8 per cent in 2040, compared to a decline from 7.4 to 3.4 per cent of the GDP in OECD countries (Dang *et al.*, 2001: 24–25).

Another common observation is that East Asia is different from the rest of the world in its lower appetite for state involvement in social-welfare efforts. Catherine Jones (1993) argues that social-security arrangements in East Asia constitute a discrete "Confucian" regime in which education is emphasized and low priority accorded to statutory social security. The dichotomization of education and social security is unnecessary as governments may, and indeed some do, emphasize both. Moreover, it is unclear how her conclusion fares in the face of recent expansion of social-security programmes in Korea and possibly Taiwan. Even in Hong Kong the programmes are not qualitatively different from their counterparts in many English-speaking OECD countries. Culture is, at best, of residual value in explaining social policies in East Asia (White and Goodman, 1998: 15).

Instead of abstracting and reducing East Asian social policies into a single defining characteristic, Paul Wilding finds at least nine common features of East Asian social policy in the literature:

> low public expenditure on social welfare; a productivist social policy focused on economic growth; hostility to the idea of the welfare state; strong residualist elements; a central role for the family; a regulatory and enabling role for the state; piecemeal, pragmatic and *ad hoc* welfare development; use of welfare to build legitimacy, stability and support for the state; and limited commitment to the notion of welfare as a right of citizenship.
> (Quoted in Holliday, 2000)

Kwang-Leung Tang (2000: 139–140) arrives at a similar six points of commonalities among the NIEs' social policies. These conclusions about the welfare state in East Asia are so general that they could just as easily be used to describe non-Asian countries. Indeed except for the centrality attributed to family (and even this is emphasized by Western conservatives), all of the features noted by these authors could readily be applied to many Western countries.

The East Asian exceptionalism in social-policy matters is often explained with reference to cultural factors. It is argued that the persistence of traditional family and community structures has meant that people in the region have not had to turn to the state for support, as is the case in Western countries (Jones, 1993; Rieger and Leibfried, 2003). A related argument is that parents in the region invest heavily (both time and money) in the education of their children who, when they grow up, look after their parents' health and social-security needs. Rieger and Leibfried (2002) are typical in their claim that familial orientation of social norms and government policy has stunted the growth of statutory social welfare in East Asia. Citing considerable "private social investment" undertaken by Asian families, Wad (1999: 33) calls for the departing from a state-centred view of the welfare state to "Confucian welfare societies" in order to understand social welfare in East Asia.

While traditional family structures are no doubt more intact in East Asia than in the west, their significance is greatly exaggerated. A comprehensive analysis of all sources of spending on social security, health, and education in Korea showed that households contributed only 12 per cent of the total in 1997, compared to 30 per cent by the government and 29 per cent by the market (Gough and Kim, 2000: Table 1). Be that as it may, families in the region are undergoing changes and governments are responding – though perhaps not as fast as some would like – with appropriate policy changes, including expansion of social security. In any event, the culture in East Asia is not as hostile to social security as is often portrayed. Even in fiercely Liberal Hong Kong, public opinion favours extensive state involvement in education, health, social welfare, and housing (Wong *et al.*, 2002: 298). Similarly, a survey conducted by the Korean government in 1996 found that 73 per cent of the respondents believed that the government was primarily responsible for looking after the poor (Jung and Shin, 2002: 275).

Cultural arguments are not the only ones that find it difficult to explain social policies in East Asia. The same is true for the industrialization thesis, which argues that industrialization, and the spread of urbanization and the breakdown of traditional forms of community and family support that accompany it, foster the origin and development of the welfare state (significant examples include Aaron, 1967; Cutright, 1965; Hage, Hanneman, and Gargan, 1989; Pryor, 1968; Wilensky, 1975). While there is no doubt that industrialization and urbanization are of central importance to social and indeed economic policy, there is no clear relationship between the level and duration of industrialization in a country and the nature of its social policies (see Castles and McKinlay, 1979; O'Connor, 1988). The earliest and most industrialized nations were not always the first or most heavily involved in social-policy matters – this is as much true for Western as for Asian nations (Ramesh with Asher, 2000; Wong, 1997: 59). Indeed, the late starters tend to establish more comprehensive programmes at an earlier stage in their industrialization than the early starters (Collier and Messick, 1975; Kim, 1996; Schneider, 1982). Hort and Kuhnle (2000) not only find similarities between East Asia and Europe, they also find that the income programmes in Asia were established at an earlier stage of economic development than was the case in Europe.

Another common explanation for the "low" social spending is the East Asian states' overwhelming emphasis on economic development, which necessarily involves neglect of social development. As Goodman and Peng (1996: 198) put it: "Very broadly speaking, welfare policy [in East Asia] has been dominated by economic rather than social considerations supported by some underlying ideas of anti-welfarism and, especially, by resistance to the provision of government-guaranteed social welfare." A more nuanced interpretation is proffered by Ian Holliday (2000), who proposes that East Asia comprises a fourth welfare regime of *productivist* welfare capitalism characterized by subordination of social policy to economic policy. This generic welfare regime is further subdivided into "developmental-universalist" (Japan, Taiwan, Korea) and "developmental-particularist" (Hong Kong and Singapore). While this is an advance on earlier formulations, it is not particularly helpful because in education (and industrial) policy sectors it is Korea and Taiwan that are particularist whereas the city-states are universalist. And it is also not clear how their productivist orientation manifests in practice. As we shall see in subsequent chapters, the NIEs do not necessarily emphasize education more than Western welfare states; nor do they always emphasize social welfare less than their non-productivist counterparts.

Bob Jessop's (1993) distinction between "Welfare" and "Workfare" States sheds further light on the distinctiveness of social policies in East Asia. Unlike welfare states' emphasis on full employment, demand management, and collective consumption, workfare states promote international competitiveness through supply-side intervention and "subordination of social policy to the demands of labour market flexibility and structural competitiveness" (Jessop, 1993: 9). The latter are better equipped to compete in a globalized economy, which explains why welfare states are gradually adopting aspects of the workfare state. In a later work, Jessop (1999), following Sum (2000), characterizes Korea, Singapore, and Taiwan as "Listian" workfare states, in which strong states rally industrial and financial capital behind national economic goals, whereas Hong Kong is a Ricardian workfare state, in which the state's role is confined to subsidizing wages through public housing. While Jessop provides few details and his overall argument is contentious, the general thrust of his argument sheds valuable light on the subject as it highlights the NIEs' emphasis on international economic competitiveness and how this has shaped their outlook towards social policy in general.

The historical juncture – the 1960s – at which the NIEs launched their industrialization drive has had a decisive impact on their social policies. It was a period when barriers to international trade had just begun to be brought down in a substantial sense and multinational firms were looking for new production sites. The East Asian states recognized the opportunity and set about taking measures to take advantage of it. Learning from the experiences of "early late" industrializers such as Germany and Japan, these "late late" industrializers were in a position to put together a social-policy package that did not hamper their international economic competitiveness. That they were starting almost from scratch was an advantage in that they did not have a constituency with vested interest in preserving the existing arrangement. But the later a country embarks on industrialization, the more effort it must make to compete with the leaders. In the case of East Asia, the recipe for catching up included measures to improve the population's education and health in order to enhance productivity, the provision of affordable housing in order to keep wage costs down, and it specifically excluded the guarantee of income security for those adversely affected by international competition, as was the case in Europe (Jessop, 2003).

Unfortunately, Jessop's argument is pitched at a high level of generalization that does not explain the differences among workfare states. As we shall see throughout the book, there are substantial differences among the NIEs' social policies that can only be understood with reference to conditions specific to each country. Thus while Jessop's analysis can enlighten us on why the NIEs emphasize education, it cannot explain why some have chosen to deliver it through the public sector whereas others have chosen the private sector. Nor can his framework explain why such large differences exist on the level of emphasis they place on social security despite similar devotion to economic growth. Answers to such detailed questions can only be discovered through more micro-level analysis of domestic politics affecting social policies.

A complete understanding of social policy requires consideration of both broad political economy and immediate political conditions. All major policy decisions are explicitly political acts and this is how social-policy development must be approached (see Amenta and Carruthers, 1988; Flora and Heidenheimer, 1981). Of all contingencies facing governments, the prospect of being thrown out of office is the most worrying and ruling politicians do whatever it takes to avert this. Their country's international economic competitiveness is an important concern for them, but it is one they can dispense with in the short run (Garrett and Lange, 1996: 51–52). Life is somewhat easier for non-democratic states – but only slightly, as they too must enjoy public support if they are to remain in office for long and rule effectively.

But political contingencies determine only the timing of the response and why governments are moved to act. To understand the substance of the policy, we need to understand the organization of the state and its relationship with key socio-economic groups (Milner and Keohane, 1996; Garrett, 1998; Swank, 1998). Policy change occurs in the context of existing programmes and socio-economic institutions that condition how policy problems are viewed and the solutions assessed. This is especially the case in "normal" times, when the rules and norms underlying them are widely accepted (Howlett and Ramesh, 1998). They have relatively less impact in "non-normal" times – such as during economic or political crisis or fundamental reorganization of the polity or economy – when established institutions lose legitimacy and conditions are propitious for measures that would not normally be possible (see Starling, 1975; Meyer, 1982). It is at such historical junctures that major policy changes or innovations tend to occur (Howlett and Ramesh, 1998). Hong Kong and Singapore have experienced less political turbulence than Korea and Taiwan in recent decades and, relatedly, have undergone fewer and shallower policy changes. In the following discussion I shall sketch out the historical and political context surrounding the development of social policies in the NIEs.

Hong Kong

Hong Kong is not the *laissez-faire* state it is often portrayed as – an image it has earned based on its economic record (see Schiffer, 1991). On the social-policy front, it has an elaborate public-assistance programme for the poor, aged, and disabled; hospital care is provided nearly free of charge to the entire population; nearly two-thirds of the population lives in public housing; and primary and junior secondary education is compulsory and provided free of charge (Lee, 2000). The early 1970s and the late 1980s to early 1990s were the periods of greatest social-policy changes and were shaped by political circumstances existing at the time.

Social policies in Hong Kong are, in their essence, remarkably similar to those found in the English-speaking world. The amount Hong Kong spends on income maintenance is lower, but this is as much a result of its relatively youthful population as of stringent means testing and low benefits. Health-care expenditures are also lower, but that may result from centralized provision and the associated efficiency. In education and housing, Hong Kong's expenditures are actually higher than in many Western welfare states.

Social policies in Hong Kong partly reflect the legacy of 150 years of British rule, but they also reflect domestic political-economic conditions. The political economy of Hong Kong is rather unusual: liberal and undemocratic but not necessarily authoritarian. It is a liberal polity with rule of law, freedom of expression and association, and protection of property rights. But it is not a democracy – there was no elected member of any kind in the Legislative Council (LegCo) until 1985 and the first direct elections did not take place until 1991. Even now, only one-third of the members are directly elected by the public and the rest by functional groups (dominated by business groups) and an Election Committee consisting of 800 members appointed by Beijing. The LegCo plays only a peripheral role in policy-making: the Basic Law reserves, as was the case under British rule, all vital powers for the Chief Executive and makes it almost impossible for the legislature to do anything more than discuss and rubber-stamp bills presented by the Executive. Hong Kong is still ruled by an elite class consisting of senior and wealthy civil servants, businessmen, and professionals (Cuthbert, 1989; Davies, 1977).

The lack of even a pretence of popular democracy in Hong Kong does not, however, mean that the government pays no attention to public opinion. Quite the reverse, as the government is acutely aware of its non-democratic base and compensates for it through extensive consultation on major policy proposals published as Green Papers and White Papers, seeking public feedback. Although business interests win out in the final instance, popular preferences are accommodated as far as possible. In more critical times, the government has also taken pre-emptive measures to diffuse political unrest.

As is well known, the government's economic strategy is one of minimal involvement, "positive non-intervention" as it prefers to describe it. For over a century, the government regarded its main responsibility as maintaining law and order for business to function. The equanimity was broken in 1953 when a devastating fire in a squatter colony rendered thousands homeless and highlighted the plight of the poor. Rapid industrialization in the 1960s and the imperatives of supporting it with a healthy and educated workforce made it all the more difficult for the government to maintain its non-interventionist position. The problem was aggravated by the political unrest that swept the colony in the late 1960s. The 1966 clashes over increases in Star Ferry fares and the 1967 pro-communist clashes with the police in which 51 were killed and hundreds wounded highlighted the volatile political situation and the need for spreading the fruits of rapid economic growth (Turner *et al.*, 1991: 49). The government acknowledged discontent among the poor as the root cause of anti-government sentiments and responded by expanding education, health, housing, and social security in the early 1970s – referred to as the "golden era" of social policy in Hong Kong.

The anxieties surrounding the negotiations between the British and Chinese governments over the colony's return to China in the mid 1980s was another difficult time and, again, the government responded by expanding its social-policy commitments. The Tiananmen Square crackdown in 1989 was followed by the same sort of uncertainty. A bus drivers' strike over pensions in 1990 and a fire in the same year that killed six "cage" people highlighted the plight of the poor aged (McLaughlin, 1993: 128). All this was in addition to the considerable anxiety over the prospects of life under Chinese rule, which prompted a substantial share of the population to consider emigrating. To reinforce the public's confidence in the future of Hong Kong and to promote a sense of belonging, the government invested huge sums on infrastructure and human-resource development, including education and health, in the early 1990s. However, an economic crisis and the conservative political instincts of Chief Executive Tung Chee Hwa and his patrons in Beijing stunted the expansion of government involvement in social security and health in the following years. But the government continues to express its commitment to expanding education and housing, though few concrete measures have actually been implemented towards their achievement

Singapore

The social-policy regime in Singapore is more austere and market-centred than in Hong Kong. Income maintenance is compulsorily funded from private contributions, but there is no redistribution even though the arrangement leaves a large chunk of the population inadequately protected. Hospital care is publicly provided but a significant portion of the costs is recovered through user charges. Almost 90 per cent of the population lives in housing built and sold by the public sector, but this has not involved a great deal of public expenditure. Education is almost entirely provided and funded by the government, but opportunities for higher education are limited.

Almost all the current social-security programmes in Singapore were established by the British in the 1950s when nationalist and communist movements posed a serious threat and the colonial government expanded social programmes to win political support for its rule. When the People's Action Party (PAP) came to office in 1959, it too was faced with social and political unrest, with the added difficulty of having to face popular elections. To neutralize the appeal of radical opposition parties and trade unions, it adopted some of the key elements of the opposition's policy offerings in conjunction with measures to attract foreign investment (Deyo *et al.*, 1987; Rodan, 1996). Although public housing was the centrepiece of its social-policy strategy, it also emphasized health and education – a policy orientation that continues to this day.

Once it felt secure in office by the early 1970s, the PAP became less enthusiastic about state support for policies that did not contribute directly to economic development. The realization in the mid 1980s that the population was ageing rapidly, which would eventually entail huge income maintenance and health-care costs, reinforced the government's determination to halt the expansion of state provision of social welfare. It had to budge from its position somewhat in the early 1990s when declining electoral support for the PAP led the government to offer welfare benefits on a piecemeal basis delivered in the form of *ad hoc* grants and tax rebates (Ramesh, 2000).

The Singapore government, unlike its Northeast Asian counterparts, has been able to successfully maintain its opposition to greater income maintenance and health-care benefits because of the unique political conditions that obtain in the country. There is a complex range of concessionary and coercive measures in place to ensure that organized labour stays out of politics except to support government policies (Anantaraman, 1990; Deyo, 1989). The government has had a close working relationship with business but is not its handmaiden: employers would prefer a lower Central Provident Fund (CPF) contribution rate, but the government has ignored such demands except during economic slumps. The government also maintains a dense network of links with the civil society, which it uses to spread its message and shape public opinion. Corporatist institutions in Singapore have been used to contain the demand for a welfare state rather than to expand it, as is arguably the case in continental Europe.

Thus Singapore has had a rock-solid political system since the late 1960s with none of the uncertainties and crises that fostered the development of social policies, especially social security, in other countries. To the extent that spending on social welfare was necessary to secure political support, it was accomplished through *ad hoc* benefits and a comprehensive public-housing policy. In the face of the ageing population, the government has tried to divest itself of as many of its responsibilities for looking after the aged's income and health as possible. Privatization of social services and the campaign for people to save for their old age and live in joint family arrangements must be seen in this light. At the same time, the government has not been oblivious of the fact that education and health-care programmes are popular with the public and so has maintained them. Housing is the government's social-policy flagship and its support for it has not waned despite near-universal ownership because of the rich political and economic dividends it yields. In any event, public housing is so deeply interwoven into the Singapore economy that any pull-back will have severe repercussions throughout the economy.

Korea

Korea has an elaborate social-policy arrangement and, among the NIEs, most closely resembles Western welfare states. It has universal pension and health-care programmes based on social-insurance principles. Pension benefits are not yet available to most people, but the promised replacement rate is respectable by world standards. Housing has attracted little government expenditure and even the regulations that existed were gradually dismantled in the late 1990s. Education is an odd case in that while the government is heavily involved in both provision and financing, private providers and, especially, private spending play a large role.

The pressures of periodic elections on authoritarian governments with slim popular support have been the main catalyst for social-policy development in Korea. Until its return to democracy in 1987, the authoritarian government lacked broad popular support, a problem it sought to overcome through what it considered would be popular measures. This was important because, unlike many authoritarian regimes, there were regular, though not entirely free or fair, elections in Korea (see Joo, 1999a; Kim, 1997; Kwon, 1998; Lee, 1997; Park, 1990).

The establishment of pensions for civil servants and military personnel in the early 1960s was in recognition of their importance to a government teetering on the brink of collapse. The Park government's role in shepherding the country to prosperity was not reflected in election results, as he barely managed to secure a majority of votes in 1967 and 1971 elections despite a booming economy and restrictions on opposition parties. It was at this point that he began to pay greater attention to social-policy issues (Ramesh, 1995). The hurried introduction of national health insurance was to compensate for the government's backtracking on its commitment to establish a pension programme and intended to marginalize the radical critics of the regime (Joo, 1999a; Park, 1997). However, the pressure to do yet more for non-business interests continued unabated.

While the ruling party won all presidential and general elections in the 1970s and 1980s, it received less than 40 per cent of the votes and won only because of a split in votes for the opposition (Lee, 1997: 6–7; Shin,

1999: 47). The late 1980s was a difficult time for the government, not only because of the return to democracy, which portended heightened political competition, but also because of labour unrest and industrial action, which sky-rocketed in 1987 after years of government-sponsored repression (Lee, 1997: 119). The uncertainties and crises were followed by the introduction of the national pension in 1988 and its expansion in the 1990s. It was also a period when the government began to seriously address the housing problem, which was particularly important for the urban voters among whom the ruling party had little support.

To say that the government expanded social programmes to endear itself to voters is not to suggest that social welfare has been a key issue in Korean elections (Kwon, 1997). Rather it saw them as pre-emptive measures to contain labour unrest and voter disenchantment (Lee, 1997). Subtle pressure from various segments of the bureaucracy subscribing to the view that a welfare state was an essential feature of a developed country also played a part in expanding social security (Kwon, 1997).

Organized labour in Korea has had a rather small impact on social policies because of low membership (it has a 25 per cent unionization rate) and high fragmentation, which makes it difficult to formulate coherent national-policy proposals (Hyug, 1992; Mo, 1996; Watson, 1998). Business too is fragmented, with several employer groups having somewhat different interests and policy positions, making it difficult to develop unified policy proposals except for knee-jerk opposition to anything that might increase cost. All in all, the government could afford to ignore the positions of both labour and business. But this did not mean that business interests were totally excluded from social-policy consideration because of the strong position of those segments of the bureaucracy dealing with economic policy, which often took a sympathetic position to business (Joo, 1999a).

Economic agencies with the government have generally opposed social policies that could divert funds away from economic development. To ensure that this did not happen, they have successfully insisted that all programmes be funded entirely from contribution by employers and employees rather than from the government's general revenues (Lee, 1997). Public-assistance programmes, which rely on the government's general budget, have been kept to a minimum in light of their opposition. Education policy also reflects their market orientation, especially at the tertiary level. The economic technocrats also see little role for the government in housing beyond providing a stable macro-economic framework and removing the impediments to market forces.

Curiously, internationalization of Korea has probably contributed to rather than hindered the expansion of social security. When Korea joined the OECD in 1996, its policies began to be increasingly judged by the standards of Western countries and were found wanting in social sectors. The 1997 economic crisis highlighted the population's vulnerability to global economic forces and prompted measures to expand health insurance, pensions, public assistance, and unemployment programmes by lowering the eligibility criteria and/or increasing the benefit amount (Shin, 2000).

Taiwan

Taiwan has all the social programmes found in Korea, but they are fragmented and afford uneven levels of benefit to different segments of the population. Its income maintenance and health-care programmes developed in an *ad hoc* manner to appease particular constituencies vital to the regime's survival. The problem with health-care financing was finally fixed in 1995 but the inadequacies of its pension system remain to be addressed despite years of deliberation. Government intervention in housing was similarly haphazard, but it later pulled back and now offers only broad, but expensive, support in the form of tax relief for buyers. Education has traditionally been an area of heavy government involvement and close planning, but this has been wound down somewhat in recent years and private providers and financing are being given a more prominent role.

Studies on Taiwan too have shown how political crises and competition faced by the ruling party Kuomintang (KMT) have shaped social policies (Aspalter, 2002; Ku, 1997; Lee, 1997; Tang, 1997). However, unlike Korea, where the government faced the possibility of losing the election, the KMT faced no serious challenge to its rule until the end of martial law in 1987. It is not entirely surprising that no major programme was established until the mid 1980s, except for those established in the 1950s when the KMT was still in the process of consolidating its rule.

The KMT experienced its first real set-back in 1986 when it lost the election for the two seats reserved for labour in the legislature (Lee, 1997; Pei, 1998). It responded by establishing the Council for Labour Affairs in 1988 and beginning to pay closer attention to labour grievances (Ku, 1997). The shift in the Democratic Progressive Party's (DPP) electoral strategy also had an effect on the government's attitude towards social policy. Given the KMT's excellent record in managing the economy, the DPP began increasingly to focus on social policy to win voter support. The KMT, in turn, responded with its own initiatives, leading to a competition between the two as to which party offered the most benefits (Liu, 1994). Much of the recent debate has concentrated on pensions because health care went through major overhaul in 1995 and housing is not a priority with the public after a decade-long oversupply. There is broad political support for education and its reform has been less controversial.

There was widespread anxiety about rising medical costs in the mid 1980s and the KMT seized the opportunity to commit itself to launching national health insurance (Lee, 1997). On pensions, however, it was usually on the back foot in responding to DPP initiatives. In the 1993 local election the DPP offered a non-contributory pension of NT$5,000 a month for the aged and made impressive gains despite KMT's hurried offer of similar benefits. In the course of the 1994 legislative election campaign, the KMT committed itself earlier than planned to the introduction of national health insurance, a pension system for farmers in 1995, an unemployment-insurance programme in 1996, and a national pension programme in the near future (*Business Taiwan*, 11 October 1993). Similarly, in preparation for the 1996 Presidential election, the government issued "The Guiding Principles of Social Welfare Policy", which promised major improvements in the social-security system and public housing for low-income families. The bidding contest over pensions reached new heights in the 1997 local election, in which KMT pushed the welfare agenda even harder than the DPP but yet suffered heavy losses (Aspalter, 2002; Pei, 1998). The same pattern of promises was repeated in 1998 legislative and mayoral elections, but this time the KMT was able to reverse its earlier losses.

The Taiwanese government has faced only feeble opposition from business or labour to its policies. Taiwan's economy is dominated by small and medium-sized business firms on whom social security laws either do not apply or are not strictly enforced. Most of the large firms are directly or indirectly controlled by the state, which limits their potential to oppose government policies. Organized labour has been similarly feeble because of KMT's tight control over trade unions until the repeal of martial law and the subsequent resurgence of trade unionism and industrial action (Chu, 1998). However, the union movement is fragmented along occupational and ideological lines, compounded by the fact that a large proportion of their members are located in small firms, making collective action difficult. But industrial disputes in Taiwan have risen continuously for more than a decade, indicating potential for severe unrest (ROC, Council of Labor Affairs, 2003). As a result of the weakness on the part of business and labour, the government has had a relatively free hand in designing social policies. The only constraint has been the key role played by the government's own economic agencies, which have constantly tried to restrain increases in government expenditure or taxes.

Geo-political and diplomatic factors also played a role in shaping the government's attitude towards social policies. As China improved its diplomatic relations with much of the world at the expense of Taiwan in the 1980s and 1990s, the KMT rulers began to view democracy and social development as the island's main attraction and its key selling point for joining international organizations from which it had been shut out. As a part of their case for joining the United Nations, they presented Taiwan as a modern state with democracy, economic stability, and a caring society (Tang, 1997: 70). By the mid 1990s, they even began to use "welfare state" to describe Taiwan, a term that is still taboo in much of the region (So and Hua, 1992: 389).

Structure of the book

This chapter started by underlining the need for studying social policies in the NIEs. It touched on the key strands in the literature on the subject and noted the need for understanding the political context in which policies are established. It then provided a quick political history of the four NIEs with reference to social policy.

The following chapter will describe the economic and demographic contexts of social policies in the NIEs. It will concentrate on overall economic indicators and their distributional impact, and the structure of public finance. The chapter will end with a discussion of demographic indicators and their impact on social policies. The chapter shows that economic and demographic developments in the NIEs pose new social-policy challenges for governments but also afford new opportunities for addressing them.

The subsequent chapters will concentrate on income maintenance, health, housing, and education policies. The focus will be on the arrangements for providing and financing each of them, and their outcomes. The study will find that the NIEs are more diverse than is often realized in that they emphasize different social policies and have different arrangements for providing and financing them. Unsurprisingly, policy outcomes also vary a great deal across the NIEs.

With respect to social policies, the NIEs may be divided into two clusters: Hong Kong and Singapore in one group and Korea and Taiwan in the other. The two clusters display sufficient intra-group similarities and inter-group differences to be described as distinct "families of nations" (Castles, 1998) or even social policy "regimes" (Esping-Andersen, 1990). This is not to deny that there are also significant differences within each group and similarities across them. Nevertheless, the categorization is useful for understanding the character and implications of social policies in the NIEs.

Drawing generalized conclusions about social polices in the NIEs is complicated by the fact that this study covers four policies in four countries. As is to be expected, the larger the number of policies and countries under comparison, the more difficult it is to generalize about them (Uusitalo, 1984). The task is made all the more difficult by the newness of social policy institutions in the NIEs and the rapid changes they are undergoing, a problem recognized by Esping-Andersen (1996) himself. Some anomalies in generalizations offered in this book are therefore unavoidable.

Social policies in Hong Kong and Singapore are, at an aggregate level, Liberal despite the fact that income maintenance, much of hospital care, education, and housing is provided by the state. The extent of state involvement is highest in education and lowest in income maintenance – the former is universally provided at negligible charge whereas the latter is subject to severe means testing. All these are consistent with a Liberal emphasis on equality of opportunity via education, and upholding the work ethics and maintaining the sanctity of the market. Involvement in health and housing promotes a healthy workforce and keeps pressure off wages and is therefore not as contradictory as may first appear. In all these respects Singapore goes much further than Hong Kong. It funds education generously and social security stingily, whereas objectives in health care and housing are realized through means other than public expenditure. As the population ages and the number of people without adequate voluntary or mandatory savings increases, education and housing expenditures will decline and income maintenance and health expenditures will expand. Over time, quite probably the city states will resemble the austere Liberal welfare state found in the English-speaking world.

Korea's and Taiwan's social policies, on the other hand, display Conservative features whereby income maintenance and health-care programmes differ by occupational groups, and benefits are tied to employment and earnings. Both countries have social-security programmes in place that will, over time, transform them into substantial welfare states in which benefits will be available as a right but without a fundamental alteration of basic class, status, or family relations. Housing does not attract the same degree of attention as other social policies and, in recent years, has been left largely to the market. Education is an odd case in that although it occupies a central place in their social-policy strategy, governments allow significant room for private providers and out-of-pocket payments, especially at the higher-education level. The social policies in Korea and Taiwan, in sum, are quite similar to those found in Conservative welfare regimes, especially in southern Europe.

2
SOCIO-ECONOMIC BACKGROUND

Social polices are shaped by, and shape, the economic and social environment in which they exist. The state of the economy affects the income level and thereby the population's capacity to maintain income and afford education, health, and housing. It also determines the government's revenues and the resources available to it to spend on social programmes. Similarly, the level of a country's economic globalization in terms of foreign investment and trade is said to be a vital determinant of a society's exposure to economic uncertainties and the level of public support residents require, and the government's ability to respond to the need through appropriate fiscal and monetary policies. The demographic composition and trends similarly affect the demand for various social-policy goods and services.

The purpose of this chapter is to analyse the economic and demographic trends in the NIE, and highlight their relevance to social policy. This chapter will concentrate largely on providing background information on these trends. Their significance will become clearer in the following chapters, when we will see that in many respects the trends in the NIEs are similar to those found in the OECD countries, but are quite different in other respects.

Economy

The economy grew and consequently income levels in the NIEs rose at a spectacular rate for almost three decades until the late 1990s, when it slowed down in some and crashed in others. As Table 2.1 shows, the NIEs' economy in 1965–1997 grew, in real terms, at a rate that was two or even three times faster than the average for the OECD countries. Growth in the 1990s was generally lower than in the previous decades, especially in Hong Kong, but still considerably faster than in the OECD countries. The rapid economic growth was reflected in improvement in the standard of living: the per capita GDP, adjusted to purchasing power, increased by over five times in Hong Kong, seven times in Taiwan, nine times in Singapore, and eleven times in Korea between 1965 and 2000. However, the economic

Table 2.1 Real GDP growth and GDP per capita

	Real GDP growth,[1] annual average, per cent			Per capita GDP, PPP international $	
	1965–1980	1981–1997	1998–2000	1965	2000
Hong Kong	9	6	3	4,843	25,153
Singapore	10	8	5	2,678	23,356
Korea	8	8	5	1,528	17,470
Taiwan	10	8	5	2,324	17,400
High income OECD	4	3	3		27,277

Sources: World Development Indicators, 2002; DGBAS, 2002; http://www.worldfactsandfigures.com/.

Note
1 Constant 1995 Local Currency Unit.

recession that began in late 1997 caused havoc in the region, reducing GDP by 5–7 per cent in Hong Kong and Korea in 1998, while Singapore's GDP remained stagnant. The year 1999 marked the beginning of wide fluctuations in the region's, indeed the world's, economy.

The higher economic growth in the NIEs enabled them to catch up with their OECD counterparts and, by the end of the century, the two city-states were in the league of rich nations. While it is common to club these countries with other "developing" countries, it needs to be remembered that their standard of living is similar to that of "developed" or "industrialized" nations.

The rapid economic growth in the NIEs has offered ample economic opportunities to their populace and unemployment has been generally low since the 1960s, even during periods of economic slowdown. In the 1980s and much of the 1990s, the unemployment rate ranged between 2 and 4 per cent, an excellent performance by world standards and considerably better than the average of around 7 per cent in the OECD countries. However, the situation deteriorated rapidly in the late 1990s as a result of the regional economic recession that began in late 1997. By 2000, unemployment had shot above 6 per cent in Korea and Hong Kong and nearly 5 per cent in Singapore. Unemployment in Taiwan remained under 3 per cent until 2000 but then shot up to 5 per cent in the following year.

The economic growth and consequent rise in income levels in the NIEs for three decades from the 1960s to the late 1990s can be attributed to fundamental structural changes in their economies. So much so that within just three decades the NIEs have gone through some of the deepest and fastest structural transformations of the economy anywhere in the world, as is evident in Table 2.2.

Interestingly, Hong Kong has gone through the deepest transformations: manufacturing formed 87 per cent of the GDP until the 1970s but

Table 2.2 Sectoral distribution of GDP by value added, per cent

	Agriculture		Industry		Services	
	1965	2000	1965	2000	1965	2000
Hong Kong	0.8[1]	0.1	86.9[1]	14.4	67.5[1]	85.5
Singapore	2.9	0.2	23.6	34.6	73.6	65.2
Korea	37.2	5.1	24.2	42.5	38.6	52.4
Taiwan	23.6	2.1	30.2	32.4	46.2	65.5
High income	7.3	1.7[2]	39.8	30.2[2]	52.9	64.9[2]
Middle income	24.0	10.3	33.3	34.0	42.6	55.7

Sources: World Development Indicators, 2002; Taiwan Statistical Data Book, 1997.

Notes
1 1980.
2 1997.

had shrunk to below 15 per cent by 2000, while services' share increased from 68 to 86 per cent. In comparison, services' share of the economy in Singapore declined from 74 to 65 per cent while manufacturing's share increased from 24 to 35 per cent. However, unlike Hong Kong and Singapore, Korea and Taiwan have a significant, albeit rapidly declining, agricultural sector. For instance, in Korea, agriculture's share of GDP declined from 37 to 5 per cent, while manufacturing's share increased from 24 to 43 per cent and the share of services from 39 to 52 per cent. Similarly, in Taiwan, agriculture declined from 24 to 2 per cent of the GDP, while manufacturing increased from 30 to 32 per cent and services from 46 to 66 per cent. As a result of this transformation, the structure of their economies is similar to those of industrialized countries, characterized by a small and declining agriculture and large and growing service sectors.

The sectoral distribution of the labour force has paralleled shifts in the distribution of GDP. Korea has gone through the deepest transformation in this respect, as the share of its labour force employed in agriculture declined from 61 to 16 per cent in less than five decades, while in Taiwan it declined from 50 to 10 per cent (Table 2.3). The profile of the labour force in these two countries is now somewhere between the high- and middle-income countries.

One of the prominent features of developing countries is the large proportion of the economically active population in non-wage employment in informal sectors. Consistent with their newly industrialized status, the majority of the economically active non-agricultural population in the NIEs now works in formal sectors and draws regular wages. Among the four NIEs, the two city-states are the most advanced in this respect, with only 12–13 per cent of the non-agricultural labour force in informal employment, which is similar to the OECD level of 15 per cent (MPFA, 2001; OECD, 2001; Singapore Department of Statistics; 2001). Informal employment is higher in the Northeast Asian states: 29 per cent in Korea

Table 2.3 Share of labour force in agriculture, per cent

	1960	1985	2000
Hong Kong	8	1	<1
Singapore	7	1	<1
Korea	61	27	12
Taiwan	50	17	8
High income OECD	20	7	4
Middle income	68	55	28[1]

Sources: World Development Indicators, 2002; DGBAS, 2002.

Note
1 1990.

and 22 per cent in Taiwan (DGBAS, 2002). There is fear, however, that economic globalization may be expanding informal employment as firms contract out services and replace permanent full-time with temporary and part-time employees. In Korea, for instance, wage labour as a percentage of the total labour force declined from 60 in 1990 to 48 in 2000 (Jung and Shin, 2002: 282–283). The relative size of formal employment has important implications for social policy, as without it governments find it difficult to operate contributory social programmes, which typically involve periodic deduction of contribution from wages.

Income distribution and poverty

Following the World Bank's (1993) finding in the early 1990s that East Asia had managed to achieve rapid economic growth with equity, there was a spate of works commenting on the positive and salutary links between the two (for example, see Root, 1996). The World Bank was wrong, as the region is highly diverse, comprising some of the least as well as the most unequal societies in the world. As is shown in Table 2.4, Korea and Taiwan have highly equal distribution of income, but that is not the case with Hong Kong and Singapore. More significantly, while all four

Table 2.4 Gini coefficient – household income

	Hong Kong	*Singapore*	*Korea*	*Taiwan*
Early 1970s	40.9 (1971)	41.0 (1973)	33.3 (1970)	28.4 (1972)
Early 1980s	37.3 (1980)	40.7 (1980)	38.6 (1980)	27.7 (1980)
Early 1990s	45.0 (1991)	41.0 (1988)	33.6 (1988)	31.2 (1990)
Late 1990s	52.0 (1996)	46.7 (1999)	31.0 (1998)	31.9 (1997)

Sources: UNU/WIDER and UNDP/SEPED (1999?); World Income Inequality Database (WIID), http://www.wider.unu.edu/wiid/wwwwiid.htm, Singapore, 1999.

Note
The numbers within parentheses indicate the year of survey.

have experienced some increase in inequality, the increase is particularly pronounced in the two city-states, where it is already high. The gini coefficient of 52 in Hong Kong is very high and should be a matter of concern for its policy-makers.

The relatively equal distribution of income in Korea and Taiwan is the result of historically unique circumstances that emerged after the end of colonial rule and the confiscation and sell-off of Japanese assets that followed. Reforms and inflation-fighting measures directed at financial wealth had similarly positive effects on the distribution of assets and income. The existence of multigenerational and extended family structure in the region – not just in Korea and Taiwan but Hong Kong and Singapore as well – also promote income equality. In such families, individuals without income (youth, women, and the elderly) tend to live with those who do have income, resulting in a redistribution of income through private transfers (Jacobs, 2000).

Income distribution in the region worsened significantly amidst economic recession in the late 1990s. In Korea, the income share of the bottom quintile declined from 7.9 to 7.2 per cent in just one year, while that of the top decile actually rose (Na and Moon, 1999). Similarly, in Singapore the poorest household quintile's share of income declined from 4.2 per cent in 1990 to 2.8 per cent in 1999, while the share of the richest quintile increased from 48.2 per cent to 49.9 per cent (Singapore Department of Statistics, 1999). In Taiwan, too, which did not go through the economic contraction experienced by the other NIEs, the gap between high- and low-income families widened from a ratio of 5.4:1 in 1997 to 5.5:1 in 1998. Hong Kong suffered the greatest deterioration in its already very uneven distribution of income.

Distribution of wealth in the region is, as is expected, far more unequal than income. In Korea, for instance, the gini coefficient was 40 for income but 60 for assets in 1988. Distribution of assets was slightly more unequal in urban areas than in rural areas, whereas income inequality was considerably higher in rural areas (Kim, 1995).

While the level of poverty in the region is low and has generally declined, it is not as low as is sometimes portrayed. The Hong Kong government does not maintain an official poverty line and therefore it does not maintain data on poverty. It is possible, however, to calculate relative poverty: about 10 per cent of the Hong Kong population in the late 1990s were living on income below one-third of the national median (HKSS, 2000). In comparison, the percentage of the Korean population living on below one-third of the national average was 8 per cent in the mid 1980s, down from 12 per cent in the mid 1960s.

In Singapore, the Population Planning Unit of the government estimated that about 5 per cent of the population was living in poverty in 1991. This was based on an unusually strict definition of poverty: US$296 for a family of four, which works out at 7 per cent of per capita GNP that year. The application of widely used international standards is likely to show a much higher percentage of the population living in poverty, as published statistics show that nearly 20 per cent of the households had income below one-half of the national gross monthly income (Singapore Department of Statistics, 1999). The income of the poor actually declined during the 1990s: the average household income of the poorest income decile in Singapore was US$204 in 1990 and US$152 in 1998, which was 12 and 5 per cent respectively of the average household income (ibid.).

On the other hand, Taiwan's poverty line since 1998 has been set at 60 per cent of the average individual consumption expenditure in the locality in question, which translates into US$350 per person in the Taipei area in 2000. Although precise data is not available to confirm this, probably around 15 per cent of the population live under the poverty line, given that the average per capita monthly disposable income for the lowest-income quintile was US$423 in that year. However, note that the definition of poverty in Taiwan is considerably more relaxed than in the other NIEs.

Public finance

The NIEs have an enviable reputation for robust management of public finance, maintaining low revenues as well as expenditures and yet achieving a healthy budget balance. Be that as it may, fiscal conditions in these countries are changing in ways that make them appear increasingly similar to the industrialized countries.

Despite modest revenues, Hong Kong's budget was always – except for the small deficit during 1983–1985 and in recent years – in surplus, reaching as high as 2.5 per cent of the GDP during the 1990–1997 period. Singapore's budget surplus was yet larger, possibly the largest in the world, amounting to 3.4 per cent of its GDP during the 1983–1989 period and 10.5 per cent during the 1990–1997 period. But much of the surplus in both Hong Kong and Singapore has disappeared in recent years. Korea, on the other hand, had a deficit totalling 0.18 per cent of GDP during the 1983–1989 period and 0.02 per cent during the 1990–1997 period. Taiwan's fiscal position has been the weakest among the four, as it has had significant and increasing budget deficit since the 1980s, with its budget

Table 2.5 Overall budget surplus as percentage of GDP

	1983–1989	1990–1997	1998–2000
Hong Kong	0.6	2.5	−0.6
Singapore	3.4	10.5	6.9
Korea	−0.2	−0.0	−1.9
Taiwan	−1.8	−6.0	−1.6
High income	−4.5	−3.2	

Sources: ADB, 2002; World Development Indicators, 2002.

deficit amounting to nearly 2 per cent of the GDP during 1983–1989 and 6 per cent during 1990–1997. Indeed, its deficit burden in the 1990s was twice as large as the average for OECD countries. Remarkably, public debate on public finance in Taiwan is dominated by talks of reducing taxes and increasing public expenditures, which will only aggravate the deficit.

Government revenues as a proportion of GDP in the NIEs used to be considerably lower than in the OECD countries but the gap has been continuously narrowing: it now amounts to 26 per cent in Korea and Singapore and a little less in Taiwan, compared to 28 per cent in the OECD. The exception is Hong Kong, where public spending's share has not risen since the 1960s and continues to be about half the level in the high-income countries.

Table 2.6 shows that, in addition, tax revenues in the NIEs form only a small percentage of the GDP, ranging from 14 per cent in Taiwan to 21 per cent in Korea. No less significantly, the tax revenues' share of GDP has remained stagnant in the city-states and increased only slightly in Taiwan. It is only in Korea that the tax revenues' share of GDP has increased substantially.

The modest tax revenues in the NIEs is confirmed by their low-income tax rates, except for in Korea, where taxes are comparable to the levels in OECD countries. The tax rates in Hong Kong are by far the lowest, with individuals paying a flat rate of 17 per cent on income over US$1,778 and corporations paying at the rate of 16.5 or 15 per cent depending on whether they are incorporated or not. However, because of the high tax threshold, 60 per cent of Hong Kong households do not pay any income tax. In Korea, the tax rate for individuals is 40 per cent on income over US$59,000 and for corporations it is 28 per cent on income over US$88,420. In Singapore, the maximum tax for individuals is 28 per cent on income over US$141,744 while the corporate income-tax rate is 26 per cent. In Taiwan, the maximum tax rate for corporations is 25 per cent. In comparison, the corporate income-tax rate is 31 per cent in the UK and 15–35 per cent in the USA.

Table 2.6 Current revenue and taxes, percentage of GDP

	Current revenue				Taxes			
	1970	1980	1990	2000	1970	1980	1990	2000
Hong Kong	–	14	14	14	–	10	10	10
Singapore	21	25	26	26	14	18	15	15
Korea	15	18	17	26	13	16	16	21
Taiwan	21	22	25	21	–	10	13	14
High income OECD	20 (1975)	23	24	28[1]	–	–	22	26[1]

Sources: ADB, 2002; World Development Indicators, 2002.

Note
1 1997.

The large difference between total revenues and tax revenues depicted in Table 2.6 is the result of significant earnings from land sales, user charges, and profits of state-owned enterprises. For instance, in 1997, non-tax revenues formed 21 per cent of current revenues in Hong Kong, 14 per cent in Korea, 34 per cent in Singapore, and 41 per cent in Taiwan. Remarkably, non-tax revenues have significantly increased their share of total revenues in Singapore and Taiwan. The diverse revenue base in Hong Kong, Singapore, and Taiwan has allowed them to maintain low taxes, leaving considerable room for increase if considered necessary in future.

The characterization of the NIEs as low-spending countries masks the significant differences among them with respect to details. Public spending's share of the GDP in Hong Kong, Korea, and Singapore is over 20 per cent, which is low compared to high-income countries. Taiwan's public spending, on the other hand, exceeds the OECD average, as shown in Figure 2.1. The patterns are relatively stable, with an upward trend in all NIEs in recent years.

The divergence among the NIEs with regard to public expenditures on social policies as percentage of GDP has narrowed over the years and now stands at just under 14 in all except Singapore, where it is less than 8 (see Table 2.7). But even the highest spending NIEs, Hong Kong and Taiwan, spend less than half of the OECD average of over 30 per cent of GDP.

There is a much greater difference among the NIEs with regard to the share of the total government expenditure (TGE) that they devote to social policies, as is shown in Table 2.8. By this measure, the largest spender is Hong Kong, which directs 64 per cent of its TGE to social policies, compared to 58 per cent in Taiwan and a little less in Korea. In

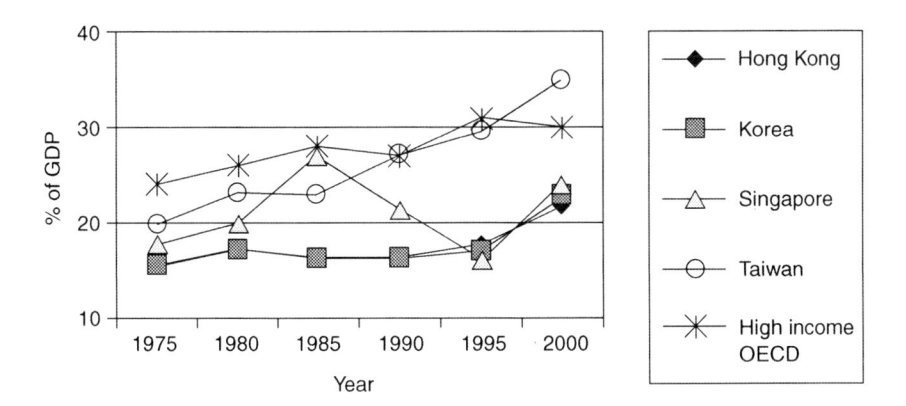

Figure 2.1 Public spending's share of GDP, 1975–2000, per cent (World Development Indicators, 2002; DGBAS, 2002).

Table 2.7 Social policy expenditures' share of GDP, per cent

	Hong Kong				Singapore				Korea				Taiwan[3]		
	1975	1985	1995	2000	1975	1985	1995	2000	1975	1985	1995	1998	1990	1995	1999
Education	2.9	2.8	3.1	4.1	3.6	5.9	3.1	4.0	2.2	3.0	3.4	3.8	5.3	4.1	4.9
Housing	2.4	3.4	3.2	4.9	1.3	1.1	1.3	2.0	0.2	0.9	0.5	0.4	0.7	0.9	1.0
Health	1.3	1.4	2.3	2.6	1.5	1.8	1.2	1.0	–	–	3.7[1]	5.9	2.1	3.4	3.5
Income maintenance	0.9	0.9	1.3	2.2	0.3	0.4	0.8	0.7	–	–	1.9[2]	3.1[2]	3.8	4.6	4.7
Total	7.5	8.5	9.9	13.8	6.7	9.2	6.4	7.7	–	–	9.5	13.2	11.9	13.0	14.1

Sources: ADB, "Key Indicators of Developing Asian and Pacific Countries 2002"; *Taiwan Statistical Data Book 2000*, various; OECD, OECD social expenditure database, 2001.

Notes
1 Includes social insurance and direct government expenditure.
2 Includes social insurance and direct government expenditure but not expenditure on retirement benefits under Labor Standards Act.
3 Includes social insurance and direct government (all levels) expenditure on pension and survivors benefits, social assistance, social relief, social welfare services, and employment service. Excludes health expenditures.

Table 2.8 Social policy expenditures' share of total government expenditure, per cent

	Hong Kong				Singapore				Korea				Taiwan[3]		
	1975	1985	1995	2000	1975	1985	1995	2000	1975	1985	1995	1998	1990	1995	1999
Education	19.2	16.7	17.6	18.8	20.2	21.6	18.9	20.0	14.0	18.4	19.5	15.9	19.5	17.2	20.4
Housing	16.0	21.0	18.2	22.5	7.1	4.2	8.1	10.7	1.1	1.0	2.4	1.9 (1997)	2.7	3.1	4.1
Health	8.6	8.5	12.7	12.0	8.5	6.5	7.6	5.1	–	–	–	–	7.9	11.4	14.8
Income maintenance	5.8	5.8	7.4	10.3	1.8	1.6	5.0	3.5	–	7.2 (1990)	11.5	13.1	13.0	15.5	19.6
Total	49.6	52.0	55.9	63.6	37.6	33.9	39.6	39.3	–	–	–	–	43.1	47.2	58.9

Sources: ADB, "Key Indicators of Developing Asian and Pacific Countries 2002"; *Taiwan Statistical Data Book 2000*, various; OECD, OECD social expenditure database, 2001.

Notes
1 Includes social insurance and direct government expenditure.
2 Includes social insurance and direct government expenditure but not expenditure on retirement benefits under Labor Standards Act.
3 Includes social insurance and direct government (all levels) expenditure on pension and survivors benefits, social assistance, social relief, social welfare services, and employment service. Excludes health expenditures.

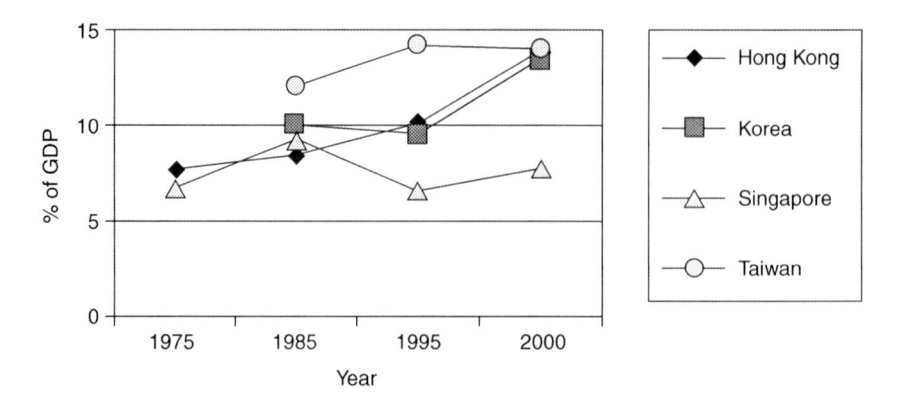

Figure 2.2 Public spending on social policy, share of GDP, 1975–2000, per cent (World Development Indicators, 2002; DGBAS, 2002).

Singapore, in contrast, only 40 per cent of the total spending is channelled to social policies. No less significantly, the social policies' share of TGE has increased in all the NIEs except Singapore.

There are some variations in the proportions of public spending devoted to different social policies in the NIEs. Education is the largest item of social-policy expenditure in all the NIEs except Hong Kong. Income maintenance is the second-largest item in Korea and Taiwan, but the smallest in Hong Kong and Singapore. Health, in comparison, is the third most expensive item in all the NIEs. Housing is the largest item in Hong Kong, the second-largest item in Singapore, third in Korea, and smallest in Taiwan.

Public-spending data must be treated with some caution, however. The biggest problem is that it leaves out mandated private spending, which is particularly large in the case of income maintenance in some countries in the region. In a substantive sense, mandated private spending is no different from tax and spend arrangements; the only difference is that receipt and disbursement in the case of the former are not channelled through the government. The compulsory employer-funded labour retirement benefits in Korea and Taiwan, and the Central Provident Fund financed jointly by employers and employees, are examples of such arrangements – their inclusion will measurably increase what we consider public spending on social policy in the NIEs.

International position

The effects of a country's international financial position are said to impact increasingly on nations' social policies. Large current-account deficit is believed to undermine investors' confidence in a country, pressuring governments to pursue prudent and generally tight fiscal policies. On this account, the NIEs have a tremendous reputation for sound foreign economic policies, which is often used to explain the absence of generous social-security programmes in the region. The reality is a lot more complex, as there are vast differences among them, shown in Figure 2.3.

Hong Kong has had a large current-account surplus since the 1970s, except for brief periods in 1980–1982 and 1996–1999. Korea's current account, on the other hand, has been mostly in deficit, except for brief periods in the late 1980s and late 1990s. Singapore has gone through the most dramatic reversal, from a large deficit in the early 1980s to a large surplus after 1995, reaching 25 per cent of GDP in 1998 and 1999. Taiwan's current account has always been in surplus, though its size shrunk gradually (but consistently) throughout the 1990s.

The current-account trends in the NIEs show that international investors would find the economic conditions in Hong Kong and Singapore appealing. Taiwan was in a similar position, but its attractiveness in this regard began to decline in the late 1990s. The large deficit in Korea until the mid 1990s, in contrast, would have made it a worrying case in international markets. These trends are not consistent with public-spending patterns in the NIEs as the governments in Hong Kong and Singapore are the smallest spenders despite their extraordinarily healthy current-account positions.

Dependence on foreign investment is said to restrict government capacity to spend on non-productive items, which is of great relevance to the NIEs because of their very high dependence on foreign capital. The NIEs were largely recipients of Foreign Direct Investment (FDI) until the 1980s, but then the situation became complicated after they became a significant source of FDI as well. A clearer picture of this change in FDI inflows and outflows is revealed in Table 2.9.

The table shows large differences among the NIEs with regard to FDI flows. In the late 1990s, FDI inflow's share of GDP ranged from around

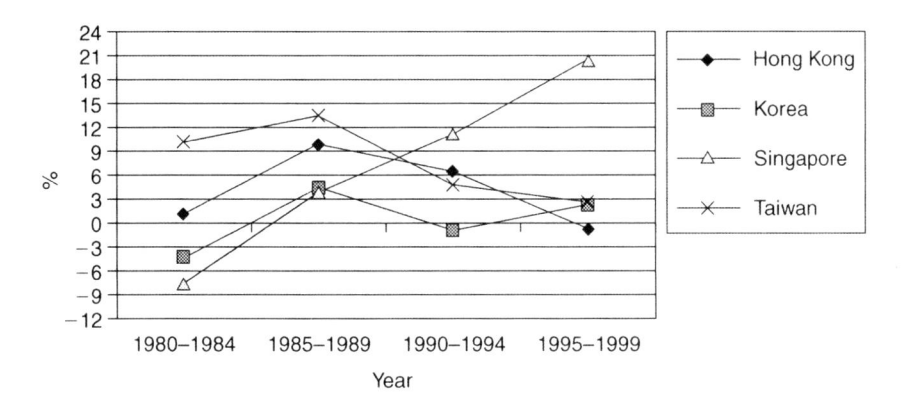

Figure 2.3 Current account balance as percentage of GDP, annual average (ADB, 2002; World Development Indicators, 2002).

Table 2.9 Foreign Direct Investment flows, annual average, percentage of GDP

	Inward		Outward		Net	
	1989–1994	1995–1999	1989–1994	1995–1999	1989–1994	1995–1999
Hong Kong	0.6	5.5	1.2	5.9	−5.3	−5.7
Singapore	9.8	10.7	3.9	5.6	6.1	4.9
Korea	0.3	1.2	0.5	1.0	−0.2	0.1
Taiwan	0.6	0.6	1.8	1.5	−1.2	−0.8

Sources: UNCTAD, *World Investment Report 2001*; DGBAS, 2002.

Note
Minus figure indicates deficit – i.e. outflow exceeds inflow.

1 per cent in Korea and Taiwan to 6 per cent in Hong Kong and 11 per cent in Singapore. The differences are only slightly less marked with respect to outflows, ranging from around 1 per cent of GDP in Korea and Taiwan to around 6 per cent in the two city-states.

Because of the difference in the amount of foreign investment flowing in and out, the net flows are quite different across the NIEs. Interestingly, Hong Kong and Taiwan have been in the peculiar position – one usually found in the developed countries – whereby FDI outflows exceeded inflows, as shown in Table 2.10. This was the result of an exodus of labour-intensive manufacturing to the neighbouring countries in the 1990s because of rising wage costs in their home countries. The net outflow of FDI from Korea until the mid 1990s, in contrast, was the result of barriers to inward foreign investment that were in place. Singapore is in a different position still, where the inflows greatly exceed the outflows despite the government policy since the 1990s to "internationalize" local firms by offering incentives for investing abroad.

The cumulative stock of foreign investment in the NIEs conveys an entirely different picture. Both the inward and outward FDI stock is largest in Hong Kong, in both absolute and relative terms, followed by Singapore. One of the reasons for the large difference across the NIEs is

Table 2.10 Trade, percentage of GDP

	1970	2000
Hong Kong	181	295
Singapore	232	341
Korea	37	87
Taiwan	70	81
High income OECD	26	79
Middle income	30	54

Sources: World Development Indicators, 2002; DGBAS, 2002.

the result of the very different lengths of time during which these countries have been the recipients and/or sources of FDI. In Hong Kong, reflecting its position as a British colony for two centuries, the current book value of inward FDI exceeds 256 per cent of GDP. Singapore has been in a similar situation, with the book value of inward FDI amounting to 98 per cent of GDP. On the whole, the two Northeast Asian states have a much shorter experience with FDI, either as source or recipient, because what Japanese FDI did exist was confiscated at the end of colonial rule.

To the extent that dependence on trade is deemed to restrict social-policy options, the NIEs would be expected to be severely restricted because of their very high degree of trade-dependence. Hong Kong and Singapore are in a class of their own, with their trade amounting to about three times their GDP. Taiwan comes in a distant third position, with its trade amounting to 93 per cent of its GDP, while in Korea trade accounts for 70 per cent of GDP. The NIEs have a much higher dependence on international trade than the average for high- or middle-income countries. In this sense, one would expect the NIEs to be far more cautious with public-spending commitments than the other countries. In reality, however, there is little relationship between exposure to international trade and social spending: the governments in Hong Kong, Korea, and Taiwan devote similar levels of GDP to it despite having very different levels of dependence on international trade.

Population

Demographic composition vitally affects the demand for different social policies, which, in turn, affects what the government does to address it. The NIEs have gone through deep demographic transition in recent decades and this has, as we shall see in subsequent chapters, decisively shaped their social policies.

The population in the NIEs grew rapidly from the 1950s to the 1970s but then the rate declined abruptly. As Table 2.11 shows, in the 1960s the population growth rate in the NIEs was two or three times higher than in the OECD countries, but the gap had narrowed by the 1980s. However, the declining trend partially reversed itself in Singapore in the 1980s and

Table 2.11 Population growth rate, annual average, per cent

	1960–1969	1970–1979	1980–1989	1990–1999
Hong Kong	2.9	2.4	1.3	1.7
Singapore	2.3	1.5	2.3	2.8
Korea	2.5	1.8	1.2	1.0
Taiwan	3.2	2.0	1.4	0.9
High income OECD	1.0	0.8	0.6	0.7

Sources: DGBAS, 2002; World Development Indicators, 2002.

in Hong Kong in the 1990s when population growth rose slightly as a result of increased immigration.

The declining population growth rate is the result of diminishing fertility rate in recent decades, as shown in Table 2.12. From a high of 3.1–4.3 in 1970, the fertility rate had declined to 1.0–1.7 in 2000. Indeed, the fertility rate in all four NIEs has been below the replacement rate of 2 for almost two decades now.

The high population growth rate until the 1970s and the sharp decline thereafter is reflected in the NIEs' demographic profile, summarized in Table 2.13. Between 1965 and 1995, the four NIEs' population increased by between 58 (Taiwan) and 76 per cent (Singapore). However, in the subsequent thirty years the population is expected to grow by only between 2 per cent (Korea) and 6 per cent (Hong Kong). In the two city-states, even the modest population increase that will occur will come from immigration rather than from natural growth.

The two interconnected developments – the sudden drop in the fertility rate and the slowing down of population growth – will have a significant impact on social policies over time. One of the effects will be that less resource will be needed for education and more for health and social security, as the NIEs gear up for an ageing population. This is confirmed by Table 2.14, which summarizes children's and the aged's share of the total population. Around two-fifths of the population in all four NIEs was aged 14 years or below in 1960, but by 1999 the proportion of this age group had halved to around one-fifth. The converse was true of the aged: those aged

Table 2.12 Fertility rate, births per woman

	1970	1980	1990	2000
Hong Kong	3.34	2.00	1.27	1.02
Singapore	3.09	1.74	1.87	1.48
Korea	4.27	2.56	1.77	1.43
Taiwan	3.70	2.51	1.80	1.56
High income OECD	–	–	1.70	1.70

Sources: DGBAS, 2002; World Development Indicators, 2002.

Table 2.13 Population, 1965–2025; number and percentage increase

	Population, million			% increase	
	1965	1995	2025	1965–1995	1995–2025
Hong Kong	3.7	6.2	7.0	66.4	5.6
Singapore	1.7	3.0	4.0	75.6	3.9
Korea	28.5	45.0	53.0	57.9	2.2
Taiwan	13.5	21.4	25.4	58.2	2.7

Sources: World Development Indicators, 2002; DGBAS, 2002.

Table 2.14 Children's and the aged's share of total population, per cent

	0–14 years		65 years and above		
	1960	1999	1960	1999	2025
Hong Kong	40.9	18.2	2.8	10.2	24.3
Singapore	38.7	18.3	1.9	5.5	20.6
Korea	41.9	21.8	3.3	6.4	15.2
Taiwan	45.4	21.4	2.5	8.3	17.1
High income OECD	27.6	18.5	9.3	14.4	–

Sources: DGBAS, 2002; World Development Indicators, 2002; US Bureau of Census, International Database, 1994.

65 years or above formed between 2 and 3 per cent of the population in 1960, but their share had increased to between 6 and 10 per cent by 1999. The baby-boom generation of the 1950s will begin to creep into the aged bracket in the early twenty-first century, when they will form between 15 (Korea) to 24 (Hong Kong) per cent of the total population in the NIEs.

In the past four decades the NIEs have gone through one of the deepest demographic transitions the world has seen, and the trend is likely to continue over the coming decades. Compared to the OECD countries, the NIEs had a disproportionately young population in 1960 but had reached a similar level by 1999. Similarly, the aged formed a disproportionately small share of the population in 1960 and even 1999, but by 2025 the NIEs would have a similar proportion of the aged as the OECD countries. It will take Singapore and Taiwan 21 years to increase the aged's share of the population from 10 to 20 per cent, compared to 25 years for Japan, 68 years for Sweden, and 86 years for the UK (Jones, 1990: 23).

The magnitude of the problem is greater than is suggested in Table 2.14 because many social-security programmes in the NIEs provide benefit at the age of 60 years rather than at 65 as is the practice in OECD countries. By the year 2000, around 15 per cent of the population in Hong Kong and 10 per cent in the other NIEs were already above the age of 60 years. The problem is compounded by the fact that women will form a disproportionately large share of the aged population, who tend to live longer but have fewer savings and suffer from a higher incidence of debilitating diseases. Heller (1999: 52) estimates that even without addition of new programmes or the expansion of existing ones, the NIEs' public expenditures on income maintenance, health, and education as a percentage of GDP will grow by between 2.8 and 4.1 per cent. The increase will take place despite the decline in education expenditures resulting from the declining birth rate.

Accompanying the declining fertility and ageing of the population is the trend towards declining household size, as shown in Table 2.15. The mean household size has declined by 21–29 per cent in the NIEs as a result of an increasing trend towards nuclear families. In Singapore, for

Table 2.15 Mean household size

	1970s	1980s	1990s	% change, 1970s–1990s
Hong Kong	4.5	3.7	3.4	−24.4
Singapore	5.3	4.7	4.2	−20.8
Korea	5.2	4.5	3.7	−28.8
Taiwan	4.8	4.4	3.7	−23.0

Sources: DGBAS, 2000; ESCAP, 1998: 69.

instance, household formation has been growing at 3.8 per year while the population has been growing at only 2 per cent. The nuclearization of families has implications not only for housing policy but also for health and social security, as it weakens adult children's ties with their parents and reduces the opportunity for care giving.

Another distinguishing feature of the NIEs is the high level of urbanization of its societies (see Table 2.16). Almost the entire population of Hong Kong and Singapore has been urban for decades. Korea and Taiwan, however, still have a significant rural population despite rapid urbanization. Korea went through the most rapid urbanization in the region, with the share of the urban population doubling between 1960 and 1980. The pace of urbanization was only slightly slower in Taiwan. By 2000, the vast majority of the population in the NIEs was living in urban areas, though in Taiwan 42 per cent of the population was still living in rural areas.

Conclusion

The chapter shows that the region has, in most years, experienced impressive economic growth rates, which made the task of governance easier but also posed new policy challenges. Economic growth was accompanied by structural transformation, which saw the swift disappearance of traditional sectors of the economy and the emergence of modern manufacturing and service industries. Employment structures changed correspondingly, with the rapid shrinking of informal employment and the expansion of paid employment.

Table 2.16 Urban population, percentage of total

	1960	1980	2000
Hong Kong	85	92	100
Singapore	100	100	100
Korea	28	57	82
Taiwan	–	47	58
High income OECD	–	76	79

Source: World Development Indicators, 1998.

Steep real increases in income also brought down poverty levels and, by corollary, the need for government poverty-alleviation measures. The only blemish on the otherwise excellent economic situation was the high and increasing income disparity, especially in Hong Kong and Singapore. The high average income in the two city-states masks the persistence of pockets of poverty, which is largely invisible because of lack of systematic official data on the subject. The Northeast Asian states have clearly done a better job at achieving growth with equity.

Economic growth also had salutary effects on government finances as it meant increasing revenues without an increase in tax rates. Government revenues both in absolute terms and as a percentage of GDP have risen continuously in all NIEs except Hong Kong. The increase was achieved without a significant change in taxes, indicating the importance of other sources of income in the NIEs. In terms of public spending, Hong Kong and Singapore are small spenders whereas Taiwan, comparatively speaking, is not, with Korea somewhere in between. The different revenue and expenditure patterns are reflected in budget balance, with Hong Kong and Singapore enjoying large surpluses in most years, Korea with a small deficit, and Taiwan with a large and growing deficit.

The different budget positions of the NIE governments is only loosely reflected in their social spending. Total public spending on education, health, housing, and income maintenance is equivalent to around 14 per cent of GDP in Hong Kong, Korea, and Taiwan, and 8 per cent in Singapore. While the share of GDP devoted to social policies has increased in all sectors in all the four NIEs except for health in Singapore, the increase has been most pronounced in Taiwan.

There are divergent trends with regard to the NIEs' international economic position, making it difficult to generalize about how economic internationalization has affected their social policies. The current accounts of Hong Kong, Singapore, and Taiwan have generally been in surplus. Even Korea's current account, which used to be in deficit, turned positive in the late 1990s. The level of their dependence on foreign investment varies from very high in Hong Kong and Singapore to rather low in Korea and Taiwan, though in the latter two it has been increasing. However, in all the NIEs except Singapore outflows exceed inflows, resulting in significant net deficit. If the outflow is the result of relatively higher costs in the host countries, and reversing the trend is an objective, then the governments in Hong Kong and Taiwan would find themselves particularly encumbered in expanding budgetary commitments to social policies.

The declining birth rate and increasing lifespan is having a significant impact on social policy in the NIEs, and the trend will accentuate further in the coming decades. Less will need to be spent on education and a lot more on health and social security, not just because the aged will exceed children in numbers but also because health and social security are more expensive responsibilities.

3
INCOME MAINTENANCE

Few topics in public policy generate as much passion and controversy as income maintenance. For some it represents the essence of what contemporary democratic citizenship is about (Marshall, 1963), while for others it epitomizes much that is wrong with liberal democracy and is a recipe for economic disaster (Brittan, 1975). In some Asian countries it is portrayed as a Western institution with no or little relevance to the region. The debate is not just among those with conflicting ideological perspectives but also among the like-minded, centring on the programmes' objectives and the instruments by which they are best accomplished.

The term "income maintenance" used here is but one among many employed to describe similar arrangements and practices. It is used to describe arrangements designed to maintain income above a socially acceptable level for the poor or preventing a sudden and large decline in the non-poor's income. This is considerably narrower than the most commonly used term, "social security", which is usually meant to include health care and child rearing as well. The most recent addition to the lexicon is the term "social protection", defined to mean "the public actions taken in response to levels of vulnerability, risk and deprivation which are deemed socially unacceptable within a given polity or society" (Norton *et al.*, 2000). The term "social safety net" is perhaps the narrowest of the available alternatives and is understood to describe mechanisms intended to provide a cushion at the point just above the rock bottom. The concept of income maintenance lies somewhere between social protection and social safety net and is the preferred term in this book.

A variety of instruments is available to governments for meeting their citizens' income-maintenance needs but they may be broadly classified into two: Defined Benefits (DB) and Defined Contribution (DC) arrangements (for review, see Gillion *et al.*, 2000; Norton *et al.*, 2000; World Bank, 1994). DB arrangements – which include social insurance and public assistance – specify the form and level of benefit that the covered population is entitled to receive rather than what they have to contribute in order to receive it. DC arrangements, in contrast, specify only what the covered population must contribute: Provident Funds (PFs) and Individual

Retirement Accounts (IRAs) are examples of this form of income-maintenance arrangement. There are, of course, other policy instruments available to governments for maintaining income, but they either maintain income indirectly or are significant only in poorer countries. Such measures include labour-market policies intended to expand gainful employment opportunities, easy credit, and the direct provision of essential goods, either free or at subsidized prices.

Social insurance is a prominent form of DB arrangement which requires contributors – usually employees and their employers though sometimes the government also contributes – to make regular contributions to a fund. The pool of fund thus accumulated is used to pay specified pension or disability benefits. The benefits may be flat or earning-related. The objective of a flat-rate scheme is to maintain a minimum level of income for the target group, usually the elderly and disabled, whereas earning-related schemes pay benefits that bear some relationship to income during the working life with the intention of preventing a sudden sharp fall in income. However, even earning-related schemes usually have some mechanism for redistributing income. All OECD countries except Australia, Ireland, the Netherlands, and New Zealand have some earning-related scheme, while many have both types of scheme. The main advantage of social insurance is that it is able to protect the working population at a relatively modest cost to the insured and (unless the government chooses to contribute) at no cost to the public exchequer. The greatest problem with insurance arrangements is that in every society there are people who are outside formal employment and are therefore outside the insurance net. The problem is particularly acute in developing countries, which tend to have majority of the labour-force engaged in non-wage employment.

Public assistance schemes, on the other hand, pay specified benefits to anyone meeting income or other criteria, such as age, disability, and pregnancy. No contribution is required in order to receive benefits, which are funded directly by the government from its general revenues. The elderly and the disabled often have separate public-assistance programmes, with no or relaxed income criterion. Public assistance arrangement is particularly suited for meeting the needs of those outside formal employment because it does not depend on regular contribution from them. However, the costs of administering an effective public-assistance scheme are high, as is the required administrative capability, which makes it difficult to employ in developing countries.

While DB has been the dominant mode of organizing a statutory social-security system for more than a century, it is DC that has been at the centre of policy debate since the early 1990s. Under the arrangement, the working population is required to set aside a specified portion of its income in a personal savings account, which becomes available for withdrawal at the time of retirement. Funds in one's account may be centrally managed by the government or by private managers chosen by the members themselves – the former being a PF and the latter an IRA.[1] DC schemes are by definition fully funded and, as such, impose no financial responsibility on the government. International economic organizations and mainstream economists prefer DC, especially of the IRA variety, because it involves a lower level of government involvement, promotes savings, boosts national capital markets, and does not adversely affect work incentives (Holzmann and Palacios, 2001; World Bank, 1994). Against such claimed benefits is the fact that DC provides little or no protection to those who have little or no income during their working life – in other words, it does not provide income protection to those who need it the most (Barr, 2002; Thompson, 2001; Orszag and Stiglitz, 1999). As a result, it can only serve as a "second" tier of income-maintenance system, though Malaysia and Singapore have PF arrangements without substantial public assistance to underpin them.

The problem of income maintenance is "modern" in that it is the result of industrialization and the accompanying social and demographic changes. Capitalist industrialization increases economic uncertainties at the same time as it weakens family and community ties that have traditionally protected individuals and families against uncertainties. The ageing of the population that often accompanies industrialization compounds the problem. Urbanization, the proliferation of nuclear families, and the changed role for women further aggravate the problem by undermining the community and family's capacity to look after the aged and the disabled at the same time that there is an increasing need for this type of care.

The NIEs began to experience the problems of income maintenance to varying degrees by the 1960s. As we saw in the preceding chapter, all four of them have experienced rapid industrialization and income growth, urbanization, smaller family units, and ageing of the population. However, the form and extent to which their governments have addressed these socio-economic trends vary considerably. In this chapter we will see that all NIEs have income-maintenance systems that provide some degree of protection for the aged. Korea has established a system that will by the end of the decade provide benefits similar to those found in advanced welfare states. Taiwan too is seriously considering proposals to reinforce its existing system but the political stalemate is delaying its adoption. The two city-states are behind in this regard, though the arrangement in Hong Kong is quite robust by regional standards and is able to cushion households against severe hardships. Singapore offers little statutory protection for its low-income households and there is no substantial effort to reinforce it, though the problems are somewhat mitigated in the short run by its still young population, low unemployment, and high income growth.

Policy history

Hong Kong

The guiding principles and parameters of Hong Kong's social-security system were defined between the mid 1940s and the mid 1960s when the government made it clear that its top concern was economic growth and that social welfare was to be provided primarily by family and voluntary agencies (McLaughlin, 1993: 110). However, the government was unable to avoid getting involved in providing income support in the aftermath of the devastation of World War II. It established the Social Welfare Office (SWO) in 1947 to provide food rations and emergency relief to the very old, disabled, and exceptionally destitute. This was followed by the establishment of the Ministry of Welfare in 1957, in a belated response to the fires that devastated a squatter colony in 1953. But just in case its objectives were misconstrued, the 1965 policy paper "Aims and Policy for Social Welfare in Hong Kong" affirmed the government's commitment to maintaining traditional Chinese values in which people looked after themselves and their families in times of need.

However, calls for expanded social-security programmes, especially for the aged, came to be increasingly heard in the late 1960s. In response, the British government sent Professor Gertrude Williams, a social-administration expert, to visit the colony and recommend changes. She proposed the progressive establishment of a social-insurance scheme for financing health care and income maintenance. A working party set up to act on the report proposed the establishment of a social-insurance scheme supplemented by public assistance, but the proposal was not put into effect (Hong Kong Government, Interdepartmental Working Party, 1967). Instead, the government established a Public Assistance Scheme (PAS) in 1971 (renamed Comprehensive Social Security Assistance Scheme, or CSSA, in 1993). The decision to provide cash benefits was a turning point, as assistance until then had been in the form of food or free medical services.

Commentators describe the 1970s as a "golden era" (Chow, 1982) or a "Big Bang" period for social-policy development in Hong Kong (Chan, 1996; Tang, 1998). The establishment of PAS in 1971 was followed by the Disability and Infirmity Allowance Schemes in 1973, renamed the Special Needs Allowance Scheme in 1979 and, again, the Social Security Allowance Scheme (SSAS) in 1993. The government also published the White Paper on "Social Welfare in Hong Kong: The Way Ahead" in 1973, expressing its commitment to providing public assistance to the poor and "vulnerable" groups, and emergency relief when necessary. The government's expanded commitment was reflected in its spending on social welfare, which increased by 65 per cent in 1974 (Tang, 1998: 62). Subsequently, several new social services for youth, family, and the disabled were added or expanded in 1977.

Yet the government was not willing to assume responsibilities that had traditionally been borne by families. The Working Party on the Future of the Elderly in 1973 recommended that "services should be aimed at enabling the elderly to remain as long as possible as members of the community at large; either living by themselves or with members of their family; rather than at providing the elderly with care in residential institutions outside the community to which they are accustomed". Similarly, the government rejected the 1979 Green Paper recommending the establishment of a semi-compulsory social-insurance scheme for sickness, injury, and death.

Later, in its 1991 White Paper "Social Welfare into the 1990s and Beyond", the government reiterated the importance of maintaining family as the main source of support but also noted its weakening as a result of immigration, relocation to suburban areas, marriage breakdowns, and so on. In his first annual address to the Legislative Council (LegCo) in 1992, Governor Chris Patten declared: "Hong Kong is not a welfare state, but we are a society that cares deeply about the state of welfare." But this was not a commitment to increasing the state's role in welfare, as the family and, to a lesser extent, employers were to continue to play the dominant role. In 1993, the government gazetted the Occupational Retirement Schemes Ordinance (ORSO) to officially recognize and regulate the voluntary occupational schemes that had gradually sprung up over the years. The principle of limited state involvement was even more clearly manifested in the launch of the privately funded Mandatory Provident Fund (MPF) in 1995.

The establishment of the MPF was the final step in a process that began almost four decades earlier. The idea of establishing a compulsory savings scheme was first mooted as early as the late 1950s, following the establishment of provident funds in Malaysia and Singapore (Macpherson, 1993: 51). The government again considered the proposal in 1966, but quickly dismissed it. The proposal was raised in the LegCo in 1975 and again in 1985–1987, but to no avail. The government was ideologically opposed to any compulsory programmes that imposed additional costs on employers (Lui, 1998: 2–3).

But proposals for setting up a DC scheme of some sort would not just go away. A motion calling for the establishment of a government-run savings scheme came to vote before the LegCo in July 1991, but was defeated by 29 votes to 11. Later in the same year, the government established a Working Group on Retirement Protection, which proposed a privately managed compulsory savings scheme in 1992. The document was put out for public consultation but was rejected by the government itself in the following year. Though the government was favourably disposed towards a privately managed scheme, it was reluctant to establish a scheme involving higher risk endemic to private management. Soon after, in

February 1993, the LegCo passed a motion urging the government to adopt a government-run scheme. But it had no binding status, and the government did not act upon it. However, the government could not entirely ignore the motion because the sentiments underlying it enjoyed broad support (Lui, 1998: 4).

The government surprised everyone when it proposed, without advance warning, a pay-as-you-go DB scheme on 15 December 1993. The proposed Old Age Pension Scheme (OPS) was to be funded from a contribution of 2 per cent of income each by employer and employee. It proposed to offer a flat benefit of US$295 per month to everyone above the age of 65 years, regardless of contribution. Business members of the Legislative Council – especially Tung Chee Hwa, who was an Executive Council member at the time – were implacably opposed to the proposal. So was the Beijing government, which saw it as the start of a slippery road to a welfare state, whereas social workers supported the proposal. There was extensive public debate on the proposal in which the government played a high-profile role in defending it. Academic economists took an unusually active role in the foray, publishing a paid advertisement in local newspapers in which they criticized the scheme and expressed their preference for a privately run DC scheme. An opinion survey showed that the public was evenly divided on the proposed OPS. After putting up a vigorous defence for a year, the government retracted the proposal in January 1995.

Two months later, the government announced a proposal for a privately managed MPF that was similar to the one it had rejected in 1993. The MPF law was passed by the legislature after little debate in July of 1995. However, the law set out only general principles that required another set of legislation to put them into effect. The second stage was more contentious, but the formalities were eventually completed in 1998 and the scheme was launched in December 2000. In its publicity materials, the government stated as a matter of fact that the MPF was equitable, because benefits would be proportionate to contribution, as well as efficient, because of its private management. These were controversial claims and certainly not as straightforward as the government suggested.

The adoption of MPF was consistent with the Hong Kong government's efforts since the mid 1990s to reduce its role in social security. After gradually but continuously relaxing the eligibility conditions for public assistance and expanding the benefits for two decades, in the mid 1990s government officials began to express concerns about the rapid growth in the CSSA caseload and expenditure. They were particularly concerned about the sharp increases in the number of people of working age applying for benefits. There was also a widespread public perception, fanned by popular media, that abuse of the system was rampant. The government ordered a review of the CSSA (but not the SSAS), which reported in December 1998 (Hong Kong Government, 1998), and the report noted tersely: "The messages that we aim to get across are 'Any job is better than no job', 'Low pay is better than no pay', and 'CSSA is a safety net and a last resort'" (Hong Kong Government, 1998). Accordingly, the report recommended various coercive and non-coercive measures to shift CSSA recipients to paid employment or even unpaid community work. It also recommended tightening of eligibility conditions and significant reductions in benefits. In a parallel move, the government began to consider imposing a means test for SSAS benefits available to the aged and disabled (*South China Morning Post*, 16 March 2000: 2).

Civil servants are a privileged lot in Hong Kong and this is reflected in their retirement benefits. They have been entitled to pensions since the early years of colonial rule and are currently governed by Pension Benefits Ordinance and Regulations 1987. The scheme is non-contributory and is funded from the government's general revenues. In 1995, the Legislative Council established the Civil Service Pension Reserve Fund (CSPRF), with an initial allocation of US$905 million to meet pension payment in the event that the government did not have the funds to pay from its general revenues; the fund has not had to be used so far.

The government is actively considering replacing the taxpayer-funded civil servants' pension with an MPF-like scheme (*South China Morning Post*, 17 January 2001). However, instead of the 5 per cent that private employers contribute, the government will contribute 25 per cent to its employees' individual accounts. It reckons that the larger contribution would still be lower than its current pension liabilities, although it does raise serious questions of equity.

Singapore

The foundations for social security in Singapore were laid during the British colonial rule and the institutions remain largely intact to this day, and indeed have been strengthened. The centrepiece is the Central Provident Fund (CPF), which serves a range of objectives in income maintenance, health, housing, and overall economic management. Singapore is also remarkable to the extent that it offers *ad hoc* benefits.

In the aftermath of the war and Japanese occupation, poverty and deprivation was widespread on the island in the late 1940s, confirmed in the social survey conducted by the newly formed Department of Social Welfare in 1947. The condition of the unemployed and the aged was particularly distressing because a significant percentage of the population at that time consisted of immigrants who did not have a family to provide support and care. In 1951, the government established the McFadzean Commission to inquire into the feasibility of a retirement scheme. The Commission emphatically rejected the provident fund on the grounds that it would not provide adequate benefits to the target population and instead recommended a contributory pension scheme paying flat subsistence-level benefits.

But the report failed to persuade the government, which went on to promulgate the Central Provident Fund Ordinance in 1953 and to implement it in 1955. The decision was based more on the colonial government's reluctance to establish a programme that might involve significant public expenditure than on a belief in CPF's greater efficiency or effectiveness. In a way, the provident fund offered just what it was looking for: something that would maintain the aged people's income without involving any public expenditure. The fact that Malaysia, with which Singapore had a common labour market, had established such a scheme in 1951 made its adoption all the more convenient (Parrott, 2000).

Soon after the CPF's launch, the government realized its limitations and established the Committee on Minimum Standards of Livelihood, headed by Sydney Caine, which submitted its report in 1957. In the same year, G. J. Brocklehurst from the International Labour Organization arrived to conduct a review of the social-security arrangements in Singapore and recommended reforms. The Caine report recommended the establishment of a contributory social-insurance scheme providing retirement, survivor, and sickness benefits, with unemployment benefits to be included at a later date. It estimated that the premium would be lower than the prevailing CPF contributions because of risk sharing and redistribution. The Brocklehurst report, which was published in the same year as Caine's, also recommended the establishment of a contributory social-insurance scheme in a phased manner, beginning with sickness, maternity, old age, disability, and survivors' benefits, later being expanded to include unemployment benefits. Both reports recommended the strengthening of the public-assistance scheme for those who could not be covered by social insurance. The Committee of Officials, established to study the two reports, presented its recommendations in 1959, largely reiterating the analysis and recommendations of the reports.

However, by 1959 the People's Action Party (PAP) was in office and it was even less keen than the colonial rulers about social insurance (Low and Aw, 1997). Instead of replacing the CPF, it gradually increased the contribution rate and expanded its functions to include provision of housing finance and, later, hospital care.

Singapore is a special case in the region because of its tenacity in resisting the expansion of state provision of income protection and because of the extent to which it has gone to encourage and/or compel individuals to meet contingencies on their own. It offers generous fiscal incentives to encourage families to take care of their aged. It also offers tax concessions to the aged if they continue working after their retirement and to the disabled if they work despite their disability. Similar fiscal concessions are available to adult children who share dwellings with their aged parents and grandparents. Moreover, it encourages families to play the lead role in caring for the disabled, and tax incentives are offered to those who look after their disabled siblings. To address the potential long-term problem of not having enough young people to look after the aged because of the declining rate of marriage and child-bearing, the government runs public campaigns and offers tax incentives amounting to US$88 million in 2001 to encourage people to marry and have many children (*The Straits Times*, 13 September 2002). Double tax deductions on donations to charities have been available since January 2002.

Similar to the efforts in other countries to establish voluntary privately financed schemes, in early 2001 the Singapore government announced the launch of a Supplementary Retirement Scheme (SRS). The scheme allows employees (but not their employers) to make voluntary contributions of up to US$6,353 a year into their personal accounts, which can be invested in a variety of financial instruments excluding property. Contributions and investment gains are exempt from taxes, but half of the withdrawal amount at retirement is subject to tax. The scheme is privately administered by financial institutions approved by the government. Businesses have demanded that they be given the option to contribute to their employees' accounts, but the government has resisted, understandably concerned that businesses will make large tax-exempt contributions in lieu of salary to their more highly paid employees. The scheme is likely to appeal to the high-income earners who are able to take advantage of tax concessions and who have a sufficient cash surplus to put away until the age of 62 years.

Korea

Article 34 of the Korean Constitution declares: "Citizens who are incapable of earning a livelihood due to a physical disability, disease, old age or other reasons shall be protected by the state." However, little was done to put the declaration into practice until the 1980s. Some income-maintenance measures were taken in the 1960s, but they were confined to looking after military personnel and public servants. Schemes for the rest of the population began to be established in the late 1980s, starting with employees of large corporations and then progressively expanding to smaller firms and finally to the informally employed. Now Korea has the entire range of social-security programmes typically found in Western welfare states.

Formal income maintenance in Korea began with the establishment of Government Employees Pension (GEP) scheme in 1960, followed by a separate scheme for military personnel in 1963 and for private school teachers in 1975. The National Welfare Pension Act, establishing a pension scheme for private-sector employees, was passed in 1973 but not acted upon until 1986, purportedly because of adverse economic conditions following the energy crisis. The National Pension Scheme (NPS) was finally launched in 1988, starting with firms employing ten or more workers, extending to firms with five or more in 1992, and to farmers and fishermen in 1995. The final expansion took place in 1999, when it included the urban self-employed, who formed nearly half of the total population. Commenting on the latest expansion, Cha Heung-bong, President of the National Pension Corp (NPC), said that the measure would "set the groundwork of an advanced welfare state, in which everybody could lead a financially stable life through his or her lifetime" (*The Korea Herald*, 24 March 1999).

Major reforms of the NPS were introduced in 1998 as a part of negotiations with the International Monetary Fund (IMF) for financial rescue package (World Bank, 2000: 8). The reforms were undertaken in the context of projections showing that the NPS would begin experiencing deficit in 2025 and the fund would be exhausted by the year 2033. A detailed study of the problem was undertaken by the National Pension Reform Board (NPRB), which recommended deep cuts in benefits, a modest increase in contribution rates, and privatization of fund management. But the government did not heed its recommendations and instead went along with the Ministry of Health and Welfare's (MOHW) recommendation for a steep increase in retirement age and contribution rates, but with only a modest decrease in benefits. Most of the Ministry's recommendations were enacted through an amendment of the National Pension Act on 31 December 1998 (World Bank, 2000: 29). The government subsequently turned its attention to the pension scheme for civil servants, which had been suffering from deficits for a long time. It took a range of measures to raise premiums and tighten eligibility conditions for benefits, although it will be a long time before the reforms begin to show discernible results.

Korea also has had an employer-liability retirement payment scheme since 1961. It originally covered only firms with 30 or more employees, expanded to 16 or more workers in 1975, and eventually to firms with five or more workers in 1989. However, nearly two-thirds of the labour-force are in informal sectors or work in firms employing fewer than five. Although it offers only a small benefit, it will remain the most significant formal source of retirement income for the aged until the NPS begins to pay full benefits in 2008.

In addition, Korea has a public-assistance scheme established under the Livelihood Protection Act of 1961, amended in 1982 and 1999. The scheme (which is now called the Basic Livelihood Security Programme) seeks to maintain a minimum standard of living, although the benefits have been too low to do that. The situation improved following the relaxation of eligibility testing and the increase of benefits in 2000. Significantly, benefits are no longer conditional upon an inability to work. The Minister of Health and Welfare described the latest amendment as a "paradigm shift ... that stresses on the government's responsibility on poverty based on the right of the recipients" (*Korea Times*, 24 August 2000).

With the passage of the Employment Insurance Act in 1993, implemented in 1995, Korea became the first country in the region to establish an unemployment insurance scheme. This was more than three decades after the government first considered, and then quickly rejected, the proposal. In the face of massive unemployment triggered by the economic crisis, the government, employers, and trade unions agreed to expand the scheme in early 1998. This was the government and employers' concession in return for the trade unions' agreement to legislative changes designed to facilitate lay-offs in specified circumstances.

The Korean government has, in addition, made efforts to keep the traditional family intact as a vehicle for providing social protection. Tax incentives, awards, and honorifices are offered to people providing care to elderly relatives (Palley and Usui, 1995: 248). Other social-welfare measures include the provision of counselling, health diagnoses, special fares for the elderly, vocational development, occupational training and guidance, housing, and social services. The government has been encouraging donations for social services since 1975, formalized in the Fund for Social Welfare Services Act 1981, but has achieved only modest success – the campaigns raised US$115 million over five years between 1992 and 1996.

Further, the government has set 2010 as the target year for achieving "welfare society" status, embodied in the document "Welfare Vision 2010" and founded on the principles of "productive welfare". The Minister for Health and Welfare clarified: "Through productive welfare, the government secures the minimum standard of living for the poor and provides assistance to the low-income class through self-support and development programmes" (*Korea Times*, 24 August 2000). The Korean government's discourse on "productive welfare" is similar in tone and content (or the lack thereof!) to the "third way" package proposed by the Blair government in Britain (Kwon, 2002: 25). While reiterating the state's role in social protection, the government also talks of free markets, work incentives, and employment flexibility (Jung and Shin, 2002). In late 2002, the government was at an advanced stage of introducing a US-style occupational pension plan. It is too early to say what, if any, impact the recent reform efforts will have on income protection in Korea.

Taiwan

The origin of many of the current programmes in Taiwan goes back to the time when the Kuomintang (KMT) still ruled all of China. Its "Social Security Principle" of 1945 commits the government to providing, among other things, poor relief and social insurance against accident, old age, death, illness, maternity, and unemployment. The 1947 Constitution contains numerous provisions related to social welfare, of which the most notable for our purposes is Article 155, which commits the government to providing social insurance for the aged and social relief for the old and disabled.

The KMT's social-security commitments were put on the backburner soon after its retreat to the island in 1949. The separate ministries for Social Affairs and Labour Affairs were immediately shrunk to departments under the Ministry of the Interior, indicating the secondary importance the government was to accord to these functions in the following decades. The situation changed only in 1986, when the KMT for the first time lost the election for the two labour representatives in the Legislative Yuan. The government responded by establishing the Council for Labour Affairs with the intention of winning back the seats. But the pressure on the ruling party continued unabated, as the opposition constantly chided the government for its inadequate social policies.

The Labour Insurance (LI) scheme was launched in 1950, as provided for in the constitution. However, it was a scheme of the provincial rather than the central government, and covered only firms with twenty or more employees, reduced to ten or more in the following year. A nationwide Labour Insurance Act was passed in 1958 and implemented in 1960. All manual workers were included in 1965, retail and farm workers employed by firms with ten or more employees in 1970, and workers in all workplaces employing five or more workers in 1979. Despite all the expansion, the scheme still covered only 52 per cent of the labour force and 22 per cent of the population in the late 1980s.

Close on the heels of the launch of LI, the Military Servicemen's Insurance Law was adopted in 1953 and the Government Employees Insurance (GEI) in 1958. Employees of private schools were covered in 1980 and dependents of government employees (for medical insurance only) in 1982. Farmers Insurance (FI) providing health (eliminated after the establishment of National Health Insurance (NHI)), maternity, disability, and funeral benefits was established on a pilot basis in 1985 and on a regular basis in 1989.

Taiwan also has a broad public-assistance scheme, established by the Social Relief Law of 1943, which was replaced by the Social Assistance Law of 1980, which in turn was replaced by the Social Assistance Act of 1997. It requires the provincial and local governments to provide public assistance to those in need. The 1980 amendment introduced income criterion – to be set by local governments – for determining eligibility, unlike the earlier law, which used *causes* of poverty such as age, youth, and disability. The 1997 amendment further relaxed the eligibility conditions for receiving benefits. Now living assistance, medical subsidy, personal accident assistance, and calamity assistance are available to everyone whose income is below the "minimum living expenditure". The 1990s saw the launch of new and expansion of existing programmes for the disabled, aged, and youth. The problem of income maintenance for the unemployed was addressed in 1999 with the introduction of unemployment insurance, which replaces 50 per cent of the income and is available for 6–16 months.

There are also compulsory employer-liability schemes, called the Government Employees Retirement and Compensation Fund (GERCF) for public-sector employees and the Labour Retirement Fund (LRF) for private-sector employees, which were established in 1943 and 1984 respectively. The GERCF used to be non-contributory for public-sector employees but changes implemented in 1996 now require employees to contribute. The LRF scheme is wholly an employer-liability programme in that it requires employers to pay a lump-sum retirement amount to all private-sector employees, except for those in certain service industries and the self- and informally employed. Amendment of the law in 1996 extended coverage to all employed persons receiving regular wages, except those whose working conditions make the application of the law difficult. However, as we shall see later, a large proportion of firms do not provide the required benefits.

The anomalies and inadequacies of piecemeal expansion of retirement programmes led the government, under constant pressure from the opposition on the issue, to consider a fundamental overhaul of the entire old-age security system in the mid 1990s. The Council for Economic Planning and Development (CEPD) published an initial proposal for a National Pension Plan (NPP) in 1995, followed by a more detailed document in 1998. It recommended the introduction of another tier of universal "basic" benefits, the "first pillar" in the World Bank's parlance. The proposed scheme was to be compulsory for everyone between the ages of 25 and 64 years who was not covered by any existing scheme; full benefits were to be available after forty years of contribution. The scheme was to be funded from monthly contributions of 10 per cent of the prevailing benefits, which in turn was set at 50 per cent of Average Consumption Expenditure. The monthly contribution and benefit worked out at US$28 and US$279 respectively in 2000. The benefits were projected to cost US$1.4 billion, equivalent to 0.4 per cent of GDP, in the first year and then to grow rapidly (Chang, 2000: 153). The government was to initially contribute to the benefits paid to those retiring without contributing to the scheme, but its contribution would decline as the current cohort of middle-aged workers retired and the size of the next cohort, who would contribute for 25–40 years before receiving benefits, began to expand. The proposed NPP was scheduled to be launched at the end of 2000, but was postponed because of the additional financial burden on the government arising from the September 1999 earthquake (*Central News Agency*, 7 February 2000).

The election of Chen Shui-bian in March 2000 and his party's election commitment to a non-contributory basic pension threw the proposed scheme off the rails. The new president preferred the payment of US$96 per month to the entire aged population not receiving benefits from any existing schemes for the aged, and not just to the low-income aged as was the case. His proposal was implemented in 2002, despite stiff opposition from the CEPD. It is a non-contributory scheme funded entirely by the government, with funds from its general revenues, lottery fund, and increase in the business tax rate from 5 to 7 per cent. 525,000 people are expected to receive the benefit in the first year of the scheme, at the cost of US$61 million to the government. It is believed that the scheme will gradually shrink as the NPP or another programme adopted in its place matures.

For the second pillar, President Chen prefers the current social-insurance schemes (with defined benefits) to be transformed into a compulsory savings scheme, called the National Pension Savings Insurance, with elements of the Defined Benefits arrangement. The contribution rate will be set at 10 per cent of the full pension benefit, which in turn will be 50 per cent of individual consumption expenditure. Of one's total contribution, 80 per cent will be deposited in one's individual account and the remainder transferred to a common balancing fund. Benefits will commence at the age of 65 years and continue until their individual account is exhausted, when the balancing fund will be used to pay benefits until death.

The proposal for the compulsory savings scheme appears to have broad support within the bureaucracy, though there are misgivings about the payment of benefits to those who have not contributed to the scheme in the initial years. The government's preference for compulsory savings is also reflected in the 2001 amendment of the Labour Retirement Fund (the employer-liability scheme for private-sector workers). The new scheme establishes an Individual Retirement Account for new entrants to the workforce as well as for those changing employment. Under the scheme, employers are required to contribute no less than 6 per cent to their employees' individual accounts; employee contribution is voluntary and is capped at 6 per cent. The accumulated amount may be withdrawn at the age of 60 years.

The Labour Insurance scheme is also being reformed with the objective of extending its coverage and offering monthly annuity rather than lump-sum payment. The contribution rate will be 5.5–6.5 per cent of the wages shared between employer and employee. After 20 years of contribution at the age of 60 years, or 15 years of contribution at the age of 65 years, members will be eligible for benefits equivalent to 0.8–1 per cent (it is yet to be decided) of the insured monthly wage for each year covered by the scheme. Thirty years of contribution to the scheme is projected to yield a monthly annuity of 24–30 per cent (depending on the benefit formula finally chosen) of one's monthly insured salary (*China Post*, 23 April 2002).

Provision

Hong Kong

For the general public in Hong Kong, public assistance (SSAS and CSSA) and compulsory savings (MPF) are the main forms of statutory income maintenance. Civil servants, on the other hand, are beneficiaries of generous government-funded pension schemes, while employees of many of the larger firms benefit from tax-assisted Occupational Retirement Scheme Ordinance (ORSO) benefits.

The SSAS is intended to provide financial assistance to the disabled and the elderly to meet a part of their essential living expenses. Those between the ages of 65 and 69 years are means tested while those who are older are not. For those subject to means testing, the monthly income limit is US$759 and asset limit is US$22,000 for single persons, and US$1,250 and US$33,000 respectively for a married couple.

The SSAS provides "normal" and "higher" levels of benefit according to age or the degree of disability. The normal old-age allowance is US$80 per month, while the higher allowance for those aged 70 years or above is US$90. The normal disability allowance is US$162 per month, while those requiring constant attendance receive US$323 per month. In 1998–1999, the average size of the monthly benefit was US$79 for the Normal Old Age Allowance; US$84 for the Higher Old Age Allowance; US$154 for the Normal Disability Allowance; and US$261 for the Higher Disability Allowance. The number of SSAS cases increased from 294,491 in 1986 to 535,452 in 2000. Of all the cases in 2000, 58 per cent were receiving higher old-age benefits, 25 per cent normal old-age benefits, and 17 per cent disability benefits (Hong Kong Social Welfare Department, 2000).

The CSSA is a means-tested public-assistance scheme for those whose income is insufficient to meet officially "recognized needs". The qualifying condition (in 2002) is income below US$335 for a single, able-bodied adult and assets below a fixed limit, ranging from US$3,077 for an able-bodied adult to US$16,667 in the case of a family of six with a disabled adult. There are three types of benefits under the CSSA: standard, special, and supplementary. The standard benefits are paid to cover the recipients' basic needs and vary widely according to the characteristics of the recipients. This ranges from US$328 per month for an able-bodied adult under the age of 60 years to US$599 for an elderly person requiring constant attendance (as of year 2002). Able-bodied single parents receive US$252 per month, while each of their able-bodied children receive US$230 and their fully disabled child receives US$392. Special grants for housing, medical care, childcare, and education is paid if warranted by individual circumstances. There is also a supplementary allowance of US$33 per month available to single parents.

The average size of the monthly CSSA benefit was US$638 in 1999 (Hong Kong Social Welfare Department, 2000). While the nominal amount of the CSSA benefit has increased over the decades, the growth was slower than the rise in per capita income: the assistance amount for single able-bodied persons as a percentage of per capita GDP declined from 12.8 in 1981, to 10.8 in 1986, to 7.4 in 1992, and then rose to 11.2 in 1998. However, the government claims that the CSSA benefits are too generous compared to low-end wages and regards the scheme as a disincentive for accepting low-wage jobs on the part of the unemployed (Hong Kong Government, 1998).

Hong Kong also has a tax-assisted voluntary occupational scheme provided by employers, called the ORSO scheme. While large firms have been establishing occupational retirement schemes for many decades – there were approximately 1,500 approved retirement schemes at the end of the 1970s (Button, 1995) – it was not until 1993 that the government began to regulate them. The 1993 ordinance requires that all schemes must be fully paid up, that is, accumulated funds must be sufficient to meet liabilities. The schemes may be of defined benefit or defined contribution types – well over 90 per cent have chosen the latter.

The ORSO schemes are intended to be replaced by MPF unless they have been granted exemption on specified grounds. Employers prefer MPF to ORSO because it requires them to contribute only 5 per cent of the wage, which is considerably lower than the amount they would typically contribute to ORSO. The number of registered ORSO schemes more than halved between 1999 and 2001 in anticipation of the launch of MPF and are expected to gradually disappear altogether.

Participation in MPF is compulsory for all employed and self-employed persons in the 18–65 years age bracket, except for those covered by a government pension or exempted ORSO schemes. Hawkers, domestic helpers and expatriates working for less than three months are also excluded. The scheme is portable and allows members changing employers a range of options to leave their accrued benefit with the existing employer or transfer it to the new employer, or deposit it with a registered MPF provider of their choice. The government prescribes a list of permissible investments for MPF and sets stringent conditions for fund management, which is understandable considering that the retirement income of members would depend on how much return the managers are able to deliver without taking unusually high risks. However, each fund must offer a range of choices, with the final choice left to individual members. To cater to members with lower tolerance to risk, fund managers are required to offer a "capital preservation product", which involves a lower risk but also lower returns.

The accumulated funds in one's MPF account may only be withdrawn at the age of 65 years, or 60 years in case of early retirement. Contribution to, returns on, and withdrawal from MPF are exempt from taxes. However, the tax treatment is not as generous as might appear because of low-income tax rates and the absence of capital-gains tax in Hong Kong. The MPF Authority projects that those currently earning US$1,282 a month (hence contributing US$128 a month to MPF) after 40 years of contribution will receive US$75,641 under conditions of a 1 per cent annual rate of net investment return and US$151,453 under conditions of a 4 per cent annual rate of net investment return (http://www.mpfahk.org/eng/employee/5a_1.htm).

The civil servants' pension scheme provides a monthly old-age pension to the maximum of two-thirds of the highest monthly salary during one's working life upon retirement (which is normally at the age of 60 years) and after at least ten years of service. The pension amount is annually adjusted according to the consumer price index (http://www.hku.hk/hkgcsb/9-2-5.htm). The scheme also provides for a disability pension equivalent to the retirement pension. Death gratuity and ex-gratia payment is paid to the nominated spouse if the deceased employee has at least two years' qualifying service and dies while in service.

Private-sector workers are also eligible for a Long Service Payment at the time of retirement. However, the amount is modest: while the actual amount determined by the length of continuous service with the firm, the maximum benefit is capped at US$1,903.

Singapore

There is little state provision of income maintenance in Singapore, except for pensions for select government officials and public-assistance for the very poor. Provision instead takes the form of regulation of employers and employees to compulsorily save for retirement.

The centrepiece in the income-maintenance system in Singapore is the CPF. Participation is compulsory for employed persons, except for foreign workers (who form a fifth of the labour force), casual and part-time workers, and certain categories of contract workers. Self-employed are required to participate in the medical component of the scheme and may participate in the overall scheme on a voluntary basis, though only a small percentage have chosen to do so.

CPF benefits consist of the sum of the members' own and their employers' contributions – amounting to 40 per cent of monthly salary but recently reduced to 33 per cent – incomes from the investments in their account, and any *ad hoc* contributions ("top-up") the government may make. Reflecting the CPF's multi-purpose role, members' accounts are divided into three separate sub-accounts: Ordinary, Special, and Medisave. The Ordinary Account holds 60–75 per cent, depending on age, of one's CPF funds. The Special Account holds 10–20 per cent, and another 15–20 per cent is channelled to the Medisave Account. Funds in the Ordinary Account earn interest at a rate tied to the rates offered by local banks, subject to a minimum rate of 2.5 per cent per annum. Funds in the Special and Medisave Accounts earn an additional 1.5 percentage points, or a minimum rate of 4 per cent per annum. The balance in the Ordinary Account is used mainly to buy housing and other investment products, whereas that in the Medisave Account is reserved for health care. The Special Account alone is exclusively for retirement, as the funds in it may only be withdrawn at the age of 55 years.

Withdrawal of one's CPF balance is permitted at 55 years of age. Since 1987, however, it has been compulsory to leave a minimum sum to ensure that members do not fritter away their savings in the early years of their retirement. The minimum sum in 2003 is US$47,000, of which half must be in cash and the rest in property. The amount is released in instalments from the age of 62 years. The member may, alternatively, use the entire sum to buy a life annuity with an insurance company or make a deposit in a bank. The balance, if any, is returned to survivors in the event of the member's death.

Before retirement, members may withdraw funds from the CPF account to purchase housing or approved investment products, or to pay for health, higher education, home insurance, and survivors' insurance. However, only the sum above the "minimum sum" may be invested in the stock markets, and usually only through approved mutual funds (called unit trusts). Such withdrawals form a large chunk of CPF funds. Indeed, of the total withdrawal of US$7.6 billion (including transfer to minimum sum) in 1999, only 14 per cent was for retirement purposes.

There has existed a publicly funded pension scheme for civil servants since the early days of colonial rule. The eligibility criteria for participating in the scheme have, however, been progressively tightened, and among the new employees only senior officials in the civil service, armed forces, judiciary, and legislature are eligible for pension. The maximum monthly pension amount is set at two-thirds of the pensionable component of the last-drawn pay for those with at least 33.3 years of service. However, all salary revisions since 1984 have been non-pensionable, as a result of which the pensionable component has fallen to only one-half of the total salary (*The Straits Times*, 5 July 2000).

The defence personnel's retirement benefits were improved considerably with the establishment of the Savings and Employee Retirement Plan Scheme (SAVER) to replace their pension scheme in March 1998. The length of employment condition (33.3 years) for receiving a full pension was believed to be inappropriate for military personnel, whose working career typically lasts only 23 years. The SAVER is a defined contribution scheme (unlike the pension, which is of a defined benefits type) to which the government contributes 13–20 per cent (depending on the length of service, rank, and whether the person is in a combat position or not) of the gross monthly salary. The amount is in addition to the contribution that the government makes to the CPF as an employer. The balance in one's SAVER account may be withdrawn at retirement between the ages of 40 and 45 years. The benefits are more generous than those available to private workers covered under CPF and are intended to encourage military officers to stay in service for 20–25 years and retire at the age of 40–45, with benefits similar to their civilian counterparts retiring at the age of 60 years.

Public assistance in Singapore is available only to those who are unable to work for a justifiable reason – age, illness, disability, or unfavourable family circumstances – and have no means of subsistence and no one to depend on. In other words, assistance is available only to "deserving" cases living in abject poverty and with no family member who may provide financial support. In 2000, the monthly public-assistance rates were US$111 (6 per cent of per capita GNP) for single adult households and US$312 for households consisting of two adults and two children.

The Singapore government also gives out cash and tax benefits on an *ad hoc* basis for various purposes. Since the mid 1990s, the government has periodically "topped up" Medisave Accounts and offered "one-off" across the board tax allowances. A rebate of 10 per cent on individual income tax was offered in 1997, 5 per cent in 1998, and 10 per cent in 1999. In 2000, the government topped up all CPF accounts by between S$500 and S$1,700, with the highest amount for low-income earners. There are many other payments the government makes towards rent and utility bills, but they are discretionary payments that do not impose long-term commitment on the government.

To encourage people to look after their family members, up to US$2,647 for each dependant (up to two) may be claimed as tax relief for taxpayers living with their dependants or spending at least US$882 a year on them. The dependant may be the individual's or spouse's parent, grandparent or great-grandparent, who is either at least 55 years of age or who is physically or mentally disabled. Members are also allowed to contribute to their parents' and grandparents' CPF accounts up to a maximum of the prevailing minimum sum requirement – such contributions are exempt from income tax.

Korea

The Korean income-maintenance system consists of social insurance, employer-liability, and public-assistance schemes. Social insurance consists of the National Pension Scheme (NPS) for private-sector workers, and separate occupational schemes for civil servants, private school teachers and military personnel. There is also an unemployment insurance scheme.

The NPS pays old-age, disability, and survivors' benefits in the form of monthly pensions to those meeting its age and contribution conditions. The full old-age pension is available upon reaching 60 years of age, but this will be raised to 61 years in 2013 and eventually to 65 years by 2033 (*The Korea Herald*, 1 April 1999). The full pension is available after 20 years of contribution, and the partial pension after 10–19 years of contribution. For those contributing for less than 10 years, contribution plus interest is returned as a lump sum. As the NPS was introduced only in 1988, and then expanded gradually, most of the current retirees and those retiring in the near future will not be receiving monthly pensions but a lump-sum refund.

The pension benefit consists of a basic pension (BP) amount and an additional pension amount (APA). The BP amount depends largely on the member's monthly income and years of contribution. The benefit formula yields a maximum pension benefit of 60 per cent (reduced from 70 per cent in 1998) of the final salary before retirement. The APA varies according to the type and the number of dependants, including whether the pensioner has a spouse, children (up to two), or aged or disabled parents (including the spouse's parents).

The Government Employees' Pension scheme promises more generous benefits, equal to 50 per cent of the final-year salary for 20 years of service plus 2 per cent of the final salary per year of service up to a maximum of 33 years. These add up to a maximum pension of 76 per cent of the final salary. The premium is insufficient to cover the generous benefits, leading to large deficits that have been covered by the government from its general revenues. The government recently tightened the eligibility conditions and benefit formula with the objective of reducing the deficit. The reforms will not, however, eliminate the large deficit (Won 900 billion in 2000) in the near future (*The Korea Herald*, 10 October 2000).

In the private sector, the Labour Standards Act of 1953, as amended in 1975 and 1989, requires firms employing five or more workers to pay a lump-sum amount equal to at least one month's average salary for each year of employment. The payment is made when an employment ceases for any reason and, as such, most of the payment is for employees merely changing jobs rather than for retirement. It is thus a severance rather than a retirement scheme. Nevertheless, this is currently the principal source of income for most retirees in Korea and will continue to be so until the NPS matures. According to a 1991 survey, employers on an average wage are paid benefits equal to 23.3 months of wages after 20 years of service and 34.4 months of wages after 30 years of service (Lee, 1997: 76). It is estimated that the scheme provides replacement income of 15 per cent of the final year's income after 20 years of service and 23 per cent after 30 years of service (An and Kim, 1994: 43). Government employees, in comparison, receive benefits equivalent to 60 per cent of their final monthly salary for each year of service (World Bank, 2000: 23).

The Employment Insurance System has three components: the Employment Stabilization Scheme to boost demand for labour; the Job Skills Development Scheme for improving labour supply; and the Unemployment Insurance Scheme. Thus, in addition to maintaining income during unemployment, it also seeks to enhance employment skills and promote employment stability though active labour-market measures. Hence the name "employment" rather than "unemployment" insurance. The scheme initially covered only employees in firms with 30 or more workers, but in 1998 was extended to firms with five or more workers, temporary workers employed for at least one month, and part-time employees working more than 18 hours a week. It still leaves out a large number of workers because of its exclusion of employees of firms with fewer than five workers (who together form about 45 per cent of all employed persons in the country), public officials, private school teachers (these two groups enjoying exceptional security of employment), new workers over 60 years of age, and all workers over the age of 65 years (International Labour Organization, 1998).

The unemployment benefit is 70 per cent (increased from 50 per cent in March 1998) of the worker's earnings during the month immediately preceding unemployment, to the maximum of W35,000 per day, which is well above the national average non-agricultural earnings (International Labour Organization, 1998). By imposing a ceiling on benefit but not contribution, the scheme allows some vertical redistribution of income. The duration of unemployment benefit depends both on the length of the insured period and on the person's age: the minimum is two months for those under 30 years of age who have been insured for one to three years, and the maximum is seven months for those over 50 years age and insured for over ten years.

Public assistance until recently was available only to persons who could not earn a living because of disability, illness, or age and, in addition, did not have family members capable of providing support. The conditions were overly stringent and their limitations became apparent during the 1997–1998 economic crisis, when many able-bodied persons found themselves unemployed or under-employed, were not eligible for unemployment benefits, but yet could not receive public assistance. The condition was finally removed in October 2000. Now, those with monthly income below the government-set minimum cost of living – equivalent to 38 per cent of the median wage earner's household income – regardless of their age or ability to work are eligible for public assistance up to the amount by which their income falls short. However, applicants must meet stringent conditions based on income, assets, and the ability of the extended family to help.

The low-income aged – those aged 65 years above and meeting the criteria set out under the Livelihood Protection Act – have also received the Old Age Allowance since 1991. The benefit is US$29 per month (in 1998) for those between the ages of 65 and 79 years and US$36 (roughly equivalent to one-half of the official poverty line) for those over 80 years. In addition, beneficiaries receive in-kind provisions of food and fuel, the average cash value of such in-kind benefits being around US$186 per month (World Bank, 2000: 2).

Since 1994, the government has offered tax exemption on contribution up to US$1,245 per year to personal pension plans, which has made them increasingly popular among the middle and upper classes. To qualify for tax deduction, the individual must contribute for at least ten years and cannot withdraw the funds until reaching the age of 55 years. Anecdotal evidence suggests a typical contribution of 2–5 per cent of salary. By June 1996, the total value of these accounts was estimated at US$13.4 billion or almost 3 per cent of GDP (World Bank, 2000: 7).

Taiwan

Taiwan is similar to Korea in that it relies on an array of social-insurance, employer-liability, and public-assistance programmes. Its social-insurance schemes are similarly divided by occupation. But, as mentioned earlier, the programmes are in the process of being changed as of late 2003.

Government Employment Insurance (GEI) covers all government employees, including those in provincial and local governments, while Labour Insurance (LI) covers all private-sector workers in firms employing more than five workers as well as workers with no definite employer if they belong to a craft union. Farmers' Insurance (FI) covers farmers over the age of 65, excluding those benefiting from other retirement programmes or owning non-farm real estate worth over US$160,000, or who have an annual non-farm income in excess of the minimum wage (US$6,118 in 1996). There is also a separate Insurance for Teachers and Staff of Private Schools (ITASPS) – employees of government schools are covered under GEI – and yet another plan for military personnel (MI). All schemes except the LI cover the dependants of the primary member.

The schemes were originally designed mainly to provide health insurance and their income-maintenance component was insignificant, but this changed with the establishment of separate health insurance in 1995, which made income maintenance their main purpose. They all provide disability, old-age, and death benefits, but the LI also provides maternity, sickness, and (since 1999) unemployment benefits, while the FI also provides a funeral allowance. All programmes pay the benefit in a lump sum and the maximum old-age benefits are available only at the age of 65 years.

The old-age benefits under GEI and ITASPS are based on the member's years of service and the salary just before retirement. The formula for calculating the benefits is complex. GEI/ITASPS benefits range from ten times the final monthly salary for contributions of ten years to 36 times for contributions of 20 years or more. The benefits were originally designed to be paid as a lump sum, but members were later offered the option of being paid monthly for the remainder of their life – the increasing popularity of the monthly payment option has ballooned expenditures (Tsui, 2002: 199). LI benefits are equal to one month's average wage in the last three years of employment for each year of contribution for the first 15 years, and an additional month's wage for each year of contribution thereafter, to a maximum of 50 months.

The employer-liability retirement schemes for government employees (GERCF) and military personnel provide retirement benefits as a lump sum or in monthly instalments. The benefits range from 75 per cent of their last income for 15 years of service to 90 per cent for 35 years of service.[2] The monthly option is more attractive as it can generate a monthly pension amount of up to 120 per cent of the final salary. The scheme for private-sector workers (LRF) provides only lump-sum payment at the age of at least 55 years to those who have worked continuously for the same employer for at least 15 years, or to those who have worked continuously for the same employer for at least 25 years regardless of age. The benefit amount is calculated by multiplying the employee's average monthly wage in the final six months of employment by the service unit.[3] The benefit for both public- and private-sector employees is exempt from taxes, as is employer contribution up to a maximum of 15 per cent of a firm's yearly wage bill.

Regardless of the law, most private-sector workers do not receive anything from LRF, as most small and medium-sized firms do not comply with the law. In 1999, only around 8 per cent of firms employing 40 per cent of all employed persons were maintaining the required scheme (DGBAS, 2000). Even then, most of the workers in firms with the scheme will not receive any benefit because of the requirement to work for the same employer for 15–25 years.

Furthermore, Taiwan has a broad public-assistance system consisting of living allowance for low-income families and students, medical assistance, and subsidy for education and festivals. The means test is quite harsh and the benefits low, despite improvements in recent years. In the mid 1990s, the public-assistance benefit rate was increased to US$115 per month for each person in medium-low income families (defined as family income of 1.5–2.5 times the poverty line) and US$230 for low-income families (family income of up to 1.5 times the poverty line). The poverty line is set at 60 per cent (it was 40 per cent until 1998) of the average individual consumption expenditure in the locality in question. By this measure, the poverty line for Taipei was a monthly income of US$350 in 2000, compared to US$282 in 1998 and US$151 in 1990. The unemployed too have been eligible for public assistance since 1993. An amount of up to US$400 per month is available for up to four months to the head of the household who loses her or his job as a result of company shutdown (*China Economic News Service*, 22 June 1994).

All aged farmers and fishermen have received allowances since August 1995, with the eligibility conditions relaxed in subsequent years. Initially, those with property assets worth over US$156,240 or those receiving pensions from other schemes were excluded, which meant that only 40 per cent of the aged population qualified for these benefits. The qualification was, however, removed in 1998 and now all aged farmers and fishermen receive a monthly stipend of US$97 without means testing.

Comparative

There are marked differences in the basic structures of providing income maintenance in the four NICs (see Table 3.1). Hong Kong relies mainly on public assistance, Singapore on provident funding, and Korea and Taiwan on social insurance, supplemented by employer liability. Public assistance is

INCOME MAINTENANCE

Table 3.1 Social security arrangements in the NIEs

	Government-financed	Compulsory savings	Social insurance	Employer-liability
Hong Kong	Public assistance: SSA and CSSA Pension for civil servants	MPF	–	ORSO – optional
Singapore	Public Assistance Pension for civil servants.	CPF	–	Supplementary retirement scheme – optional
Korea	Public Assistance Additional benefits for aged poor Grants to social insurance schemes	–	Separate schemes for military, civil servants, private-sector employees, self-employed	Labour Standards Act – compulsory
Taiwan	Public Assistance Additional benefits for the aged Grants to social insurance schemes	–	Separate schemes for military, civil servants, private-sector employees, self-employed	Labour Standards Act – compulsory, but many loopholes

available in all NIEs, though Hong Kong is the only one that uses it as the primary instrument. Social insurance patterned after the Japanese system (which in turn is similar to the German system) is the key income-maintenance mechanism in Korea and Taiwan. Singapore used to be the only country among the four NIEs that relied mainly on provident fund, but now Hong Kong has followed it, though it will be many years before it begins to play a significant role. Taiwan is in the throes of establishing a compulsory savings scheme and there are talks of establishing one in Korea too, though the likelihood is remote in the near future.

The employer-liability schemes in Korea and Taiwan are unusual in that they are mandatory. Such schemes in Hong Kong and Singapore are voluntary, as is normally the case in the industrialized economies. What further distinguishes the schemes in Korea and Taiwan is that only the employer is required to make the entire contribution – again unlike the situation in the industrialized economies, where the contribution is shared between the employer and the employee.

Public assistance is the primary source of statutory income maintenance in Hong Kong and the public source of last resort in the other NIEs.

However, the conditions attached to receiving benefits vary greatly, as is shown in Table 3.2. Singapore has by far the harshest conditions, whereby to receive public assistance one needs to be able to demonstrate abject poverty and no capacity to earn income in addition to a lack of family members able to provide financial support. Hong Kong has rather relaxed conditions for the aged and the disabled but harsh conditions for the rest. There is no means test for those above 70 years of age, and those between the ages of 65 and 69 years need to be on an income of less than 38 per cent of per capita GDP to receive SSAS benefits. In contrast, CSSA requires one to be on an income of less than 17 per cent of GDP to receive benefits. Taiwan's is a comparatively generous system, which pays benefits to those with an income of up to 33 per cent of per capita GDP; there is no means test for aged farmers and fishermen. The Korean public-assistance system is the least stringent among the four NIEs in that all those with an income below 35 per cent of per capita GDP are eligible for benefits.

The conditions for receiving benefits under the social-insurance schemes in Korea and Taiwan vary considerably by occupation and are therefore difficult to compare. However, generally speaking, the requirements for receiving retirement benefits are somewhat more relaxed than in the industrialized economies. This probably just refects the privileged position of the workers covered by the existing schemes.

The value of income-maintenance benefits also vary tremendously across the NIEs. As Table 3.3 shows, the benefits are not always as low as is commonly believed, and in some instances the income they generate is considerably higher than the replacement income of 40 per cent recommended by the ILO Convention 102 (1952). The public-assistance scheme for the poor in Hong Kong is the most generous in that the benefits may rise to as

Table 3.2 Key qualifying conditions for public assistance

	Aged	*Low-income*
Hong Kong	Monthly income below US$758 (38% of per capita GDP) for singles aged 65–70 years. No means test for 70 years and above	Monthly income below US$335 (17% of per capita GDP) for a one-person family
Singapore	Unable to earn for a justifiable reason, no income, and no family able to support	
Korea	>65 years	Monthly income below US$269 (35% of per capita GDP)
Taiwan	No means test for aged farmers and fishermen	Monthly income below US$558 (33% of per capita GDP) in 2000.

INCOME MAINTENANCE

Table 3.3 Income maintenance benefits

	Public assistance, amount as % of per capita GDP[1]	Social insurance, maximum amount	Compulsory employer liability, maximum amount
Hong Kong	Aged: 40–45, depending on age	–	–
	Poor: 16–30, depending on age, physical condition, etc.	–	
Singapore	Poor: 6 for singles, including aged	–	–
Korea	Aged: 4 for 65–79-year-olds	GEI and MI: 76% of final salary, monthly	One month average salary for each year of employment
	Poor: 15 maximum	NPS: 60% of final salary after 40 years of contribution, monthly	
	Aged poor receive both		
Taiwan	Aged farmers and fishermen: 8	GEI: 36 times the final monthly salary, lump-sum benefit	Government employees: 106 times the final monthly salary, may be paid in monthly instalments
	Poor: 16	LI: 50 times the average monthly salary in last 3 years of employment, lump-sum benefit	Private employees: 45 times the final monthly salary, paid as lump sum

Notes
Provident funds in Hong Kong and Singapore are omitted because the benefits equal one's contribution plus returns.
1 Amount actually paid is usually lower because of various conditions for benefits.

much as 30 per cent of per capita GDP. A similar scheme in Singapore is the least generous in that the benefits are only 6 per cent of per capita GDP. The situation is a lot better in Korea and Taiwan, where the poor can expect to receive as much as 16 per cent of per capita GDP in benefits.

Social-insurance and compulsory employer-liability programmes exist only in Korea and Taiwan. Social-insurance for the aged is meaningful only in Korea but is yet to mature and provide full benefits, while the one in Taiwan is not universal and provides only patchy benefits, though the benefits for government employees are exceptionally generous. The employer-liability scheme in Taiwan, however, is the one that is most inequitable, in that the benefits for government employees are many times higher than those available to private-sector workers. In fact, most private-sector workers receive nothing at all from the employer-liability scheme.

Financing

Hong Kong

The government's general revenues are the main source of financing for statutory income maintenance in Hong Kong, but this will gradually change as the MPF matures. The government's expenditure on income maintenance increased by more than 10 times between 1985 and 2000, from US$334 million to US$3.6 billion. The composition of the expenditure also changed considerably: the CSSA formed only 40 per cent of the total income-maintenance expenditure in 1985, but by 2000 its share had risen to 64 per cent, while the SSAS's share fell from 57 to 19 per cent. The CSSA expenditures are expected to continue to rise in the years to come despite government efforts to tighten eligibility and reduce benefits because of increasing poverty, unemployment, and single-parenthood. The expenditure on programmes related to emergency relief, law enforcement, injuries compensation, and traffic accident victims' assistance has remained negligible over the entire period.

Public expenditures on the pension schemes for government employees have risen fast, increasing from US$95 million in 1998 to US$1.2 billion in 2000. This was a rise of 31 per cent over two years, compared to only an 8 per cent increase in the number of pensioners, indicating that the recipients were receiving larger payments (Hong Kong Government, 2000). Although much of the scheme is still largely funded by the government, government employees have been required since 1993 to contribute 3.5 per cent of their salary to the Surviving Spouse and Children's Pensions Scheme (Hong Kong Government, 2000).

Participation, and the level of contribution, in ORSO schemes is voluntary for employers. Employers typically contribute 10 per cent of their employee's salary to the scheme and later deduct the contribution amount from their taxable income. Employee contribution, if any, is also exempt from income taxes. In 1999, all ORSO schemes together received US$3 billion in contribution, of which 76 per cent was by employers and 24 per cent by employees. The schemes held US$18 billion in assets, of which 42 per cent was in defined contributions and 58 per cent in defined benefits schemes. Of all the schemes, 73 per cent had an asset size of less than US$257,700, and 92 per cent of less than US$1.3 million, a modest sum for a retirement scheme (http://www.mpfahk.org/eng/orso/7_5.htm).

The MPF scheme requires the contribution of 10 per cent of wages, divided evenly between employee and employer, except for the self-employed, who contribute only 5 per cent. The minimum monthly income for contribution is US$513 and the maximum is US$2,564. For an employee with a monthly salary below the minimum, the employer pays its share but not the employee. Contribution by both employers and employees are tax deductible, up to US$1,540 per year for the employee and up to 15 per cent of the salary for the employer (http://www.mpfahk.org).

Expenditure on social services has increased over the years and stood at US$1.2 billion in 2000, which was about one-third of the government's total social-welfare expenditure. A significant proportion of the social services is directed through voluntary agencies in Hong Kong: 22 per cent of the government's recurrent welfare expenditure in 1998–1999 was allocated to 184 non-government organizations providing social services of various kinds (Hong Kong Government, 1999).

Singapore

The government's main income maintenance expenditures are, mostly, on civil servants' pensions and, to a lesser degree, on public assistance. There are also large sums involved in the various tax incentives for social purposes, but their true magnitude remains unknown.

The Singapore government, according to official statistics, spent US$286 million on social security in 1997. The actual expenditure is considerably smaller because official data include many "community development" and "sports" expenditures. If one looks only at the expenditure of the Family Support Services Division[4] – the unit dealing with income maintenance – the amount spent on income maintenance was only US$116 million in 1997 (Singapore Government, various years).

The official data on social-security expenditures does not, however, include the relatively large sum spent on pensions for government officials: US$487 million in benefits in 1999 and US$119 million a decade earlier (Singapore Government, various years). It also excludes the contribution of US$121 million to the SAVER scheme for military personnel in 1999. The expenditure on civil servants' pensions is thus twice as much as the amount the government spent on income maintenance for the general population. The expenditures are likely to grow much larger before they will begin to decline as a result of the recent tightening of eligibility conditions. To ensure that pensions were not eroded in the future by adverse economic or political circumstances, in 1995 the government established a separate trust fund financed from the general budget, which had accumulated a balance of US$6.2 billion by 1999.

The CPF is entirely funded by the workers themselves and their employers. The CPF contribution rate began with 5 per cent each in 1955, creeping up to 10 per cent each in 1970, and reaching the peak of 25 per cent each in 1984. In 1986, the employers' contribution was reduced to 10 per cent to ease business costs in the face of economic recession. In subsequent years the rate for employers was gradually pushed up while that for employees was pushed down slightly, until it reached 20 per cent each in 1994. The government has maintained 40 per cent of wages, shared equally by the employer and employee, as the target CPF contribution rate, but in 2003 the rate was reduced to 33 per cent, with the employer contributing 13 per cent, and the employee contributing 20 per cent. To reduce the cost of hiring older workers – whose continued employment is vital in a labour-scarce economy – in 1988 a lower contribution rate was set for workers older than 55 years and one yet lower for those over 60 years.

The CPF received US$7.5 billion in contributions in 1999 and the total accumulated balance stood at US$52 billion. Since the amount withdrawn from CPF is really one's personal fund, similar to one's savings in a bank except that CPF is compulsory, it is not counted as "public expenditure". In 1999, 63,974 members reaching the age of 55 years withdrew or reserved in their minimum sum account a total sum of US$760 million, an average of US$11,972 per member (CPF Statistics, http://www.cpf.gov.sg/cpf_info/home.asp). CPF withdrawal amounts are to cover the entire period of retirement. Considering that the average life span in Singapore is 76 years, the simple monthly amount per member living up to the average age after the age of 55 years is only US$48.

Korea

Total government expenditure on income maintenance[5] increased by 179 per cent in real terms between 1990 and 1998, at constant 1995 prices. The increase was, of course, even more spectacular at current prices, from US$3.3 billion to US$9.9 billion (OECD, 2002). The largest share of the expenditure is, as expected, towards old-age benefits: 46 per cent of the total in 1990 and 62 per cent in 1998. However, nearly 72 per cent of the total old-age benefits in 1998 were accounted for by benefits for civil servants, military personnel, and school teachers, though this was a decline from 96 per cent in 1990. In future, expenditure on unemployment benefits is projected to increase rapidly, but pension expenditures will increase yet more rapidly, especially after 2008 when the first group of NPS members becomes eligible for full pensions.

The contribution rate for the NPS is 9 per cent of the wages (it was 3 per cent until 1992 and 6 per cent until 1998), shared evenly between employer and employee. The contribution rates for the self-employed, farmers, fishermen, and the voluntarily insured was 3 per cent of the standard monthly income – defined as the average monthly income of all insured persons – until June 2000. Then it was raised by 1 percentage point and will be raised by 1 percentage point each year until it reaches 9 per cent in the year 2005. The government subsidizes one-third of the premium for poor farmers and fishermen, and they themselves pay the remainder. The contribution rate for the schemes for government employees, school teachers, and military personnel has also increased over the years: the combined total rate was 4.6 per cent when the scheme was established in 1960 but it now stands at 17 per cent, shared equally between employer (that is, the government) and employee. For school teachers, however, the premium is shared three ways between the employer (30 per cent), the employee (50 per cent), and the government (20 per cent).

The NPS's annual revenues increased from US$5.4 billion in 1994 to US$8.4 billion in 1998, of which 71 per cent was from contributions and the remainder from investment returns. Total expenditures – which were for the most part refunds of members' contributions – were only 18 per cent of total revenues over the five years, leaving the fund with an increasingly large surplus. By 1999 the scheme had accumulated a reserve of about US$39.5 billion, which is more than 10 per cent of Korea's GDP and is projected to reach 70 per cent of GDP by 2030. In fact, the reserves may reach 100 per cent of the GDP if the contribution rate is increased to match the benefits promised by the scheme, which it must or else it will begin to run deficits by 2037 and will be completely depleted by 2049 (World Bank, 2000: 6). The National Pension Corporation has proposed that the premium be gradually doubled to 18 per cent by 2033 to avert collapse. If the government does increase the premium, the resulting size of the fund would be unprecedented in the international experience for a public pension fund and would make it one of the largest players in the international capital markets.

The financial position of the schemes for civil servants and military personnel is worse than the NPS as a result of low contribution rates combined with generous benefits. Indeed, the scheme for military personnel began to experience deficit in 1972 and has had to rely on transfers from the government to meet its obligations. The main problem is that military personnel retire early (around 45 years of age), and their premium is not high enough to pay pensions over three to four decades of retirement (Yoo, 1993: 492–493). The scheme for civil servants also began to run deficits in 1999 and will peak at 3 per cent of GDP in 2030, when it will start declining as a result of the recent reforms (World Bank, 2000: 23). It is still too early to assess the financial situation of the scheme for the urban employed, but its deficit is likely to be large because of under-reporting of income and the difficulties in assessing income.

The employer-liability retirement scheme requires payment of a sum equivalent to one month of final salary for each year of employment and is entirely funded by employers. However, employers are not required to make monthly contributions to a separate account and usually make the payment from their operating revenues. The total employer payment towards this scheme amounts to 8.3 per cent of gross wages (World Bank, 2000).

A combined maximum premium of 3 per cent of wages (1.5 per cent until February 1998) is allowed for the three components of the Employment Insurance System. The current premium is 0.3 per cent of wages for the Employment Stabilization scheme, and 0.1–0.7 per cent (depending on the size of the firm) for the Job Skill Development scheme: both premia are paid entirely by employers. The Employment Insurance scheme is funded by a premium of 1 per cent of wages (0.6 per cent until 1998), split evenly between the employer and employees.

The unemployment scheme too is running in deficit: in 1998 it received US$679 million in revenues but spent US$670 million (Korea, 2000). While in this instance it was the result of increased unemployment following the economic crisis, the trend may well continue because of the higher incidence of unemployment that may result from the government's policy of promoting labour-market flexibility.

Taiwan

Public spending on income maintenance in Taiwan consists of expenditures from the general revenues of the central, provincial, and local governments as well as social-insurance funds. However, the data for the period up to 1985 include a variety of items unrelated to income maintenance (Ku, 1998: 34). Even after that period, social-insurance data are maintained in such a way that income maintenance is often inseparable from health. Another problem is that published data usually exclude expenditure from employer-liability programmes, which seriously underestimates public expenditures on income maintenance.

Keeping the data limitations in mind, total public expenditure on income maintenance and social services has grown rapidly since 1950. Government expenditures (at all levels) on social welfare increased at an average annual rate of 42 per cent during the 1950s, 19 per cent during the 1960s, 17 per cent during the 1970s, 19 per cent during the 1980s, and 17 per cent during the 1990s (Ku, 1997: 42–43; DGBAS, 2000a). Accordingly, net public expenditures on "social welfare"[6] increased from US$9 billion in 1992 to US$14 billion in 1999.

A disproportionately large share of the public expenditure on income maintenance is, more than in Korea, directed at civil servants, military personnel, and school teachers: their employer-liability pension alone amounted to 42 per cent of the total in 1999. In comparison, social insurance (including GEI and MI) and social welfare services attracted 26 per cent each of the government's total social-security expenditure in 1999, whereas public assistance attracted only 5 per cent (DGBAS, 2000). The government and military personnel's pension would have attracted a yet larger share, were it not for the reforms adopted in the 1990s. Requiring employees (including school teachers and the military) to contribute to their Government Employees' Retirement Fund alone saved the government about US$4.7 billion during the 1996–1999 period. As a result of the changes, total government expenditure on income maintenance (excluding NHI) declined from US$12 billion in 1996 to US$2 billion in 1999.

The overall decline took place despite an increase in transfers to social-insurance programmes during the period.

The social-insurance schemes are meant to be entirely funded by contributions from employers and their employees, but this is not the case in reality as the schemes run large deficits. The current insurance premium is 6.4 per cent of the monthly "insured" salary (which is approximately 80 per cent of the total salary) for GEI, 8 per cent for MI, and 4.75 per cent for ITASPS; the premium for dependants is 3–5 per cent of the primary member's income.[7] The LI premium is set at 6.5 per cent of the insured monthly salary and 2.55 per cent for FI; the LI premium is only 5.5 per cent for those not covered for unemployment. Different schemes require different sharing arrangements between the government, employers, and employees.

The government subsidizes the premium for most of the insured to varying degrees. As an employer, it pays 65 per cent of the premium for GEI members and officer-grade members of MI, and the entire amount for soldier-grade members of MI. For ITASPS members, the employer and the government each contribute 32.5 per cent of the total premium, while the employee contributes the remaining 35 per cent. For LI members, the government pays 10 per cent of the total, while the employer pays 70 per cent and the employee 20 per cent. In the case of self-employed members of LI, the government pays 40 per cent of the premium and the remainder is paid by the insured. It also pays 70 per cent of the premium for FI members. In 1995, the premium subsidies cost the central and local governments US$1.3 billion (DGBAS, 1996: 13).

In addition to premium subsidy, the government pays for the huge deficits that many of the schemes incur. In 1995, revenues formed only 65 per cent of the GEI's expenditure and 44 per cent of FI's expenditures (DGBAS, 1996: 11). The deficit was covered by the government transfer of US$272 million to GEI and US$555 million to FI. The LI, on the other hand, had a surplus amounting to 11 per cent of the revenues in 1995, but it is suspected that the surplus does not fully account for the accrued liabilities. It is estimated that the premium needs to be set at 21.9 per cent for MI and 15.5 per cent for GEI (and not the current rates of 8 and 6 per cent respectively) for the schemes to be able to pay entitlements without incurring deficit.

The employer-liability GERCF is funded from contributions of 8.8 per cent of the "basic" salary (which is roughly 20 per cent lower than the actual salary received); the premium is 10.8 per cent for school employees and 12 per cent for military personnel. Of the total premium, the employee pays 35 per cent and the remainder is borne by the employer, that is, the government. The scheme used to be paid entirely from the government's general revenues but it is now self-financing and, indeed, in surplus. However, the contributions are insufficient to meet the obligations in the long run and it is estimated that the GERCF will begin to incur current-account deficit in 2010 and that the fund will be totally depleted by 2020 (Personal Interview, January 2003).

The LRF, which is the private-sector counterpart of GERCF, is funded from the contribution of 2–15 per cent of wages, to be determined and paid entirely by employers. Not surprisingly, most firms have chosen to contribute 2 per cent and yet most do not pay it. The contributions amounted to US$513 million in 1990 and US$1.7 billion in 1999, while the benefit payments amounted to US$350 million and US$874 million respectively, leaving a cumulative balance of US$6 billion in the fund.

Expenditure on public assistance also increased during the 1990s to US$1.3 billion in 1997, but then fell to US$800 million in 1998 and the slide continued in subsequent years (DGBAS, 2000a). The decrease in the late 1990s was triggered by the establishment of the NHI. Earlier, medical assistance formed a major chunk of public-assistance expenditure, but this chunk is now quite small. Of all public-assistance programmes, Living Allowance for the Low-Income Families is the largest component, followed distantly by schemes for the aged, disabled, and aged farmers (ROC, Ministry of Interior, 1999). The total spending on social services grew from US$449 million in 1981 to US$2.2 billion in 1993, and then to US$3.6 billion by 1999 (DGBAS, 2000a).

Comparative

The four NIEs differ vastly in the funding arrangements for their income-maintenance programmes, as is evident in Table 3.4. Singapore has the simplest arrangement: for most people, the employers and employees equally contribute to the CPF. The government only funds civil servants' pensions, which is a small but expensive scheme, and public assistance, which is a small and inexpensive scheme. Hong Kong has a similar arrangement, except that its public-assistance scheme reaches a larger share of the population and pays higher benefits than its counterpart in Singapore. Korea and Taiwan, in contrast, rely primarily on social-insurance contributions, supplemented by substantial government subsidies towards premiums and the deficits incurred by the schemes.

The contribution requirements are the lowest in Hong Kong and the highest in Singapore. Programmes in Hong Kong used to be funded largely by the government, but the launch of MPF, which requires a total contribution of 10 per cent of income, has changed that. In Singapore, employees and their employers normally contributed up to 40 per cent of the former's income, but the rate was reduced to 33 per cent in 2003. The total contribution requirement for most workers in Korea is, or soon will be, 9 per cent of income. In Taiwan, the total contribution rates vary considerably: 4.7 per cent for private school teachers, 6.4 per cent for government employees, 6.5 per cent for private-sector employees, and 8 per cent for military personnel. More peculiarly, the government pays some

Table 3.4 Funding arrangements of income maintenance programmes

	Name of programme	Funding source
Hong Kong	SSAS; CSSA; Civil servants' pension	Government's general revenues
	MPF	Employer: 5%; employee: 5%
	ORSO	Employer and/or employee: amount varies
Singapore	Public assistance	Government's general revenues
	CPF	Employer: 13%; employee: 20%
	Civil servants' pension	Government's general revenues
Korea	Public assistance	Government's general revenues
	NPS	Employer: 4.5%; employee: 4.5%. Self-employed: 5% (9% from 2005)
	Government employees and military	Employer: 8.5%; employee: 8.5%
	Private school teachers	Employer: 3.5%; employee: 8.5%; government: 3.5%
	Retirement payment	Employer, from operating reserves
	Unemployment insurance	Employer: 0.5%; employee: 0.5%
Taiwan	Public assistance	Government's general revenues
	Labour insurance	Employer: 4.5%; employee: 1.3%; government: 0.6%. Self-employed: 3.9%; government: 2.6%
	Government employees' insurance	Employer: 4.6%; employee: 2.2%
	Military insurance	Employer: 5.2%; employee: 2.8% for officers. Government pays the entire 8% for non-officers
	Private school teachers' insurance	Employer: 1.54%; employee: 1.66%; government: 1.54%
	Farmers' insurance	Farmer: 0.77%; government 1.78%
	Government employees' retirement fund	Employer: 5.2%; employee: 2.8%
	Labour retirement fund	Employer: 2–15% (usually 2%)

Note
Per cent refers to share of monthly wage or income.

portion of the premium contribution for schemes that are supposedly self-financing. In addition, the governments in both Korea and Taiwan cover the deficit incurred by the social-insurance schemes.

The total amount of public expenditure on income maintenance in current prices during the 1980–1997 period grew the fastest in Hong Kong (2,143 per cent), followed by Korea (1,947 per cent), Taiwan (1,142 per cent), and Singapore (525 per cent). However, as a result of differences in the starting point, Taiwan is by far the largest spender, devoting almost 24 per cent of total government expenditure (TGE) on income maintenance, which is three times the figure of 9 per cent of TGE spent in Hong Kong and Korea, and twelve times the 2 per cent of TGE spent in Singapore.

Public expenditure on income maintenance has increased in absolute terms in all four NIEs over the past 25 years. As a proportion of the GDP too, it has grown in Hong Kong, Korea, and Taiwan, which is remarkable because the size of the GDP itself grew rapidly. Between 1975 and 1999 the share increased from 0.9 to 2.3 per cent of the GDP in Hong Kong, from 1.3 (1990) to 3.1 per cent in Korea, and from 1.5 to 5.7 per cent in Taiwan. The share in Singapore has experienced sharp fluctuations but generally remained unchanged. But even the highest ranking, Taiwan, spends less than one-third of the average of 17 per cent of GDP spent on income maintenance by OECD countries. As a share total government expenditure, Taiwan is the largest spender on income maintenance, followed by Korea, Hong Kong, and, distantly, Singapore. Indeed, the share devoted to income maintenance in Taiwan is nearly as high as the OECD average.

The data in Table 3.5 must be treated with some caution, however, as it conceals the fact that the GDP and TGE themselves grew rapidly during the period. For instance, between 1986 and 1997, the GDP in current prices grew by 340 per cent in Korea, 264 per cent in Singapore, and 184 per cent in Taiwan. Even in Singapore, income maintenance expenditures grew by 213 per cent in current prices during the period, but were dwarfed by yet faster GDP growth. Moreover, the data for Korea and Taiwan do not include mandatory employer-liability schemes, which involve substantial expenditures, though no reliable data is available. The table also says nothing about the pension scheme that has been put in place in Korea but is not yet paying benefits. Exclusion of tax incentives from expenditure calculations is another limitation of the data. For

Table 3.5 Public expenditure on income maintenance as percentage of GDP and total government expenditure

	% of GDP				% of TGE			
	1975	1985	1995	1999	1975	1985	1995	1999
Hong Kong	0.9	0.9	1.3	2.3	5.8	5.8	7.4	10.2
Singapore	0.3	0.4	0.8	0.3	1.8	1.6	5.0	1.6
Korea	–	1.3 (1990)	2.0	3.1 (1998)	–	7.2 (1990)	11.5	13.1 (1998)
Taiwan	1.5[1]	3.0[1]	4.6	5.7	7.6[1]	13.3	15.5	19.6

Sources: ADB, 1999 and 2002; IMF, 2000; ROC, 2000; OECD, 2002.

Note
1 Includes "public housing and community development" and "environment protection".

instance, the tax exemptions applicable to CPF contributions amounted to US$2.6 billion (or 2.8 per cent of GDP) but are not included in the expenditure data (Asher, 2002: 104).

The data also raise broader questions of how to interpret compulsory contributions to provident funds, which is the main scheme in Singapore and will become important in Hong Kong in the future. To the extent that they are individual savings, albeit compulsory, they cannot be regarded as public expenditure. This has the effect of significantly lowering Singapore's income-maintenance expenditures. The problem cannot be overcome by simply treating all provident fund withdrawals as expenditures in any given year because the amount is meant to cover the entire period of retirement and not just the year in which it is withdrawn.

Outcomes

Hong Kong

On the face of it, Hong Kong has a comprehensive social-security system providing a secure safety net for all those whose income might fall below a certain level. However, stringent criteria set to screen out the "undeserving poor" and the low benefits reduce their income-maintenance potential.

While 13.5 per cent of the population was receiving some form of public assistance in 2002, the beneficiaries consisted largely of the aged and disabled. Of all CSSA and SSAS cases that year, 72 per cent related to old age and another 14 per cent to disability (Hong Kong Government, 2003). The low representation of the poor and the unemployed among the public-assistance recipients is the result of tough means testing for CSSA benefits but not for SSAS, which is readily available to the aged and the disabled.

The total number of CSSA cases increased quite slowly in the 1970s and 1980s but rapidly in the 1990s, especially after 1997. However, while the growth has been rapid, the share of the population receiving the benefits was still small: only 4.4 per cent in 2002, compared to 1.2 per cent in 1990 and 0.3 per cent in 1971. Much of the growth was driven by increases in unemployment, single-parent, and low-income cases. Of all the CSSA cases, the unemployed's share increased from 4 to 16 per cent over the 1993–2002 period, low-income cases from 1 to 4 per cent, and single-parent cases increased from 6 to 13 per cent (Hong Kong Government, 2003). As a result of the changes, the combined share of aged, disabled, and ill-health cases declined from 85 per cent of the total caseload in 1993 to 66 per cent in 2002, while the caseload for the unemployed, single parents, and low income increased correspondingly.

Public-assistance benefits are deliberately kept low to encourage recipients to leave public welfare (Wong, 1997: 59). The basic public-assistance rates were 24–25 per cent of the median income during the 1970s, but had fallen to 20 per cent by 1986, 15 per cent by 1993, and only 11 per cent by 1998 (Hong Kong Human Rights Commission, 1994). A survey in 1994 found that the CSSA recipients were spending 70 per cent of their income on food alone, and yet their food expenditure was lower than is desirable, not to mention their need for other necessities (Brewer and Stewart, 1997: 84).

The MPF may also be less adequate than the government has led the population to believe. In 2001, 18 per cent of the working population were outside MPF either because they were excluded from the scheme or because they had not joined despite the legal requirement (MPFA, 2001). A significant proportion of those covered may, even after decades of contribution, find the scheme inadequate because of low salaries in their working life. The consulting firm appointed by the government estimated – based on the assumption of an annual economic growth rate of 7 per cent and average annual real investment returns of 5 per cent – a replacement rate of only 17.5 per cent after 30 years of contribution and 36.5 per cent after 40 years of contribution (Hewitt Associated and GML Consulting, 1995). To get a replacement income of 53 per cent, the real annual investment returns will need to be 8 per cent and will need regular contribution to for 40 years. For most people, especially women, MPF is thus unlikely to be sufficient to last through retirement (Lee, 2001).

At the same time, the benefits provided by different schemes are significantly unequal. For instance, the CSSA benefits are higher for the aged than for the working poor and the unemployed, and the benefits are highest for civil servants. But there are large disparities even among civil servants because of the highly unequal wage structure. The 10 per cent lowest-paid government employees received only 1 per cent of total benefits paid in 1998–1999 (<http://www.hku.hk/hkgcsb/9-2-5.htm>).

The ORSO schemes covered about 25 per cent of the labour-force in 1999 but the share fell to 17 per cent when MPF was launched and the slide is expected to continue in the coming years. A disproportionately large percentage of the workers covered by ORSO belong to the management ranks or are employed in multinational corporations (MNCs) (*South China Morning Post*, 12 August 1998). Moreover, they typically provide inequitable benefits, replacing 80 per cent of final income for senior executives and only 40 per cent for non-executive employees. The fact that they are tax-exempt, which means those on higher salaries receive greater benefits, compounds the inequity.

Income-maintenance problems in Hong Kong are aggravated by the weakening of the informal system of social protection. According to a 1993 survey, just over 62 per cent of the respondents agreed that the aged could rely on their children for income (Brewer and Stewart, 1997: 84). More significantly, only 5–10 per cent of the elderly were in a position to rely on their own savings after retirement, though the majority would prefer to be financially independent (Lee, 1999: 13).

The vast majority of the elderly in Hong Kong continue to live with their children, however. In 1996, only 22 per cent of the elderly were living alone or only with their spouse, while 44 per cent were living with their children and another 17 per cent lived in three-generation families (Chow, 2000: 159). The high percentage of elderly people living with their children and/or grandchildren must, however, be seen in the context of high housing prices, which make it difficult for adult children to form their own household.

The incidence of poverty among the aged is high: about 25 per cent of the population over 65 years of age were living below the poverty line in 1996 (Ho, 1996). One-third of the elderly remain in employment until the age of 70 years and one-tenth until the age of 80 years (Mok, 1994, cited in Tang, 1997: 69). Of the working elderly, 16 per cent were earning less than US$250 per month (Hong Kong Human Rights Commission, 1994).

Singapore

Singapore has an unusual and arguably the most inadequate system of income maintenance among the four NIEs. Its main scheme, the CPF, has near-universal coverage and high contribution rates, yet it falls well short of providing adequate protection to a significant proportion of its members. In fact it is possible to make a case that income-maintenance function is peripheral to CPF. Of the total CPF withdrawal of US$7.7 billion (including transfer to minimum sum) in 1999, only 14 per cent was for retirement purposes.

The average sum withdrawn at the age of 55 years in 1999 was under US$11,000 (CPF statistics, http://www.cpf.gov.sg/cpf_info/home.asp). In the same year, 19 per cent of the active CPF members in the 50–55 years age bracket had a balance of under US$29,412 (*CPF Annual Report* 1999: 75). Estimates of CPF's replacement rate range from 25 to 35 per cent (Lim, 2001; Wong and Park, 1997; McCarthy *et al.*, 2002). These rates are less than half of the two-thirds of the last-drawn salary that is usually regarded as the minimum for maintaining one's standard of living. It is projected that 60–70 per cent of the 50–55 years age group will not have sufficient funds in their account to meet the minimum-sum requirement in 2003 (Lim, 2001: 374). The problem of inadequate income during old age is especially acute for women, who live longer, suffer from a higher incidence of debilitating illnesses, have lower income, and have a smaller CPF balance (Lee, 1999; Shantakumar, 1995).

Moreover, wages in Singapore are highly unequal and this is reflected in workers' current CPF contributions and the amount they will eventually draw on. About 17 per cent of the contributors in 1999 were earning less than S$1,000 a month and are unlikely to have sufficient funds in their CPF account when they retire (Singapore Department of Statistics,

2001). This is in addition to the unemployed and those excluded from the CPF.

Inadequate income maintenance on the part of the CPF is the result of several factors. The low returns that members earn on their funds is a significant reason for this: between 1983 and 2000, the CPF provided average annual returns of only 1.8 per cent, which was lower than the growth in GDP and income (Asher and Newman, 2002: 58). The government has encouraged people to earn higher returns by investing directly in the financial markets, but the results have been disappointing, as a majority have actually lost money (*Business Times*, 4 January 2001). The second reason for the low replacement income is the many pre-retirement withdrawal schemes for housing, health, education, and so on. While these are worthwhile purposes, they reduce the value of funds available for retirement. Cardarelli (2000) estimates that the removal of housing withdrawal alone would double the CPF replacement rate. The third, and most important, reason is the absence of any redistributive mechanism inherent to personal savings schemes. Those on low income or with intermittent employment history have little in their fund to withdraw when they reach retirement age.

Public assistance, which is normally the first line of defence in countries with defined contribution arrangements, is small and of declining significance in Singapore. The number of persons receiving public assistance declined from 2,867 in 1988 to 2,070 in 1998, forming 0.1 per cent and 0.05 per cent of the population respectively (Singapore Department of Statistics, 1998). This is hardly surprising considering the strict criteria for receiving benefits. Again unsurprisingly, the aged form an increasing share of the public-assistance recipients.

The *ad hoc* assistance periodically offered in Singapore is inefficient as well as inequitable. Because the incentives are announced intermittently, individuals are not able to plan their saving and spending behaviour. Moreover, the rebates are usually available to all, not just to those who need them. In fact the vast majority of Singaporeans cannot benefit from tax rebates because almost two-thirds of the adult population does not pay any income tax. For those who do pay taxes, benefits increase with the marginal rate of tax, allowing the high-income taxpayers to benefit more than the lower-income taxpayers.

On the household front, the share of one-person households increased from 5.7 per cent of all households in 1980 to 8.2 per cent in 2000 (Singapore household survey 2000, http://www.singstat.gov.sg/C2000/c2000keyind.pdf). The 2000 census found that only 6.6 per cent of the elderly (over 65 years) were living alone and 13.9 were living with spouses but without children (*Singapore Census Of Population*, 2000, advance data release no. 6). Although hard data are not available to confirm this, it is likely that there is considerably higher incidence of poverty among the aged.

Korea

The income-maintenance system in Korea ostensibly provides comprehensive protection on a nearly universal basis but this is not entirely the case in reality. The share of the labour-force covered by all retirement insurance schemes increased from 5 per cent in 1985 to 39 per cent in 1995, and then rapidly to 73 per cent by 2000. The non-covered consist largely of part-time, temporary, and household workers. However, not everyone covered by the schemes is actually insured: the insured formed only 54 per cent of the labour-force. In other words, a lot of people who should be covered are not so in reality for various reasons (OECD, 2003: 56). Worse still, a significant proportion of the self-employed insured under-report their income, which will reduce the pension they will eventually receive.

Significantly, only a small proportion of the covered population qualifies for benefits and it will be many years before the majority of the elderly will receive substantial pension benefits. In 1995, only 13.7 per cent of the elderly population – mostly civil servants, military personnel, and school teachers – received pensions from the various insurance schemes (Kwon, 1999: 6). Even in 2015, less than half the population will be receiving a pension because of the limited coverage until 1995.

The average monthly pension amount in 1995 was US$1,271 for civil servants and US$1,483 for private school teachers – these amounts were more than four times the amount in 1985 (National Pension Corporation, 1997: 29). These are large benefits, amounting to 140 per cent and 164 per cent of the monthly per capita GDP. As mentioned earlier, the NPS is not yet paying pension benefits except for lump-sum refunds. But when it does start providing full benefits, its target replacement rate of 60 per cent would be comparable, and in many instances superior, to those found in advanced welfare states.

The mandatory retirement allowance is not, as mentioned earlier, necessarily for the retired but is available to anyone leaving an employer after two years of service. In any event, more than half of the total workforce (including the self-employed) work in firms with fewer than five employees and are hence outside the scope of the law. Moreover, most of those covered do not work for the same firm for long enough to earn entitlement to a substantial lump-sum payment at the time of retirement. In 1997, only 40 per cent of the employed in firms with ten employees or more had been with the same firm for five years or more, and only 4 per cent for 20 years or more (Korea National Statistical Office, 1999). Unsurprisingly, two-thirds of the labour-force receives no benefit from the scheme. The increasing labour-market flexibility will only compound the problem.

The combined benefits of the NPS and retirement-allowance scheme – roughly half of those covered by the NPS work in firms where retirement allowances are also mandatory (World Bank, 2000: 4) – for a worker with 35 years of accrued rights would produce a replacement rate of around 85 per cent of the final salary. This is extremely high by international standards (World Bank, 2000: 7). The replacement rate is even higher for government employees, school teachers, and the military.

Notwithstanding the expansion of unemployment insurance in the late 1990s, it covers only 70 per cent of all wage and salary earners. Not all those eligible for it join the scheme, as the total number of actually insured forms only 51 per cent of the Korean wage and salary earners. The stringent qualifying conditions for receiving benefits further limit its income-maintenance potential: only 16 per cent of the unemployed in 2002 were receiving the benefit (OECD, 2003: 111). Nevertheless, the average size of the benefit per claim increased from US$130,525 in 1996 to US$154,000 in 1998, while the average duration of receipt of the unemployment benefit increased from 85 to 126 days (Cho, 1999).

The Livelihood Protection Scheme covered 2.6 per cent of the population in 1997, but the share rose to 4.2 per cent amidst economic recession and relaxation of eligibility conditions, declining to 3.2 per cent by 2001 (Jung and Shin, 2002: 280–281). The eligibility conditions are tough, however, which is reflected in the fact that only 55 per cent of those living below the official poverty line were actually receiving public assistance (Martin and Torres, 2000: 285). Indeed, less than 10 per cent of the retired population receives public assistance (OECD, 2003: 55). Moreover, public-assistance benefits in Korea are quite low relative to incomes and wages: in 1997, the cash transfer paid to needy persons aged 65–79 years was approximately 6 per cent of the average Korean wage and 4 per cent of the national per capita income (World Bank, 2000: 2). Even combined, the livelihood-assistance and old-age-allowance benefits is only 50–55 per cent of the official poverty line (Kwon, 1999: 9).

The inadequacy of the system is reflected in a survey of the elderly in the early 1990s, which showed that only 4 per cent of the respondents cited statutory schemes as their main source of income (Choi, 1996b). Children were the main source of income for 44 per cent of the respondents, earnings from work for 38 per cent, and savings and property income for 7 per cent. High dependence on children should be viewed in light of the fact that 73 per cent of non-elderly respondents said they would prefer to live separately after their children's marriages (Choi, 1996b: 7).

A survey conducted in 1990 showed that the incidence of poverty among the elderly was more than three times higher than for persons below 50 years of age (World Bank, 2000: 3). Poverty is higher and increasing in households headed by the aged: 12.6 per cent of those above 60 years of age were poor in 1974, but their share had increased to 25.5 per cent by 1990.

There is a high dependence on family for support among the elderly when the families themselves are undergoing nuclearizaton. The share of three- or four-generation households fell from 29 per cent of total population in 1960 to 12 per cent in 1995. But even when adult children live separately from their parents, most still accept responsibility for financial and other forms of support for their aged parents (Palley and Usui, 1995: 243). However, the increasing number of women participating in occupational and social activities is making it increasingly difficult for them to continue caring for the elderly as they have done traditionally (Choi, 1996b: 8).

Taiwan

Notwithstanding the fact that no major income-maintenance programme has been announced in almost five decades, and despite the continuing political stalemate over it, the existing programmes have gradually matured and expanded in coverage. But the benefits they provide are patchy and highly unequal.

Two-thirds of the population aged 25–64 years were covered by some income-maintenance scheme in Taiwan in 1999 and almost half of those over 64 years of age were receiving some income support from the government. However, the schemes provide vastly different levels of benefit: the replacement rate is only 20 per cent for LI, while it is 72 per cent for GEI (Tsui, 2002: 200–201). The actual amount of the benefit varies even more markedly, because it is based strictly on salary and years of service, though this is somewhat mitigated by the relatively equal distribution of wages in Taiwan. The average amount of old-age benefit (paid in lump sum) in 2001 was NT$1.3 million for GEI members and NT$0.7 million for LI members. More significantly, the disparity between the two schemes has increased: between 1976 and 2001, the average amount of GEI old-age benefit increased by almost 16 times, compared to 13 times for the LI.

The benefit formula for employer-liability schemes (GERCF and LRF) is such that public employees receive twice as much in benefits as their private-sector counterparts. In the majority of cases, the private-sector workers receive nothing, either because of non-compliance by employers or because of an eligibility condition that requires them to work with the same employer for at least 15 years. It is therefore not surprising that less than 10 per cent of the retirees in Taiwan receive benefits under the scheme (Lee, 1997: 77).

The unemployment-insurance system, the latest addition to the income-maintenance system in Taiwan, has grown rapidly since its establishment in 1999. The number of persons receiving benefits from the scheme increased from 39,471 in 1999 to 611,640 in 2002, while the total value of benefits received increased from NT$516 million to NT$10,204 million. The average value of benefits received per beneficiary per year also increased, amounting to 3.0 and 3.7 per cent of per capita GDP.

Government expenditure on income maintenance is highly skewed towards government employees. Almost 75 per cent of the central government's total welfare expenditures in 1991 went to military personnel, government employees, teachers, veterans, and retired members of parliament, while the disadvantaged received only 3 per cent (Ku, 1997: 58). It is estimated that in 1991 the handicapped on average received NT$8,595, whereas military personnel received NT$25,853 and government employees NT$28,253.

The share of all the households considered poor by official criteria has remained within the 0.8–0.9 per cent range since the 1980s and the share receiving public assistance for low-income families in the 0.5–0.7 per cent range (DGBAS, 2000a). This suggests that a significant proportion of the poor do not receive public assistance and there has been little improvement in this regard despite relaxation of eligibility conditions. However, the average value of benefit increased from NT$1,511 per month in 1990 to NT$8,137 in 1998, with the largest increase occurring in 1994 when it more than doubled over the previous year (*Monthly Bulletin of Statistics*, various issues). The share of the aged population receiving old-age allowance was 35 per cent in 1998, but this is likely to have increased after the removal of asset and income testing for farmers (http://140.129.146.192/dgbas03/english/bulletin/).

Transfer payments from social assistance and social services have had an increasingly positive impact on reducing income disparity in Taiwan: they reduced income inequality by 0.04 per cent in 1980 and by 0.36 per cent in 1996. Much of the reduction was the result of subsidies to farmers because the majority of them are poor. Social-insurance transfers, in comparison, increased inequality by 0.5 times. The main problem here is the pension benefits for government employees, who receive considerably larger amounts, which increases the income gap (Jao, 1998).

Despite the expansion of statutory income-maintenance programmes for the aged, public schemes are a source of only a small, albeit growing, part of the aged's income. Of their average monthly income of NT$2,807 in 2000, only 15 per cent came from pensions, and another 12 per cent from other public transfers, while 47 per cent came from children (ROC, Ministry of Interior, 2000). Fourteen years earlier, in 1986, only 1.2 per cent of the income came from public transfers, while 66 per cent came from children.

There is a high level of poverty among the elderly in Taiwan, especially among those not living with their children. The share of the elderly population living in poverty increased from 9 per cent in 1969 to 22 per cent in 1996 (Chang, 2000: 51). Nearly 25 per cent of the elderly population in 1991 had income of less than half the national median; it was 53 per cent among those living alone with a spouse, but only 15 per cent among those living with their children or other family members. Similarly, the poverty rate among elderly women living alone is three times (74.5 per cent) higher than for the total elderly population (24.7 per cent) – if 50 per cent of the national median disposable income is regarded as the poverty line (Smeeding and Saunders, 1998: 36). Shared living arrangements are thus a key income-protection mechanism for the aged in Taiwan. Fortunately for them, most elderly people do live with their children. Only 8 per cent lived alone and 19 per cent lived with spouse only, while 73 per cent lived with other family members (Smeeding and Saunders, 1998: 34).

Comparative

Outcomes of income-maintenance programmes are difficult to compare because of the absence of commonly agreed criteria for evaluation. Even if there were such criteria, it would be difficult to apply them because rarely is micro-data, especially for countries outside the OECD, available in comparable form. Nevertheless, coverage rates and replacement rates are commonly used for comparing social-security programmes. But even coverage is not as simple to calculate as it may first appear. Public-assistance schemes ostensibly cover the entire population, but the eligibility conditions may be set so strict as to exclude almost the entire population. Contribution-based systems too may in reality cover fewer than the data suggest because members may not contribute for a period long enough to qualify for significant or any benefit.

The social-insurance scheme in Korea and provident-fund schemes in Hong Kong and Singapore have near-universal coverage. Those outside the system are for the most part unemployed, part-time workers, informal workers, and foreign workers, but these add up to a lot of people: nearly half of the working population in the case of Korea (Jung and Shin, 2002: 285) and yet more in Taiwan. The social-insurance scheme in Taiwan has a somewhat lower membership, reflecting the patchy nature of its programmes and the large informal sector. The employer-liability schemes in

Table 3.6 Coverage of income maintenance schemes for the aged, per cent

	Social insurance membership, % of labour-force	Compulsory savings scheme membership, % of labour-force	Employer liability scheme membership, % of labour-force	Public assistance beneficiaries, % of population
Hong Kong (2000)	–	78	<25 (ORSO)	11
Singapore (1998)	–	63[1]	–	0.05
Korea (2001)	88	–	–	3.2
Taiwan (1999)	66 (share of working-age population)	–	40 (% of employed workforce)	0.5

Note
1 Includes only members currently contributing.

the NIEs, as elsewhere, have incomplete coverage and are usually available only to the better-off segments of the labour-force.

The higher percentage of the population receiving public assistance in Hong Kong compared to the other NIEs not only reflects the relatively less stringent means test but also that it is the main social-security scheme in the territory. This is in contrast to Singapore, where the strict means test allows few to qualify for benefits. The lower percentage of public-assistance recipients in Korea and Taiwan, despite their relatively less strict qualifying conditions, is probably a reflection of low-income inequality in the two countries.

There are immense differences in the levels of benefits both within and across states, as is shown in Table 3.7. For the general public, the benefits are most generous in Korea and Taiwan and least generous in Singapore. However, in all countries civil servants and military personnel as a group

Table 3.7 Average income maintenance benefits, percentage of per capita GDP

	Name	Benefit	Notes
Hong Kong	SSAS	4	Average amount of normal old-age allowance in 2002. Aged poor also receive CSSA
	CSSA	34	Average benefit payment in 1998
	Civil servants' pension	71	1998 (estimate)
Singapore	Civil servants' pension	119	1999, based on the scheme's average expenditure per pensioner
	CPF	2.4	1999, derived by dividing US$10,672 (the average amount withdrawn at the age of 55) by 21 (the average number of years Singaporeans live after the age of 55 years)
	Public assistance	6.6	1999 (for a single-person household)
Korea	GEP	9.3	1998
	NPP	0.2	1998 (the amounts consist largely of refunds)
	Public assistance	16.5	Maximum amount
Taiwan	GEI	21	1999, derived by dividing the average annual benefit by 16 (the average number of years Taiwanese live after the age of 60 years)
	LI	9	
	Public assistance	12.2	Average amount of benefit paid as assistance for low-income families
	Employer-liability		May be as high as 200% for government employees and a lot less for private employees – data on amount actually paid is not available

are a lot better looked after than the general public. This is particularly true in Singapore and Taiwan, where their pension amount is higher than the per capita income.

Of all income-maintenance schemes in the NIEs, only the NPS in Korea has explicit redistributive goals; for others the benefits are equal to the contribution, though the Taiwanese schemes do impose both floor and ceiling levels, which provides for some redistribution. Provident funds in Hong Kong and Singapore are distribution-neutral, as one receives strictly according to what one contributes.

The inadequacies of the statutory income-maintenance schemes are significantly offset by the family structure in the region. However, while an overwhelming majority of the aged in the NIEs still live with their children (see Table 3.8), there is a distinct trend towards living in nuclear households.

The changing family structure is reflected in the decreasing reliance on children for income, as shown in Table 3.9. In Taiwan the declining significance of children has been more than offset by the increase in income from public transfers, but this has not been the case in Korea because the statutory schemes are not yet paying full benefits. The aged's condition is likely to be worse in Hong Kong and Singapore, where the weakening of the family structure has not been replaced by compensatory social-security schemes.

Table 3.8 Share of the aged (65+ years) living with children, per cent

	1980	1995
Hong Kong	82.2	80.8
Singapore	–	73.7 (2000)
Korea	59.2	77.1
Taiwan	74.1	64.0
Japan	72.0	60.8
UK	–	8.4
USA	–	14.8

Sources: Jacobs, 2000: 12; *Singapore Census Of Population, 2000*, advance data release no. 6; Lee *et al.*, 2000.

Table 3.9 Main income sources of the elderly[1]

	Korea		Singapore	Taiwan	
	1988	1994	1986	1993	2000
Earnings and property	33.1	44.5	27.6	44.7	–
Children	63.7	44.3	85.8	53.2	47.1
State pension and assistance	3.0	3.5	16.4	1.6	12.3

Sources: Kwon, 1999: 10; Lee, 1999.

Note
1 60 years and above.

The effects of inadequate savings and lack of sufficient public transfers to compensate for it, coupled with changing family structure, is reflected in high and increasing levels of poverty among the aged (Table 3.10). In Korea, 56 per cent of the elderly in single-person households and 31 per cent in two-person households live in poverty. In Taiwan, the corresponding share is 36 and 31 per cent respectively (Kwon, 1999: 16). In Hong Kong, a smaller share – 25 per cent – of the aged population live in poverty. While comparable data is not available for Singapore, around 37 per cent of the poorest income decile on the island consists of elderly households, up from only 16 per cent in 1990 (www.channelnewsasia.com, 9 February 2001). Clearly, children are unable or unwilling to transfer sufficient income to their elderly parents to keep them out of poverty. These figures are higher than in OECD countries, where 14 per cent of the aged in the mid 1990s were living in poverty, defined as 50 per cent of the population's median disposable income (see Table 3.10). The increasing poverty among the aged in the NIEs is a worrying trend because of the rapidly ageing population and the inadequacies of the income-maintenance programmes for them.

Conclusion

The NIEs have the complete range of income-maintenance programmes typically found in Western welfare states, except for unemployment benefits, which in a substantial sense are available only in Korea. Other than that, there are vast differences among them with respect to the mechanisms they employ and the level of security they provide.

With respect to their mechanisms for providing social protection, Hong Kong relies primarily on public assistance, Singapore on provident fund, while Korea and Taiwan employ social insurance supplemented by public assistance. The inherent advantages and disadvantages of these mechanisms are evident in the schemes that exist in the NIEs. Public assistance schemes in all four NIEs, but especially Singapore, impose stringent eligibility conditions and provide meagre benefits and, as a result, probably only prevent extreme hardship. Singapore's CPF typifies the limitations inherent to defined contribution schemes: it provides inadequate income protection to the bulk of the population despite high contribution rates.

Table 3.10 Percentage of the elderly population living in poverty, 1996

Hong Kong	25
Korea	26
Taiwan	22
OECD	14

Sources: Ho, 1996; Kwon, 2001; OECD, 2000: 58.

The social insurance schemes in Korea and Taiwan, on the other hand, offer benefits and impose eligibility conditions comparable to those found in advanced welfare states. But the benefits they offer are closely tied to employment, which disadvantages the unemployed and those employed in low-wage jobs. However, the problem is mitigated somewhat by relatively comprehensive public assistance schemes that exist in the two Northeast Asian countries.

With respect to financing, the NIEs depend heavily on private contributions by employees and their employers. Instead of paying for income maintenance from its general or earmarked tax revenues, governments in the region often require employers and/or employees to provide income support or to partially or entirely pay for it. Indeed, this is argued by Kwon (1997) to be a vital distinguishing characteristic of the East Asian welfare system. In the case of Korea and Taiwan, private funding takes the form of contribution to social-insurance and employer-liability schemes, whereas in Singapore and (to a lesser extent) Hong Kong it takes the form of contribution to provident funds. Only in Hong Kong are programmes for the general population financed largely from the government's general revenues.

The principle of private financing is not, however, applied to state employees, who receive government-financed benefits immensely superior to those available to the rest of the population. Separate from the issue of huge expenses is the issue of equity. There is no defensible reason why civil servants and military personnel need more income protection than other workers. What is particularly troubling is that the schemes are regarded as an ongoing budgetary commitment, which shields them from the scrutiny normally applied to public programmes.

Politicians' proclivity to set low social insurance premiums and high benefits – as is the case to varying degrees in Korea, Taiwan and much of Europe and South America – has made Defined Contribution arrangement an attractive option in policy circles. However, it is often forgotten that DC is inherently limited in its capacity to provide income support to those with poor employment record or in low-wage employment, as the case of Singapore clearly shows, and as is projected for Hong Kong (Mok, 2000). Provident fund as the primary mechanism for maintaining the aged's income works only if it is built on a robust public assistance scheme, as is the case, to some extent, in Hong Kong.

We see broad similarities in the income maintenance systems in Korea and Taiwan on the one hand and in Hong Kong and Singapore on the other hand. Social protection in the two Northeast Asian states is available as a matter of right and benefits are closely tied to employment. In comparison, the government largely regulates private provision of income protection in Singapore and, to a lesser extent, Hong Kong. The latter has had a comprehensive, albeit highly targeted, income support system based on public assistance but is trying to move in Singapore's direction whereby individuals rely more on their own savings.

4

HEALTH

The problems that necessitate state intervention in health care are in many respects similar to those in income maintenance: industrialization, increasing income, and ageing of the population increase the need for health care at the same time as weakening of traditional support structures reduces the community's capacity to meet this need. In fact in some respects the problems manifest in graver forms in health. Industrialization requires a healthier workforce because of higher costs of employee absenteeism and difficulties of replacing skilled labour at short notice. Industrialization and ageing of the population also manifest in different epidemiological patterns: infectious diseases are increasingly replaced by cancer and cardiovascular ailments, which are more debilitating and often too expensive for all but the wealthy. Advancements in medical technology and the increasingly higher skills of the staff required to operate it aggravate the costs. It is not possible for democratic societies to ignore the health-care needs of individuals who cannot afford it because of widespread belief that it is something that must be available to all regardless of ability to pay. It is for these reasons that governments, willing or not, are pressured to intervene earlier and more extensively in health care than in income maintenance.

The central question in health policy thus is not whether the state should intervene in the health sector but the form and extent this intervention should take. Specifically, there are fundamental differences among policy-makers and commentators alike over how and to what extent the state should supplant, rather than just supplement, the market in the provision and financing of health care.

Those preferring the maximum role for the market tend to be influenced by mainstream economic thinking in which health is just another service – albeit one that is vital, with large positive externalities – which ought to be privately sold and bought like any other commodity. Even when such thinkers admit a role for the state, they would prefer it to be confined to correcting market failures and providing health cover to the poor. But even then, they would confine the state's role to the minimum. Peaboy *et al.*'s (1999: 25) caution is typical of this line of thinking: "Direct government provision of services is often the most expensive approach, because it eliminates incentives for efficiency, distorts the parallel private sector, often prevents the private market from entering, and is subject to fraud and waste." Their faith in the market's efficiency rules out of hand the possibility that the state could actually be a more efficient mechanism in the health sector. Many economists supplement the efficiency argument with the claim that confining the role of the state to the minimum is more equitable because it allows the government to concentrate its limited resources on the poor (World Bank, 1987).

Pitted against the market-centred conception of health care is the view that health is a merit good, for which the state has the responsibility to ensure provision in adequate quantity. Those with this view make their case just as much on the basis of the weaknesses of the market mechanism as on the superiority of the state. They argue that health care is characterized by features that make it difficult, indeed impossible, for the market to function efficiently. They cite evidence that the private health operators are less cost-efficient than non-profit operators (the evidence comparing private and public facilities is conflicting) and are more likely to overservice (Bennett, 1997: 100–102). They also object to the market-centred approach on the grounds that it undersupplies public goods and ignores those without the ability to pay. The higher-income opportunities in the private sector are alleged to draw scarce medical personnel away from the public sector, to the detriment of those unable to pay for private care (Berman, 1997: 113).

The state-centred view claims that centralized public provision is both more efficient and equitable (for evidence supporting the efficiency of a centralized system, see Abel-Smith, 1992; Pfaff, 1990; Schieber *et al.*, 1991). Its proponents claim that conventional health economics seriously underestimates the value of public provision and the efficiency benefits of competition from public hospitals (Hammer and Berman, 1995: 47). On the financing side, they argue that proposals to concentrate public resources only on the poor are politically naïve because they undermine popular support for the public system; the poor's best chance is universal availability. The effects of user charges on health care are not as straightforward as is claimed by their proponents (for review of the empirical literature on the subject, see Gertler and Hammer, 1997). It is also argued that while increased private-sector funding appears to lower costs for the government, it increases aggregate costs for society as a whole. As Evans (1997: 427) sums up: "International experience over the last 40 years has demonstrated that greater reliance on the market is associated with inferior system performance – inequity, inefficiency, high cost, and public dissatisfaction. The United States is a leading example." He goes further and argues that the privatization of health care is driven by those who are likely to benefit from it: health care providers, drug companies, private insurers, and wealthy and healthy consumers. Notwithstanding the reservations, an international consensus has emerged that market-based solutions are best suited to resolving health-care financing problems (Scheil-Adlung, 1998).

The debate between those who prefer private provision and financing and those who would rather have the state provide and finance health care is somewhat spurious, however. Provision of health care requires significant state intervention in the form of either direct delivery or regulation of private providers because of the providers' ability to control demand as a result of consumers' ignorance of their own health-care needs. Similarly, the various peculiarities of the health-care market makes some degree of collective financing unavoidable because of the enormous costs of many essential treatments. The key question thus is the form and extent to which, rather than whether, the state should be involved in the health sector. Discussion in this chapter will show that the NIEs employ a range of alternative combinations of state and market mechanisms for providing and financing health care with varying outcomes.

The central argument of the chapter is that Hong Kong and Singapore have, more by historical accident than design, the most attractive health-care systems in the region. The key to their superior performance at modest cost is centralized public provision of hospital care while still leaving room for private competition. The comprehensive health insurances in Korea and Taiwan do provide people adequate access, but without appropriate controls over providers' behaviour they may have allowed costs to escalate to levels that are unsustainable in the long run. The study suggests that governments should go beyond their obsession with controlling the demand for health care and pay at least as much attention to its supply.

Policy history

Hong Kong

The British colonial administration confined itself mainly to meeting the medical requirements of the European community until the 1930s and did little to address the health problems faced by the general population. Civil servants, the middle and top rungs of whom were almost exclusively British, were particularly privileged, as they were entitled to free medical care as far back as 1902 (Gauld, 1996: 73). The local population relied, by tradition and through lack of choice, entirely on their family when in need of support, though some basic hospital services were funded by Chinese charitable organizations and clan associations (Brewer, 1993: 95).

The government's attitude towards health began to change gradually in the 1930s. Following the 1929 Report by Dr Wellington (the first Director of Medical and Sanitary Services), in 1936 the government centralized administration of government hospitals and dispensaries, took measures to inspect hospitals, opened first-aid centres, and launched quarantine and vaccination programmes. There was reluctance, however, to develop anything more than basic facilities. Mission hospitals and local Chinese associations helped to partly fill the gap left by inadequate government facilities (Chu, 1994: 220). In 1938 the government announced a plan to provide 2,500 additional beds in order to reduce the 3,300 estimated shortfall, but the war interrupted its implementation (Gauld, 1996: 75).

The sudden influx of a million refugees following the Chinese Civil War, and the overcrowding and unsanitary living conditions it created, led the colonial government to play a more active role in the provision of health services. However, efforts were focused mainly on providing primary care and quarantine services to combat epidemics and high mortality rates (Chu, 1994: 220). A five-year plan for the 1960–1965 period prepared by the Medical and Health Department in 1959 called for greater state involvement in provision and financing of health care. While the government agreed to implement the plan, it did little in practice. Health moved into the foreground of the government's policy horizon in the following decades, reflected in the publication of four comprehensive reviews of the health system and proposals for reform in the following decades: 1964, 1974, 1986, and 1999.

The first White Paper on health, "Development of Medical Services in Hong Kong" (1964), defined the government's health-policy objective as "providing, directly or indirectly, low cost or free medical and personal health services to that large section of the community which is unable to seek medical attention from other sources". It recommended greater emphasis on prevention of communicable diseases, promotion of children's health through better maternal care and childcare, and tackling the serious shortage of hospital beds. The government accepted the recommendations and took follow-up measures in the forms of expanding public health-care clinics and hospitals.

The government's emphasis on primary care became increasingly inappropriate as infectious diseases came to be replaced by modern diseases requiring lengthy and expensive treatment. The government established a Medical Development Advisory Committee in 1973, which produced a White Paper entitled "Further Development of Medical and Health Services in Hong Kong" in 1974. The White Paper emphasized the need for a shift in focus from primary care to hospital-centred curative services and decentralization of health-care delivery (Chu, 1994). It recommended an increase in hospital beds to 5.5 beds per 1,000 population as the long-term goal, and to generally improve the hospital and ward environment. It also proposed dividing Hong Kong into four regions supported by regional health-service management centres organized around one major hospital. The government accepted and largely implemented the proposals. The increased government involvement in providing free or virtually free in-patient care without means testing, similar to the National Health Service in Britain, continues to this day (Liu and Yue, 1998).

The full implications of the heavy government involvement in provision of in-patient care became apparent in the 1970s with the increasing incidence of cancer and cardiovascular diseases. The increasing costs they involved alarmed the government, which led it to search for less costly long-term solutions. The government appointed W. D. Scott to review the management of the hospital system in 1985 with the objective of utilizing public resources more efficiently and containing costs. The report, "The Delivery of Medical Services in Hospitals", recommended the establishment of an independently administered hospital system with each hospital management responsible for its operations within a broad framework laid out by the government. It also recommended measures to reduce costs and recover a greater portion of the hospital costs from fees.

The Hospital Administration (HA) was finally established in 1991. Its foundation marked the onset of efforts to "corporatize" health-care delivery in Hong Kong. Although the financial relationship with the government remained the same, individual hospitals became responsible for their own operation. To allay fears that the move was a step towards privatizing health care, the Working Party on Primary Health Care in its 1990 report, "Health For All The Way Forward", reiterated the principle that "no one should be prevented, through lack of means, from obtaining adequate medical treatment" – the principle was subsequently incorporated in the Hospital Authority Ordinance. The tension between corporatizing public hospitals while maintaining government control and ensuring universal access continues to this day.

The government's reform efforts until the 1980s concentrated on the provision rather than financing of health care. This changed with the publication of a consultation document, "Towards Better Health", in 1993, in which the government mooted the idea of increasing private financing of health care. In January 1994, the government approved in principle the introduction of semi-private beds in public hospitals and the promotion of voluntary insurance. A pilot scheme of semi-private beds was accordingly launched in five hospitals and completed in 1996, but no further action was taken to regularize it.

In October 1997, the new Chief Executive of SAR announced in his maiden policy address that the government would carry out a comprehensive review of the existing health-care system. It commissioned a team led by William Hsiao from Harvard University's School of Public Health to study and recommend reform of the health-care system in Hong Kong. The team submitted its report, "Improving Hong Kong's Health Care System: Why and For Whom?", popularly known as the Harvard Report, in 1999.

The report's assessment of the current system was quite positive. It concluded that the existing system was equitable as well as efficient and that there was broad community satisfaction with the quality of services. However, it predicted a 50 per cent rise in public medical expenses by 2010 and projected that public-health expenditures would increase to 3.4–4.0 per cent of GDP by the year 2016, taking up 20–23 per cent of the total government budget. The centrepiece of the report was the proposal to target subsidies and to establish two new financing schemes: Hospital Security Plan (HSP) and Medisage. The former was a low-cost insurance scheme for specified chronic illnesses (similar to Singapore's Medishield in many respects), while the latter was a compulsory individual health-savings account to which employees and their employers would contribute. Again, Medisage was similar to Singapore's Medisave except that the fund could be used only after the age of 65 years. It further proposed that up to 30 per cent of charges in public hospitals should be recovered from patients. It also recommended increased choice for consumers with regard to doctors and greater freedom for doctors regarding the fees they charged.

In late 2000, the government published a consultative document called "Lifelong Investment in Health" in which it rejected the proposed HSP and all but rejected Medisage. The HSP was rejected on the grounds that it was a compulsory insurance scheme that would increase labour costs, impose intergenerational burden, and promote overuse. Instead, it proposed a Health Protection Account (HPA), which was to be a personal savings account to which everyone would contribute 1–2 per cent of their income from the age of 40 to 60 years. The balance in one's account would be available for withdrawal only after the age of 65 years and only to pay for health care at rates applicable at public hospitals. However, it proposed to study the scheme further before announcing its decision.

Singapore

Singapore, similar to Hong Kong, was a British colony and shares many features in common with it. The British had established a reasonably well-developed health-care system in which public and private care co-existed and the arrangement continues to this day. In the 1950s, the government became increasingly involved, without much discussion or planning, in the provision of in-patient care through public hospitals. In part this reflected the National Health Service in Britain, where hospital care was available to all without means testing. The PAP government that took office in 1959 continued and indeed expanded the arrangement in its bid to maintain popularity with voters. The large financial implications of publicly provided hospital care became increasingly clear in the 1970s as trends of population ageing and epidemiological transition became apparent, prompting the government to search for alternative mechanisms for health-care financing (Aw and Low, 1997; Phua, 1990).

After briefly toying with the idea of establishing public health insurance, the government firmly rejected it in 1982 on the grounds that third-party payment would lead to over-supply by producers and over-use by consumers. The National Health Plan, announced in 1983, instead initiated a range of privatization measures designed to reduce the share of expenditures borne by the government and to encourage consumers to assume greater responsibility for their health care. At the same time, the government reiterated its commitment to providing heavily subsidized service to those who could not afford it.

The establishment of the Medisave within the CPF in 1984 was the first of the series of measures towards reducing the government's involvement in the financing of health care. The scheme compulsorily covers the entire workforce, including the self-employed. It requires compulsory saving of 6–8 per cent of one's monthly income, depending on age, to be used for payment for hospital care of the account holder and his/her immediate family, except siblings. However, it cannot be used to pay for out-patient care, except for some specialist care, and there are limits on the amount that can be withdrawn each day and for each procedure. The exclusions and ceilings are intended to allow accumulation of funds to pay for expensive in-patient care when needed. Since savings in one's Medisave are one's own money, it is expected that people would spend them cautiously.

In the same year that Medisave was established, the government announced a plan to grant greater autonomy to government hospitals in managing their operations. Operational autonomy was intended to lead to greater competition, which in turn was expected to lead to greater efficiency, lower costs, and higher standards.

In 1990, the government established a publicly managed but voluntary health-insurance scheme called Medishield. It covers hospitalization expenses for surgery and out-patient treatment for specified "serious" illnesses. Its establishment, despite the government's opposition to social insurance, was in response to the realization that most Medisave accounts did not have sufficient funds to pay for illnesses with expensive treatment costs. Premium is kept low (S$12–136 per year for the basic scheme) by imposing a large number of exclusions and a severe co-payment requirement to avoid the moral hazards associated with third-party payment schemes. As a result of the exclusions and restrictions, the basic Medishield scheme pays only, for example, 5 to 27 per cent (depending on the class of ward chosen) of the total surgical costs of colorectal cancer or heart transplant; the remainder is paid for by the individual from his or her Medisave account and/or out-of-pocket (Tan, 1997: 300–302).

The Health Review Committee's report of 1992, issued as a White Paper in the following year, supported expansion of the role of the private sector and greater competition among health-care providers, both public and private. At the same time, it acknowledged that "Market forces alone will not suffice to hold down medical costs to the minimum.... The government has to intervene directly to structure and regulate the health system" (Singapore, 1993: 3). It called for greater government involvement in controlling costs, managing the supply of doctors, and governing key operations of subsidized hospitals. In the following years, measures were taken to control the introduction of technology and specialist disciplines in government hospitals, impose price caps in public hospitals, exclude expensive treatment from public schemes, and tighten the supply of doctors (Barr, 2001: 714).

The realization that there was a segment of the population that could not afford even subsidized health care led the government to establish a public-assistance scheme called the Medifund in 1993. It is an endowment trust fund built on US$59 million contribution from the government. To prevent dissipation of the fund, only income from the fund is used to pay bills of those unable to afford hospital care. Under the scheme, patients in the lowest-class wards at public hospitals and out-patients needing expensive services may apply for a complete or partial waiver of their bills. To receive assistance, applicants need to pass a means test administered by the hospital.

Korea

The Korean health system is patterned after Japan's, which in turn was inspired by the German system. The end of Japanese rule was followed by an increasing influence of American medical practices, mainly in the form of an increasing role of private provision and financing.

The passage of the Medical Insurance Act in 1963 marked the beginning of a significant shift in health policy. The Act provided for a voluntary insurance scheme financed from equal contribution by employees and their employers, with the government paying for the administrative expenses. Without sufficient incentives or coercion, it is not surprising that only 20 insurance societies were established under the Act (NFMI, 1997: 5). A private member's bill providing for compulsory health insurance was passed by the legislature in 1970, but it was never implemented due to government opposition. The Minister of Health argued that there needed to be major improvements in national income and the state's finances, along with medical resources, before Korea could have national health insurance (Park, 1997: 353).

National Health Insurance (NHI) finally came about in 1977 when health insurance was made compulsory for firms employing 500 or more employees, followed by its extension to school employees in 1979. Health-insurance coverage to other workers was expanded in phases: the membership threshold for private firms was reduced to 300 employees in 1979, 100 in 1981, 16 in 1983, and 5 in 1988. The final expansion took place when the rural self-employed were covered in 1988 and the urban self-employed in 1989. The schemes for the rural and urban self-employed (inappropriately referred to as "regional schemes") cover more than half the population as they include anyone not covered by other health-insurance schemes or Medicaid (discussed on p. 109). The insured population belonged, as in Germany and Japan, to non-profit insurance societies based on region, occupations, and large firms, each with its own administrative and premium structure. The NHI not only insures the members, but also their dependants, which is defined rather liberally: indeed around two-thirds of all insured are dependants of primary members. Only daily wage-earners with less than one month of continuous employment and the unemployed continue to be excluded from health insurance.

Those not covered by NHI are eligible for Medicaid, which is a means-tested public-assistance scheme. It is available at three levels – 100, 50, and 33–60 per cent of the medical bill – depending on the claimants' level of poverty. More than half of all Medicaid beneficiaries fall in the 33–60 per cent aid bracket.

In the face of escalating health-care costs and financial problems faced by the schemes for the self-employed, the government established a high-powered Health Care Reform Committee, chaired by the prime minister in 1996, which published its report in December 1997. The Committee recommended integration of the 350 separate health-insurance societies into a single national scheme, reform of the pricing scheme for medical equipment and pharmaceuticals, and separation of prescription and dispensing of drugs. The implementation of the plan proved more problematic than the government had anticipated but it was eventually put in place despite massive protests The new National Health Insurance Corporation (NHIC) responsible for the entire insured population was established in 1998, though it was not until July 2000 that schemes for private-sector workers were brought under its aegis. A uniform premium structure came into effect in 2002. A new organization, the Health Insurance Review Agency, was also established to review reimbursement claims independently from insurers and providers.

Other aspects of the reform proved more problematic, especially the separation of the prescribing from the dispensing of drugs. The common practice of prescribing drugs by pharmacists and selling of drugs by doctors was believed to have led to the over-use of drugs and so the government decided to separate the two functions (De Geyndt, 1991: 8). The medical profession, after reluctantly agreeing to the separation, reneged on its commitment because it saw the move as depriving its members of a significant source of income. Following a violent strike by doctors and the arrest of the strike leaders, the dispute was finally resolved after the government agreed to increase doctors' fees by 25 per cent in phases – at the cost of US$1.9 billion over two years – reduce intake by medical schools, and increase wages for medical interns and residents (*Korea Times*, 16 August 2000).

Taiwan

The origin of the current health system in Taiwan goes back to the late nineteenth century when the Japanese colonial government systematically stifled traditional Chinese medicine and tried to replace it with Western medicine (Hsiao *et al.*, 1990). However, the efforts were haphazard and the government did little more than licence practitioners. Physicians could set up practice anywhere and most prescription drugs could be bought over the counter. Substantial changes were introduced only in the 1990s, when the establishment of National Health Insurance (NHI) necessitated regulation of services, charges, and payments.

On the financing side, Labour Insurance (LI), established in 1950, and the Government Employees' Insurance (GEI), established in 1958, were largely health-insurance schemes, though they provided modest cover for other contingencies as well. In the beginning the health-care benefits were modest, but this changed when in-patient benefits were made available in 1958 and out-patient benefits in 1970 (Lin, 1997: 71). Farmers were brought under social insurance in 1985, at first on a pilot basis and finally on a regular basis in 1989.

The introduction of the new programmes paralleled massive increases in health-care costs, which put an enormous strain on those not covered by insurance. This is reflected in the fact that between 1975 and 1993 the average monthly private expenditure on health increased by over twelve times, compared to only an eight-fold increase in average monthly earnings (Lin, 1997, 112). The Taiwanese sought to cope with the increasing burden of health-care costs by finding ingenious ways of joining social-insurance schemes, the premium for which was rising less rapidly than health-care costs. Those excluded formed occupational unions or declared themselves to be farmers – both categories were eligible for health-insurance, as we shall see soon – for the sole purpose of securing health-insurance cover (Lin, 1997: 113). By the 1990s, most people had found a way of securing health-insurance cover except for those who needed it the most, the young and the aged. The problem was only partially ameliorated by the launch of health insurance for the poor in 1989.

At the same time that the people were feeling the increasing burden of health care, the government too was faced with ballooning deficits incurred by GEI and LI. The problem was compounded by the government's inability to increase the premium because of its weak standing in a rapidly changing political environment – it was politically expedient to simply cover the deficit from public coffers (Lin, 1997: 69).

The government established a task force on social-welfare programmes in 1984, which in a report two years later recommended the establishment of an NHI programme by the year 2000. The target date was later advanced to 1995 and the scheme began operating in March of that year.

It was a peculiar scheme in that it differentiated between different segments of the population for the purpose of determining contribution rates, a legacy of the existing schemes. It was also unusual in that it involved varying levels of government contribution to the insureds' premium. The scheme also imposed severe co-payment requirement to curb demand, but the measures did not prevent increasing the deficit, which had to be funded by the government.

Provision

Hong Kong

Although private hospitals exist and are indeed lightly regulated, it is the public sector that dominates in-patient care in Hong Kong. There is also a third group of not-for-profit private hospitals, known as "subvented" hospitals, but they are tightly regulated and almost entirely funded by the government – they are for all practical purposes government hospitals and are treated as such in this book. The provision of out-patient care, in contrast, is dominated by the private sector.

Of all medical doctors in Hong Kong, 45 per cent are working in the public sector and the rest in the private sector. While private doctors account for 85 per cent of all out-patient consultation, their public counterparts provide much of the specialist consultation (Harvard Team, 1999). The share of all hospitals in the public sector increased in the 1960s and 1970s before stabilizing at around 88 per cent. Public hospitals in Hong Kong account for approximately 88 per cent of hospital beds, 92 per cent of total bed days, and most of the preventive and rehabilitative care (Grant and Yuen, 1998: 181).

The admission and occupancy rates in public hospitals have gone up, especially since 1991. Bed occupancy rates in public hospitals have been over 80 per cent, compared to only around 35 per cent in private hospitals and nursing homes. The low occupancy in private hospitals is no doubt a result of their high charges: the median total charge for private hospitals for a stay of three days was found to be US$1,269, which was close to one month's earnings of an average full-time employed worker. The physicians' charges (especially surgeons' fees) are usually many times more than the hospital charges (Harvard Team, 1999).

Beds in public hospitals are divided into three categories: general, semi-private, and private wards. However, the private and semi-private wards contain less than 2 per cent of all beds and are used mainly by civil servants, who pay a reduced rate. In-patient fees for general wards amounts to US$9 per day, revised according to a rise in the average operating cost of all HA hospitals. Charges in semi-private wards are ten times as much and yet more in private wards, but even these are lower than the comparable charges in private hospitals. Pensioners, civil servants (and their eligible family members), and public-assistance recipients receive free or nearly free care at public hospitals.

Singapore

The government is heavily involved in providing health care in Singapore. The large state presence in health care is, in the government's own words, to "cater to the lower income groups who cannot afford the private sector charges, and also to set the benchmark for the private sector on professional standards and charges" (http://www.gov.sg/moh/mohiss/hlthfin.html). In reality, public hospitals cater for a lot more people than just the lower-income groups.

The government owns and operates 13 of the 26 hospitals on the island. However, public hospitals are considerably larger than their private counterparts and contain 81 per cent of all beds, a small decline from 84 per cent in 1980. Public hospitals enjoy considerable autonomy in operational matters. The public facilities (including government out-patient clinics) employ 49 per cent of all doctors, a significant increase from 45 per cent of the total in 1980.

Public hospitals in Singapore offer a choice of different classes of ward accommodation, ranging from one-bedded room (Class A) to a dormitory with ten or more beds (Class C), at different prices. The different wards provide equivalent clinical services but different levels of comfort and physician choice. More significantly, patients in Class A wards pay the full cost whereas charges in other classes range from 80 per cent in Class B1 to 20 per cent in Class C; the rest is subsidized by the government. Thus, the choice of ward class involves not only a choice of the level of comfort but also the level of subsidy because the two are linked. The result of the different subsidies is that while the average size of in-patient bill at the National University Hospital was US$403 per day in a Class A ward in 1999, it was only US$52 per day in a Class C ward (http://www.gov.sg/moh/mohiss/hosbill.htm).

While there is no means test for the subsidized wards, it is expected that those who can afford better-class wards will do so to receive better non-clinical services. Moreover, there is a cultural stigma attached to admission to Class C wards, which discourages people from using them. In recent years, only about 20 per cent of hospital beds have been in Class C wards, a sharp decline from 80 per cent in the early 1980s (Purcal, 1995: 62). The decrease in the number of beds in the more subsidized wards was prompted partly by a decline in consumer demand and partly by the government's own wish to reduce its health-care expenditure by cutting back on these more subsidized wards.

Fees in private hospitals are considerably higher than in public hospitals' Class A wards, which are similar to private hospitals in the sense that they also do not receive subsidy. Thus, compared to the US$403 per day charge in the Class A ward of the University Hospital, the average daily cost at Gleneagles Hospital, a leading but not the most expensive hospital, was US$891. It is hardly surprising that patients choose public hospitals even when they are choosing non-subsidized hospital treatment. It is also not surprising that the private hospitals' share of total hospital admission has declined somewhat: from 25 per cent of the total in 1997 to 22 per cent in 1999 (http://www.gov.sg/moh/hfacts/hfacts-gen.html#ghe). A variety of reasons explain the higher charges at private hospitals, including higher levels of comfort, lack of economy of scale, and the incentive for over-servicing in order to maximize profit.

The government provides only a quarter of out-patient care and the rest is provided by the private sector. Users pay a nominal charge at government clinics, and the aged and students pay even less. Visits to government clinics as a share of all visits have been declining since the early 1980s. However, these clinics serve as a price benchmark for private clinics and offer a viable alternative to those who may find private services unaffordable.

Korea

In contrast to the two city-states, the provision of health care in Korea is heavily and increasingly dominated by the private sector. The share of hospitals in the public sector declined from 35 per cent in 1975 to 5 per cent in 1994 (Yang, 1997: 66). The decline was equally rapid with regard to beds: beds in public hospitals (including non-profit private hospitals) accounted for 53 per cent of total in 1977 (the year the NHI was introduced), but only 13 per cent in 1997. The share would be yet smaller if non-profit private hospitals were classified as private providers, whose market behaviour is similar to that of private providers. Public hospitals in recent years have been confined to areas involving public health and safety issues, such as tuberculosis and psychiatric hospitals.

Not only are most health-care providers in the private sector, there is little government regulation governing their behaviour regarding location, the quality and type of service they provide, or the level and nature of competition among them. Substantive regulation of providers includes the number of beds an institution must have to be called a hospital and the fees they charge (OECD, 2002a).

The NHI pays for the full range of in-patient and out-patient services, medication, preventive care, ambulances, and nursing. Traditional medical therapy was covered in 1987 and medicines prescribed by pharmacists in 1989. However, insurance does not cover such services as plastic surgery, many types of dental care, many expensive new procedures, and the treatment of narcotics abuse and self-inflicted wounds. There is also no cash benefit except when medical expenses exceed US$442 per month.

The number of total bed-days in hospitals in Korea increased from 27 million in 1989 to 43 million in 1998, even though the average length of hospitalization remained constant. The average length of stay in hospitals in 1998 was 16 days in national hospitals and 11 days in private hospitals, indicating that the former may have a higher incidence of critically ill patients. The bed-occupancy level declined from 79 to 66 per cent over the same period, though this has fluctuated by a big margin (Korea, 1999).

Taiwan

Taiwan's medical system reflects the market-driven nature of its economy with privately owned medical centres and hospitals accounting for a large and increasing share of total health services (Hsiao et al., 1990: 13). The public sector's share of all hospitals was only 15 per cent in 1998, while its share of out-patient clinics was 5 per cent. However, public hospitals tend to be larger and accounted for 33 per cent of all hospital beds in 1998, a sharp decline from 42 per cent in 1985. With regard to physicians, the share in the public sector increased somewhat, from 21 per cent in 1985 to 23 per cent in 1998 (ROC, Department of Health, 2000).

The NHI pays for most in-patient and out-patient services, dental services, prescription drugs and Chinese medicine, psychiatric services, laboratory and X-ray services, pre- and post-natal care, and physical examinations for adults over 40 years of age. However, it does not cover treatment for drug addiction, plastic surgery, in-vitro fertilization, and other procedures and treatments routinely excluded from health insurance in other countries. Maternity care in shared wards is covered, but only for the first two children.

Consumers have the freedom to visit any public or private facility they wish, but must pay an additional fee of US$1.60 to visit district hospitals without a referral and US$3.25 for visiting area hospitals without a referral. However, the Taiwanese continue to prefer larger medical facilities and are willing to pay the extra cost involved.

Comparative

The ratio of doctors to population is broadly similar across the four NIEs, as shown in Table 4.1. The ratio of hospital beds to population has also increased, except in Singapore where it has declined apparently as a result of the excess capacity that existed earlier. While the ratio for both hospital beds and doctors in the NIEs is considerably lower than the OECD average, there is no evidence of an overall shortage. It may well be that the small geographic size and high population density in Hong Kong and Singapore makes it possible for them to intensively utilize their health

HEALTH

Table 4.1 Physicians and hospital beds, per 1,000 persons

	Physicians		Hospital beds	
	1970	Late 1990s	1970	Late 1990s
Hong Kong	0.7	1.3	4.2	4.7
Singapore	0.7	1.6	3.7	4.9
Korea	0.5	1.3	0.5	4.8
Taiwan	0.5	1.4	1.6	5.6
High income OECD	1.4	2.8	9.4	7.4

Sources: World Bank, 2002; DGBAS, 1999.

resources. Even Korea and Taiwan are geographically compact places where much of the rural population lives relatively close to an urban centre. Having said that, there is a shortage of health-care facilities and personnel in rural areas in the two Northeast Asian states.

There is significant difference across the NIEs with respect to the distribution of physicians and hospital beds in public and private medical facilities, as shown in Table 4.2. Less than half of all physicians in all NIEs work in the private sector, reflecting the predominance of general physicians, who tend to be concentrated in the private sector. Specialist doctors, in comparison, are concentrated in the public sector.

The situation is very different with regard to hospital beds. At one extreme is Hong Kong and Singapore, where more than 80 per cent of all beds are in the public sector. At the other extreme is Korea, with only 23 per cent of beds in the public sector, and Taiwan, with 33 per cent. More remarkably, the public sector's share has declined by a large margin in Korea and Taiwan as a result of government efforts to reduce involvement in the provision of health care. As we shall see later in this chapter, the predominance of private hospitals in combination with national health insurance may have been a significant contributor to rising health-care costs in Korea and Taiwan.

Table 4.2 Share of total physicians and hospital beds in the public sector, per cent

	Physicians		Hospital beds	
Hong Kong	–	45 (1996)	88 (1980)	88 (1996)
Korea	–	–	53 (1997)	23 (1994)
Singapore	45 (1980)	49 (1998)	84 (1980)	81 (1999)
Taiwan	31 (1993)	48 (1998)	42 (1980)	33 (1999)

Sources: DGBAS, 2002; Grant and Yuen, 1998; Yang, 1997; Singapore Department of Statistics, 2001.

HEALTH

Financing

Hong Kong

Total health expenditure in Hong Kong increased at an average annual rate of 16 per cent during the 1990s. This was a faster growth rate than that of GDP, which rose by only 13 per cent each year over the same period. As a result, health expenditure's share of GDP increased from 3.7 per cent in 1990 to 4.6 per cent in 1997 (Harvard Team, 1999b: table 1.3).

At the same time, per capita health-care expenditure grew at an average annual rate of 14 per cent, increasing from US$550 in 1990 to US$1,152 in 1996, a cumulative increase of 108 per cent. In constant HK$ (1990) terms, however, it increased by only 40 per cent (Harvard Team, 1999b: table b).

Much of the growth in health-care expenditure has been in the public sector, where it more than tripled between 1989 and 1996, compared to a 2.5 times increase in private health expenditures (Liu and Yue, 1998). Of total health expenditures, the public sector accounted for 54 per cent in 1996–1997, up from 48 per cent in 1989–1990[1] (Harvard Team, 1999b: table d1). The share of total government expenditures devoted to health increased similarly from 11 to 14 per cent over the same period.[2]

Government health expenditure consists mainly of spending on public and aided hospitals, which provide heavily subsidized services without means testing. Patients pay a nominal flat fee of US$9 per day for hospitalization, which is waived in the case of hardship. In 1996, the HA waived slightly more than one-third of its in-patient fees (Grant and Yuen, 1998: 119). Pensioners, civil servants, and recipients of public assistance receive free or nearly free services in public hospitals and out-patient clinics. It is not surprising that the cost recovery rate from user charges in HA hospitals is only 2 per cent in acute care wards (Liu and Yue, 1998).

Outpatient services in government clinics are heavily subsidized: the public pays a flat rate of under US$5 for general out-patient treatment and under US$6 for specialist out-patient consultation. In addition, CSSA recipients, who represented 11 per cent of all patients attending government clinics in 1996, receive free service in government clinics. The cost-recovery rate in government clinics is 19 per cent for general out-patient services and 10 per cent for specialist out-patient services (ibid.). However, as mentioned earlier, government clinics form only a small part of the out-patient care system.

Private health expenditures as a percentage of total private consumption expenditure declined in the late 1980s, from 4.1 per cent in 1986 to 3.5 per cent in 1989, before growing to 4.8 per cent by 1997 (ibid.). Private payment is the main source of funding for out-patient services as well as pharmaceuticals. Private health expenditures are largely from out-of-pocket, as only a small percentage of the population is covered by private insurance: 18 per cent of the population in 1991 and 21 per cent in 1998 (Harvard Team, 1998). Group-purchased insurance, which is offered mostly by large firms, formed 84 per cent of all who were covered by private insurance (Grant and Yuen, 1998: 123).

Singapore

The Singapore government sums up its health-care-financing system as "based on individual responsibility, coupled with government subsidies to keep basic health care affordable. Patients are expected to pay part of the cost of the medical service that they use, and pay more when they demand higher levels of service in terms of comfort and ward amenities" (http://www.gov.sg/moh/mohiss/hlthfin.html). To put the principle into practice, it has established an elaborate financing system consisting of direct expenditure by the government, regulated private expenditure from the Medisave and Medishield schemes, and out-of-pocket payments.

Singapore is one of the smallest spenders on health in the world and, more remarkably, the share of the GDP devoted to it has actually declined over the past forty years. In the early 1960s, national health expenditures formed around 4.5 per cent of GDP, but then they began to decline and have hovered around 3 per cent of GDP since 1985. In 1999, Singapore spent about US$2.5 billion, or US$792 per capita, on health (http://www.gov.sg/moh/hfacts/hfacts-gen.html#ghe).

The government's expenditure on health as a percentage of national health expenditure ranged between 37 (in 1975) and 52 per cent (in 1968) until the mid 1980s, when it declined and began to fluctuate in the 25–29 per cent range. But its share began to rise again in the late 1990s and had risen to 42 per cent by 1999.

Government expenditures on health include subsidy to public hospitals and out-patient clinics, capital expenditures on the Ministry of Health, and the cost of providing medical care to state employees. Class C wards in public hospitals are the main vehicles for delivering subsidized health care to the general population. As mentioned earlier, patients pay only 20 per cent of the cost of service in Class C wards, and 35, 50, and 80 per cent respectively in B2, B2+ and B1 wards. The subsidy to public hospitals amounted to US$360 million in 1999 (Singapore, 2000: 17). Those unable to pay even for lower classes and highly subsidized service in public hospitals may request a partial or total waiver, which used to be funded from the government's general revenues but is now funded indirectly through Medifund. The government also provides 50 per cent of the public out-patient clinics' operating costs (*Straits Times*, 17 July 1996: 22). Individual patients pay a modest sum for out-patient treatment, and students and the aged pay even less.

Private health expenditures in Singapore take the form of indirect payment through Medisave or Medishield or directly from out-of-pocket. However, Medisave and Medishield form a rather insignificant share of the total spending. In 1999 formed only 8 per cent of the total health expenditure (Singapore, 2000: 17), which is hardly surprising given the limitations on its use. Similarly, Medishield payments formed only 1.2 per cent of the total health expenditure in 1999, which is again unsurprising given the restrictions the scheme imposes. The average size of the Medishield payment was US$415 per claim in 1999.

Over the years, the health-care burden on Singaporean households has increased continuously. Household expenditure on medical services as a percentage of the total household expenditure increased from 2.7 in 1975 to 4.5 in 1995, and then rapidly to 5.8 in 1999 (Singapore, 1999).

Korea

The country's national health expenditure amounted to US$26 billion in 1997 (declining to US$16 billion in 1998 in the wake of the economic crisis), which was a sharp increase from US$5.7 billion in 1987 (OECD, 2000a; OECD, 2001). More significantly, it increased at an annual average of 7.5 per cent during 1990–1998, compared to the inflation rate of 6.0 per cent and GDP growth of 5.8 per cent (*Korea Times*, 10 May 1999). National health expenditure's share of GDP increased, accordingly, from 2 per cent in the 1970s to 4.2 per cent in 1987, rising to 6.0 per cent in 1997 (it then fell to 5.0 per cent in 1998). In per capita terms, national health expenditures increased from US$228 in 1987 to US$870 in 1997 (declining to US$730 in 1998). While the level of national health expenditure is not large by OECD standards, the pace at which it increased during the 1990s was the fastest in the industrialized world (OECD, 2002a: 21).

Public expenditure on health increased from US$2.1 billion in 1987 to US$7.6 billion in 1998 (OECD, 2002a).[3] Its share of total expenditures increased correspondingly from 36 to 45 per cent; the rest was funded from out-of-pocket payments, unlike many other countries (for example the USA) where private spending is derived largely from private insurance. About three-fifths of the public expenditure is derived from social insurance and the remainder from the government's general revenues. As a share of total public spending, government expenditure on health increased from 9.4 to 12.4 per cent between 1987 and 1997 (but declined to 9 per cent in 1998). About 60 per cent of the government's direct health expenditure (that is, excluding social insurance) was towards health insurance, largely as premium subsidies for the self-employed, while another 27 per cent was devoted to Medicaid.

Health insurance is funded largely from premiums contributed by employees and their employers. The premiums used to vary considerably across the schemes, but a uniform premium of 3.9 per cent of income came into effect in 2002. The premium for the self-employed takes into account a range of factors, including property, income, age, and sex. The premium is split evenly between employers and employees, except that the government contributes 20 per cent of the premium for private school teachers (the employer pays 30 per cent), 46 per cent for the rural self-employed, and 34 per cent for the urban self-employed. Government subsidies, much of which went to the self-employed, formed 7 per cent of the total health-insurance revenues in 1988 but this figure had risen to 19 per cent by 1999.

The insurance schemes' expenditures began to exceed revenues in the mid 1990s and they began to experience varying levels of financial difficulties. Between 1994 and 1998, the schemes' expenditures increased by 20.5 per cent each year on average, while contributions increased only by 12.2 per cent. In 1999, the various schemes suffered a combined deficit of US$604 million, despite the legal requirement for the schemes to be self-sufficient. The deficit was the largest for a scheme for private-sector employees, but it was projected that in the future it would be the scheme for the self-employed that would have the largest deficit. A significant reason for the self-employed scheme's deficit is non-reporting (almost 28 per cent of the insured did not report income in 1999) and under-reporting of income (*Korea Times*, 22 September 1999). It was projected that without reform the NHI's deficit would soar to US$3 billion by 2004 (*Korea Times*, 23 February 2000). Recent reforms are believed to have reversed the trend and the government is committed to eliminating the deficit altogether.

Despite the large and growing expenditures by the government and insurance schemes, out-of-pocket payment continues to form the largest source of health-care financing. Out-of-pocket payments are required even for covered services: 20 per cent for in-patient services and 30–55 per cent for out-patient care, and 30–40 per cent of the dispensing and drug cost at pharmacies, in addition to a flat fee of about US$4 for each unit of service. In 1996, out-of-pocket payments formed 59 per cent of national health expenditures (compared to 72 per cent in 1980), 66 per cent of out-patient expenditures, and 44 per cent of in-patient expenditures (Young, 1999; Korea, 1996: 237).

Taiwan

The country has witnessed spectacular increases in national health expenditures, rising from US$8.2 billion in 1991 to US$15.8 billion in 1999, which in per capita terms was an increase from US$416 to US$717 (ROC, Department of Health, 2000). The expenditures grew at an average annual rate of 11 per cent in current NT$ terms between 1991 and 1999, compared to a 9 per cent average annual growth for the GDP. As a result,

HEALTH

the national health expenditures' share of GDP rose from 4.6 per cent in 1991 to 5.4 per cent in 1999.

The government's budget, compulsory insurance (NHI), and out-of-pocket spending by individuals are the main sources of health-care financing. The three have grown at different paces over the years, leading to a realignment of their respective shares. The compulsory insurance's share of total health expenditure increased from 36 per cent in 1991 to 56 per cent in 1999. At the same time, the direct government expenditures' share declined from 16 to 9 per cent, while the private payments' share declined from 49 per cent to 35 per cent. However, taking both insurance and direct government expenditures into account, public expenditures' share of the national health expenditures increased from 51 per cent in 1991 to 65 per cent in 1999 (ROC, Department of Health, 2000).

While the NHI's contribution rate is set at 5.2 per cent of income (it was 4.25 per cent until 2000), the formula by which it is shared among the employer, the employee, and the government varies by occupational group. The insured are divided into six categories and thirteen sub-categories by occupations and employment status. The government's share of the contribution varies across occupational groups, ranging from nil for the high-income professionals and the self-employed (except farmers and fishermen) to 100 per cent for low-income families and retired veterans. For most private-sector employees, the government contributes 10 per cent of the total and the employer 60 per cent, while the employee pays 30 per cent. For public-sector employees, the government contributes 60 per cent (except for private school employees, for whom the government and the employer each pays 30 per cent) and the employee 40 per cent. Farmers and seamen pay a flat rate equivalent to the average premiums for all NHI members – they pay 30 per cent and the government pays the rest. Members of occupational unions and public-assistance recipients also pay a flat rate, but they pay 60 per cent of the amount while the government pays the rest. Veterans and their dependants pay the flat rate too, but the government pays the entire premium for the veterans and 70 per cent for their dependants. Each NHI member is also required to pay a premium for his or her dependant family members, to the maximum of five, at the same rate as the primary member.

Receipts from premiums contributed by employers, employees, and government subsidy formed 33, 39, and 28 per cent respectively of the NHI's total revenue of US$8.5 billion in 1999 (ROC, Department of Health, 2000). But its expenditure that year amounted to US$8.9 billion, resulting in a deficit that was paid for by the government. The scheme has increased user co-payment to reduce its deficit and may have to increase the premium in the next round of actuarial assessment.

In addition to paying a premium, the insured are required to make co-payment at the point of service. For out-patient visits, the co-payment ranges from NT$50 at local clinics and district hospitals to NT$100 at regional hospitals and NT$150 at medical centres. The objective of differentiated rates is to encourage people to visit their local general physician, though this has not worked in practice because those who prefer higher-level facilities are willing to pay the extra amount from out-of-pocket. For in-patient care, the co-payment ranges from nil to 30 per cent (subject to a ceiling of NT$20,000 per admission and NT$34,000 for the entire calendar year) depending on the length of hospitalization. Since 1999, there is also co-payment for drugs, which ranges from nil to NT$100 depending on the cost of drugs. The government provides subsidies to cover user charges for the poor. Co-payments recovered 5 to 13 per cent of the out-patient costs, depending on the type of the institution, and about 6 per cent of in-patient costs in 1998 (http://www.nhi.gov.tw); this is likely to have gone up recently as a result of an increase in co-payment rates.

As one would expect, private payment used to be the largest source of health-care expenditure but this declined following the introduction of NHI. Yet health's share of total household-consumption expenditure increased from 6.0 per cent in 1990 to 7.6 per cent in 1995, and then further to 8.6 per cent in 1999 (DGBAS, 1999). This is because of the extension of insurance coverage, which required insurance payment from those sections of the population not paying before, and various co-payments that the insured have to make at the point of service. On average, households pay 50 per cent more on health care than was the case during the pre-NHI period but in return receive comprehensive insurance coverage (Tsay, 1998: 98).

Comparative

The health-care financing arrangement in the region displays two distinct patterns. Korea and Taiwan rely on statutory health insurance, while Hong Kong and Singapore rely on direct government subsidy to public hospitals and out-patient clinics (see Table 4.3). The insurance schemes in Korea and Taiwan are supposed to be self-financing, but in reality the government contributes significant sums towards subsidizing premiums and deficits. Singapore also has a compulsory savings scheme (Medisave) and a voluntary health-insurance scheme (Medishield) but they play a small role in the overall financing of health care. Hong Kong is seriously considering establishing a compulsory savings scheme similar to Singapore's Medisave but allowing withdrawal only during old age. Regardless of the financing arrangement, out-of-pocket payments form half or more of total health expenditures in the NIEs. As mentioned earlier, this is the result of heavy co-payment requirements (except in Hong Kong) and the small state presence in the provision of out-patient services in the two city states.

Health-care expenditures in the NIEs, as indeed elsewhere, have risen faster than the consumer price index. This is the result of greater reliance

Table 4.3 Health care financing in the NIEs

	Government financed	Compulsory savings	Social insurance
Hong Kong	Public hospitals and government out-patient clinics	Health protection account (proposed)	
Singapore	Public hospitals and government out-patient clinics – subsidy varies by class of ward	Medisave	Medishield (voluntary, but high take-up rate)
Korea	Medical aid Subsidy towards insurance premium and insurance funds' deficit		National health insurance
Taiwan	Subsidy towards insurance premium and insurance funds' deficit		National health insurance

on the latest technology, which tends to cost more, and the economic and political power of health-care professionals to increase the price of their services faster than productivity increases. Increasing consumer expectations exert further pressures on costs. Table 4.4 depicts the massive increase and divergent patterns in per capita health expenditures in the NIEs. Hong Kong is the largest spender per capita, followed by Singapore, Taiwan, and then Korea. The ranking is consistent with the expectation that health-care expenditures depend on income levels: Hong Kong is the richest country in the region and Korea the poorest. However, Singapore's placement conceals the fact that its per capita income is similar to

Table 4.4 Per capita national health expenditures, US$

	Late 1980s	Late 1990s
Hong Kong	548	1,153
Singapore	218	807
Korea	228	870
Taiwan	403	671
High income OECD	1,797	2,907

Sources: De Geyndt, 1991; Shin, 2000; Kalisch, 1998: annexe, 99; World Bank, 2002.

Note
National expenditure converted to US$ at prevailing exchange rate.

(and by some measures exceeds) Hong Kong's, yet it spends 43 per cent less.

A different picture emerges when we look at the total health expenditures as a percentage of GDP (see Table 4.5). By this measure, Korea is the largest spender, followed by Taiwan, Hong Kong, and, distantly, Singapore. But even Korea spends a much smaller share of its GDP on health than the OECD average of 8 per cent. Hong Kong and Singapore are remarkable because they rank among the richest countries in the world yet spend less than the minimum of 5 per cent of GDP recommended by the World Health Organization.

Yet another picture is revealed when we look at the growth patterns in Table 4.5. Singapore experienced the largest increase in per capita spending on health but as a share of GDP it actually declined because income grew faster than health expenditures. Hong Kong's per capita spending increased at the second-fastest rate and the share of GDP spent on health grew at the fastest rate among the four NIEs. Korea is a special case because the share of GDP spent on health grew only modestly despite the fact that it spends the largest share, indicating that its health spending was high even before the period being considered here.

The distribution of total health spending again reveals interesting patterns. Unlike many countries, both developed and developing, around the world that experienced a decline in the public sector's share of health spending during the 1980s and 1990s, the four NIEs experienced varying degrees of increase. Table 4.5 shows that the largest private spending on health is in Korea, which might be surprising given its universal health insurance but not if it is remembered that the NHI imposes huge co-payment requirements and excludes a large number of services. In many ways Taiwan is similar to Korea, in that its NHI also imposes large co-payments and exclusions, but this is offset somewhat by its substantial subsidy towards insurance premiums. Hong Kong has witnessed a modest

Table 4.5 National health expenditures in the NIEs, per cent

	Total health expenditures, % of GDP		Government's share[1] of total health expenditure, %	
	Late 1980s	Late 1990s	Late 1980s	Late 1990s
Hong Kong	3.7	4.6	48	54
Singapore	3.1	3.0	41	42
Korea	4.2	6.0	36	45
Taiwan	4.6	5.4	51	65
High income OECD	8.8	10.8	60	56

Sources: De Geyndt, 1991; Shin, 2000; Kalisch, 1998: annexe, 99; World Bank, 2002.

Note
Includes social-insurance expenditure.

decline in the share of private health expenditures, though by some measures it has increased by a small margin. In any event, most Hong Kong residents receive virtually free in-patient treatment, the most expensive component of health care. The variation in the respective shares of the public and private sectors is the result of the pricing behaviour of private providers who dominate the out-patient services and pharmaceuticals sectors rather than of a shift in government policy. Singapore is an interesting case because the private sector's share increased rapidly in the late 1980s and early 1990s but receded somewhat in the late 1990s.

Outcomes

Hong Kong

Health care in Hong Kong is largely adequate and all those who need care get it, though not as promptly or at as high a level of comfort as they might wish. There is ample supply of public in-patient and out-patient facilities, which are available to all regardless of ability to pay. There are of course non-monetary costs involved in accessing health care at public facilities. The average waiting time at public out-patient clinics is two hours, while the waiting period for non-emergency surgery is nine months – the government has set a target of reducing the waiting time to one hour and four months respectively (http://www.info.gov.hk/hwb/english/PA99/).

The health system is relatively equitable in terms of financing: the lowest income quintile spends 1.8 per cent of household income on health whereas the highest quintile spends 2.4 per cent (Harvard Team, 1999). Moreover, there are only small differences in the rates of both in-patient and out-patient visits in different income quintiles. The government's health expenditures too are largely equitable. In 1996, the poorest quintile attracted 25 per cent of Hospital Authority's in-patient expenditures, compared to 16 per cent for the richest quintile. The government was the largest source of finance for in-patient services for all quintile groups, while for out-patient services it was the largest source only for the poorest quintile (Harvard Team, 1999b). However, the continuation of the privileged access enjoyed by civil servants and the superior ward classes available to them are inequitable and a blemish on an otherwise fair system. While lower-income households are more likely to use subsidized public facilities, even the top income group uses public facilities for both out-patient and in-patient services. The political implications of this are significant, as use of public facilities by upper-income groups ensures political support for the public system.

None the less, health status in Hong Kong varies by class. The Harvard Team found that 11 per cent of the lowest income group (with a monthly household income below US$1,282) suffered from bad health, compared with only 3 per cent of the highest income group (households with an income above US$5,128).

Hong Kong's accessible and equitable health-care system has been achieved at a rather modest cost, as described earlier. The concentration of public subsidies on in-patient care, which is expensive, has fostered a system that is both efficient and equitable. Centralized provision in public facilities reduces scope for supplier-induced demand and duplication of facilities, thus reducing overall costs. There are, of course, some who prefer private provision and call for a reduction in the extensive role that the government plays in the health sector in Hong Kong (Hay, 1992).

The reform efforts currently underway are unlikely to make a significant difference in the way health care is provided and financed in Hong Kong. Even if the proposed Health Protection Account is established, it is unlikely to make much of an impact except to mobilize some additional resources. Based on Singapore's experience with Medisave, one can surmise that the proposed contribution rate is too low to allow the accumulation of sufficient funds to pay for long-term care of the aged.

Singapore

Heavy government involvement in the provision of in-patient and, to a lesser extent, out-patient care ensures that the entire population has access to subsidized health care of reasonable quality. At the same time, the government has a complex range of direct and indirect measures in place to curb demand for health care and to control costs. Users are required and/or encouraged to pay from out-of-pocket, Medicare, and Medishield.

Medicare, the compulsory savings scheme for medical expenses, covers two-thirds of the labour-force; the excluded are for the most part foreign workers. Subscribers to Medishield, which is a public but voluntary health-insurance scheme, account for under half of the labour-force. Non-subscription to Medishield is particularly high among the aged, the segment of the population most in need of it: 25 per cent of those aged 61–70 years do not subscribe to the scheme (Prescott and Nichols, 1997: 7).

Hospital admission has declined continuously in Singapore, falling from 0.09 per person per year in 1980 to 0.08 in 1999. The average length of hospitalization has also declined constantly: from 24.6 days in 1965, to 10 in 1980, and 7.5 in 1999 (Singapore, 1999).

Targeting of subsidy, without administratively costly means testing, and large government involvement in the provision of health care have kept a lid on costs. The government plays a significant role, though largely through guidance, in what doctors and hospitals charge for their service. Government dominance of hospital care also has efficiency benefits in the form of economy of scale. The availability of reasonably good services at subsidized prices imposes immense pressure on private hospitals to remain competitively priced. Unlike in many countries where public hospitals are stigmatized, those in Singapore offer viable choice to consumers, forcing private providers to target the small niche for the affluent that value hotel-type service frills.

On the financing side, the government has established an elaborate system to raise private funds for paying for services through schemes such as Medisave, Medishield, and out-of-pocket payments. However, notwithstanding the compliments heaped by Singaporean and foreign observers (Lim, 2002; Pauly, 2001), Medisave and Medishield play a rather insignificant role in the overall financing of health care, together accounting for less than 10 per cent of total health expenditures. Reliance on Medifund, on the other hand, has increased, though it still involves only a modest sum, a total of US$7.2 million, or US$108 per beneficiary, in 1997 (Singapore, 2000: 18).

While no study is available, one may reasonably surmise that government spending on subsidies is egalitarian because a large proportion of the expenditure is directed at public hospitals. However, Medisave and Medishield are likely to have replicated or even worsened the overall distribution of income in Singapore.

Korea

The key component in the Korean health system is the compulsory health-insurance system covering almost the entire population. In 1999, 92 per cent of the Korean population was covered by health insurance, with the remainder covered by Medicaid (Korea, NHIC, 1999). Beneficiaries of the Medicaid scheme as a percentage of the population increased from 5.6 in 1980 to 9.2 in 1990 but then began to decline, reaching 4.4 in 1995 and 2.8 in 1998 (MOHW, *Yearbook of Health and Welfare Statistics 1999*).

There is evidence that utilization of health care increased after the advent of universal health-insurance coverage. Health-care utilization during the 1985–1999 period increased by 54 per cent for in-patient care and 108 per cent for out-patient care. In 1999, the utilization rate was 0.09 cases per person for in-patient care and 5.89 cases per person for out-patient care (Korea, 2000). As one would expect, the rate for those above 65 years of age was almost five times that of the rest of the population. The increase in the utilization rate has been accompanied by increasing incidence of insurance claims as well as a larger size for each claim. The number of health-insurance claims increased by 84 per cent between 1992 and 1999, while the payment for each claim increased on average by 88 per cent for out-patient care and by 70 per cent for in-patient care (Korea, NHIC, 1999). No less significantly, claims for drugs per person increased by 432 per cent during the same period.

The universal insurance alone cannot be blamed for the sky-rocketing health-care expenditures in Korea, however, but rather its combination with private provision. The prevalence of profit-driven private providers with the security of reimbursement from insurance funds promotes over-servicing, evident in the high use of prescription drugs, especially injected drugs, which attract higher rates (Yang, 1991: 125). Further evidence of this is the world's highest incidence of Caesarean delivery in Korea, especially in private hospitals where 38–39 per cent of all deliveries are by Caesarean section, compared to 28 per cent in public facilities (Yang, 1997: 70). It is not coincidental that Caesarean procedures involve a hospital stay of 7.2 days on average, compared to 2.9 days for normal delivery. Another reason for the high health-care costs in Korea is the fragmented health-insurance system, which hampers the realization of economy of scale. The result is that administration constitutes 10–16 per cent of the schemes' premium income, compared to 1.5 per cent in Canada and similar to the 10 per cent in the USA (Yang, 1997: 63–64). The amalgamation of insurance schemes in 2000 is expected to have improved the situation in this regard. However, until recently the government's cost-control measures targeted demand through co-payment and the exclusion of services and only recently did it shift its attention to the supply side and put measures in place to control the providers' behaviour. The government has introduced a payment schedule whereby hospitals are paid rates based on costs at the most efficient hospitals, and has banned hospitals from selling drugs.

The Korean health-care system also suffers from inequities, largely because of the co-payment requirement, which restricts the poor but is too low to inhibit the affluent (Peaboy *et al.*, 1995: 37; Yang, 1991: 126). The existence of separate insurance societies, each with its own premium, was a source of inequity as rural dwellers and lower-income private-sector workers often paid a larger proportion of their income, but this ended with the establishment of a national scheme in 2002 (Kwon, 2003). Medicaid only partially offsets the inequities of the Korean health-care system, as the completely free component of the scheme is availed by only 1.6 per cent of the population, a small proportion of the 9.8 per cent of the population that live under the poverty line (Yang, 1997: 74). Access to health care is significantly lower for those living in rural areas: only 4.2 per cent of medical doctors and 8 per cent of hospital beds are located outside urban areas, but they serve about 24 per cent of the Korean population (Young, 1999).

Opinion surveys reveal a high level of dissatisfaction with the health services, despite the large resources devoted to it. A 1995 survey found that 61 per cent were moderately or very dissatisfied with the medical services they had received. Long waiting times for treatment, unsatisfactory treatment, and high medical fees were ranked as the three most important reasons for dissatisfaction (Korea, 2000). Recent reforms have done little to allay public dissatisfaction, as is evident from opinion surveys conducted following the reforms (*Korea Herald*, 4 July 2001).

Taiwan

The percentage of the population covered by statutory health insurance expanded dramatically after the launch of NHI in 1995. Compared to 1993, when only half the population was covered by some public-health insurance, nearly the entire population was covered by NHI in 1997. However, enrolment is lower for the aboriginal population and for residents of mountain areas and outlying islands: 84 per cent and 90 per cent respectively in 1997 (www.nhi.gov.tw/achievement.htm).

The establishment and expansion of NHI has been accompanied by a tremendous increase in the utilization rate and Taiwan is now believed to have one of the highest rates in the world (http://www.nhi.gov.tw). In 1999, the utilization rate was 0.12 per person per year for in-patient services and 15.1 visits per person per year for out-patient services (cens.com/nhi/what.htm). The number of out-patient visits increased by 60 per cent between 1995 and 1999, while the number of in-patient days increased by 104 per cent. However, the average length of hospitalization declined by 8 per cent, from 9.4 to 8.7 days, during the same period (ROC, Department of Health, 2000). NHI alone does not account for the increased utilization, as the out-patient visitation rate was a high 13.5 before its introduction (Lin, 1997: 462).

The average cost of out-patient visits increased by 16 per cent between 1995 and 1999 while the average cost of in-patient care increased by 26 per cent. It would be a mistake, however, to point the finger exclusively at NHI, because costs began to sky-rocket much before its launch. Taking a longer-term perspective, per capita expenditure increased at an average annual rate of 16 per cent during 1980–1994 and by only 9 per cent during the 1994–1998 period. The rising expenditure is more likely to be the result of combining NHI with the expansion of private health-care provision.

The NHI has many features that promote equity. The government subsidizes the entire premium for low-income families and 70 per cent of the premium for farmers, who tend to have significantly lower income than the rest of the population (Chiang 1997: 229). The establishment of the NHI evinced a larger increase in utilization for low-income groups. Within a year of its establishment, visits to physicians increased by 41 per cent among the middle-income groups and 37 per cent among the low-income group, compared to 11 per cent among the upper-income groups (Cheng and Chiang, 1997: 91). Yet the NHI also has some seriously regressive features. Co-payments, which comprise a fixed amount rather than a proportion of income, constitute a greater percentage of the lower-income groups' income (Tsay, 1998: 94). However, since the government pays the entire premium for low-income groups, NHI has the overall effect of reducing income inequality by 4.3 per cent (Tsay, 1998: abstract).

Compared to the poor public perception of health insurance in Korea, there is broad support for the NHI among the Taiwanese. Surveys show that more than 75 per cent of the users were happy with the NHI in 1997, which was a large jump from the 33 per cent before its establishment in 1995 (Hu and Hsieh, 1999).

Comparative

The different arrangements for providing and financing health care in the NIEs are reflected in their different health-care outcomes. Not surprisingly, utilization of health care varies greatly across the NIEs. Table 4.6 shows that Hong Kong has the lowest incidence of utilization of both in-patient and out-patient care and Taiwan the highest. Indeed in Taiwan the rate of in-patient care utilization was four times higher than in Hong Kong, and in the case of out-patient care it was 100 times higher. Singapore is closer to Hong Kong and Korea is closer to Taiwan in the utilization of both in- and out-patient care. Ageing of the population, greater incidence of chronic illness, and higher income levels, which lead the population to demand a higher level of service, have all contributed to the increasing utilization in the NIEs. However, the largely private provision of health care coupled with social insurance financing have also contributed to the particularly high utilization rate in Korea and Taiwan.

Higher utilization of health care, combined with improvement in nutrition, education, public health, and medical technology, is reflected in the population's health status, shown in Table 4.7. The infant mortality rate in

Table 4.6 Health care utilization rate, per person per year, late 1990s

	In-patient	Out-patient
Hong Kong	0.03	0.15
Singapore	0.08	–
Korea	0.09	5.89
Taiwan	0.12	15.1

Sources: Liu and Yue, 1998; HOHW, 1999; Singapore Statistical Highlights, 1999; www.nhi.gov.tw/achievement.htm.

Table 4.7 Infant mortality rate and life expectancy

	Infant mortality rate per 1,000 persons		Life expectancy at birth, years	
	1970	Late 1990s	1970	2000
Hong Kong	19.4	2.9	70.0	80.0
Singapore	19.7	2.9	68.0	78.0
Korea	46.0	8.2	60.0	73.0
Taiwan	22.7	6.4 (1995)	–	76.0 (1996)
High income OECD	22.0	5.8	71.0	78.0

Sources: World Bank, 2002; DGBAS, 2000.

HEALTH

the four NIEs has declined by a large margin and in the case of the two city states the rate is actually superior to that of most OECD countries. A similar picture emerges from data on life expectancy, which in all four NIEs was lower than in high-income OECD countries in the 1960s, but the gap had been closed by the mid 1990s and Hong Kong actually achieved a longer life span. Women in the NIEs on average live six years longer than their male counterparts, which is same differential in the OECD countries.

There is no point denying the inadequacies of the infant mortality rate and life expectancy as indicators of health outcome, but without agreement on better indicators (Smith, 2002), they should suffice as approximate measures. The graph in Figure 4.1 compares health status and the share of resources devoted to health care across the four NIEs. The best possible outcome would be one in which a country would have both low total expenditures and a low infant mortality rate. The graph shows that Singapore has achieved the best health-care outcomes at the lowest cost, followed by Hong Kong and Taiwan, with Korea in last place.

Income levels partially explain the different performance of the health-care systems in the four NIEs: the two city states enjoy the highest income levels and it is to be expected that they have the best health status. However, income levels tend to be positively related to health-care expenditures, although that is not the case in the NIEs: the two city states have the highest income but the lowest expenditure as a share of GDP. Moreover, contrary to findings of a positive relationship between public spending on health and health status (Gupta *et al.*, 1999), the varying level of public spending on health does not explain the varying performance because this is low in Korea as well as in Singapore, with two very different outcomes. Nor is the level of private spending significant because it is,

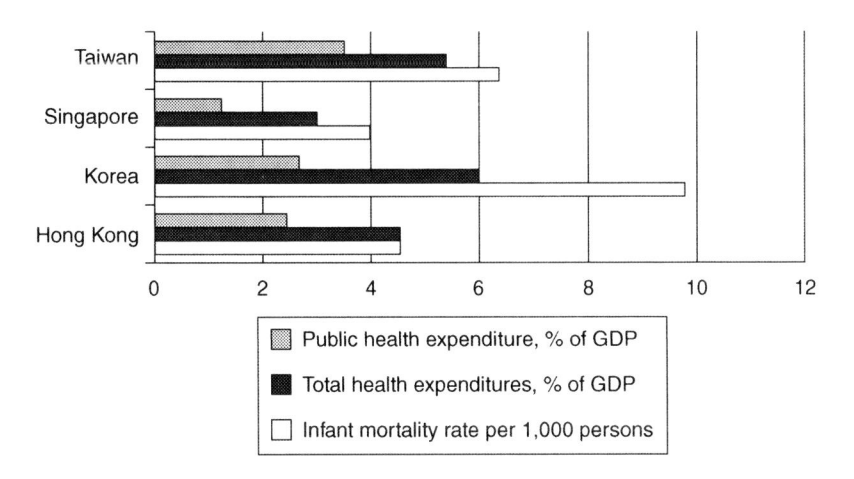

Figure 4.1 Health expenditures and infant mortality rate (based on Tables 4.5 and 4.7).

again, low in both Korea and Singapore. Notwithstanding comments by some observers (Lim, 2002; Pauly and Goodman, 1995; Pauly, 2001), the Medisave being buttressed by Medishield also does not explain Singapore's superior performance, because these schemes form only a small part of its overall financing system (Barr, 2001: 709; Hsiao, 1995; 2001). In any event, Hong Kong has achieved only slightly inferior outcomes without a similar scheme.

The different arrangements for provision of health care comes closest to explaining the differences in the NIEs' health-policy performances. In contrast to Korea and Taiwan, where health care is provided mostly by the private sector, in both Hong Kong and Singapore in-patient care is provided largely by the government. Centralized public provision of acute care, which is the most expensive component in health-care expenditures, may be more efficient because it allows economy of scale, avoids duplication, and, most significantly, avoids the incentive for over-servicing (Hammer and Berman, 1995). Global budgetary allocations characteristic of the system also have the effect of rationing supply and thereby expenditures. There is extensive empirical evidence that government-provided and tax-financed health-care systems have been more effective in controlling costs (Elola, 1996: 242).

Conclusion

In many respects, the NIEs have gone through experiences typical for most countries. In the early stages, communicable diseases were the main health problem and this was reflected in their policy focus on public health rather than on curative services. By the end of the 1960s, non-infectious diseases had replaced communicable ones as the predominant health problem and the policy focus shifted accordingly. But the newer ailments were relatively expensive to treat, compounded by the ageing of the population, whereby a growing share of the population requires increasingly expensive health care in the final years of their life. Governments in the NIEs, as in other countries, tried to meet the rising demand for health care by increasing health-care resources, but they quickly realized that it was not possible to provide health care in quantity and at the quality demanded by the population without major increases in taxes, which for various reasons were difficult to impose. They turned their attention to financing issues in response, which in Singapore and, to a lesser extent, Hong Kong took the form of higher user charges, whereas Korea and Taiwan resorted to social insurance, which seemed an easy way of mobilizing additional resources.

There is surprisingly large government involvement in the provision of health care in Hong Kong and Singapore, but not so in Korea and Taiwan. The two Northeast Asian states concentrate on the public financing of health care through compulsory insurance, which co-exists with the largely private provision of health care. The different arrangements partially reflect the legacy of British rule in Hong Kong and Singapore and the extension of the National Health Service arrangement it involved, whereas Korea and Taiwan were influenced by the social-insurance arrangement that existed in Japan.

The NIEs spend a relatively small percentage of their GDP on health care compared to both developed and developing countries. Only Korea's total expenditure on health is higher than would be predicted from its income level (Griffin, 1992: 60), while Singapore's is extraordinarily less. The difference between the largest and smallest spender cannot be explained by sources of finance because private payments make up the largest source of financing in both Korea and Singapore.

The two countries with the best outcomes at rather modest costs are Singapore and Hong Kong, and what they have in common is the provision of in-patient health care largely by the public sector. The arrangement allows the city states to realize the benefits of public provision in the most expensive component of health care, in-patient services. The case of Singapore is particularly innovative because it does not significantly compromise individual choice, which is regarded as important by middle- and upper-income groups. The system of private provision of in-patient care coupled with third-party payment through NHI in Korea and Taiwan, on the other hand, has played a major role in escalating health-care costs.

Singapore may well have the most sophisticated system of financing and, especially, provision. Its Class A wards, which are operated on a complete cost-recovery basis, compete directly with private hospitals, thus forcing the latter to match their level of service and charges. At the same time, by leaving the luxurious end of the service to the private sector, the health system accommodates the demands of the upper-income families who desire better frills and are willing to pay for them. However, the admiration for its Medisave scheme that one finds in international policy circles these days is misplaced in that the scheme plays a rather small role.

Korea and Taiwan are illustrations of the danger of combining fee-for-service with insurance. They are also examples of how demand-management techniques such as co-payment and user charges do not work in this sector: health-care expenditures have sky-rocketed despite large co-payment requirements. Indeed, making individuals pay some portion of the cost at the point of service seems to have had little impact on Korea, Singapore, or Taiwan, as Hong Kong has fared no worse even without significant user charges in public hospitals.

Similar to income maintenance, health-care policy in the NIEs also displays two clusters. Hong Kong and Singapore are characterized by public provision and private financing, whereas Korea and Taiwan are characterized by private provision and social insurance financing.

5
HOUSING

The significance of housing extends beyond the issue of shelter, as it has a strong bearing on the nation's social and economic welfare. While the problem itself is essentially about providing a roof over people's heads at an affordable cost, its causes and many of its consequences touch on an array of economic, political, and health issues. But this is not entirely reflected in the housing literature, which has traditionally underestimated the complexity of the problem and the solutions to it.

The economic significance of housing is reflected in the fact that housing investment typically forms 2–8 per cent of GNP (7–18 per cent if the associated services are included) and 10–30 per cent of gross capital formation (World Bank, 1993a: 10). Studies show that each dollar of housing investment generates two dollars of economic activity in other sectors, and each additional job in housing construction creates two other jobs (World Bank, 1993a: 34). It is a major reason for households to save, and thus affects the nation's overall savings behaviour and eventually its macro-economic conditions (Miles, 1994).

Housing's social significance is most manifest in the population's health. Ill-health in developing countries has been found to be strongly associated with inadequate shelter, poor ventilation, lack of facilities for solid-waste disposal, air and noise pollution, and over-crowding (Weil, 1990: 124). Poor housing conditions are likely to affect the educational performance of children as well. Housing assets are also a major source of income security for the aged and the extent to which these should be taken into account in the calculation of social-security benefits is the subject of much debate in policy circles.

The main problem with housing is affordability – prices are often simply too high compared to income for a significant proportion of the population. Rapid urbanization and inflation have a particularly adverse effect on housing affordability. The problem is especially acute for immigrants from rural areas who tend to be poor and without kinship or social networks in their new surroundings.

Housing affordability is determined by price, which in turn is determined by demand and supply. Housing demand is a function of demographic conditions (rate of urbanization, household formation, and the like) and macro-economic conditions affecting household income. It is also affected by property rights, availability of housing finance, taxes, and subsidies. Housing supply, on the other hand, is determined by availability of land, infrastructure, building materials, and, no less significantly, the organization and resources of the construction industry. Both the demand and supply of housing is affected by government regulations and institutional legacy of housing provision and financing in a country (World Bank, 1993a: 13–14).

While the market forces of demand and supply are paramount in determining affordability, there is considerable scope for state intervention to improve the situation. States can improve affordability in various ways, most commonly through direct provision, subsidy to producers, subsidy to buyers, or a combination of the three. Each of these themselves can be of different types (Haffner and Oxley, 1999: 148). However, complicating the government's ability to address housing problems are the often conflicting expectations and actions of consumers, producers, financial institutions, and the various levels of government. There is a constant conflict between the interests of those who own property and those who would like to – and the government has the nearly impossible task of reconciling them. Efforts to satisfy potential buyers often disadvantage and alienate the existing owners whose prime objective is price appreciation of their assets.

In the face of seemingly insurmountable problems, governments in recent years have scaled back their involvement in the housing sector (Priemus, 1997: 549). Particularly, they have reduced public-sector production and are concentrating more on assisting private producers and homebuyers. "In general, the move has been away from the role of government as producer, to a new role as enabler, facilitating and encouraging housing activities by the private sector" (World Bank, 1993a: 10). This "enabling" strategy is endorsed by the World Bank and mainstream economists, to the horror of those who distrust the market and would prefer the state to play the lead role.

Another recent policy trend is a shift away from an emphasis on rental housing and towards ownership. Although ownership does offer numerous advantages to both individual and society, it is not as unproblematic as it is often made out to be. It confers different levels of wealth on different sections of the population. The sale of public rental housing that often accompanies emphasis on home ownership further marginalizes the poor who remain in public rental housing (Chan, 2000: 31). While ownership itself does not promote inequality, it does so when governments subsidize purchase without restricting or taxing capital gains when the property is sold. It is also an inflexible form of tenure, which restricts labour mobility and imposes high costs on those whose financial conditions change (Priemus, 1997: 553).

The sources and ramifications of the housing problems in the NIEs are similar to those of rapidly developing societies everywhere. Urbanization and increasing population and household formation promote a demand for housing, as does growth in income. The increasing demand may not be fully met, however, because of government regulation, limited land supply, poor infrastructure, or inefficient financial system. The excess demand causes price inflation, which aggravates the situation by promoting speculative activities among those seeking windfall profits. All these conditions existed in all four NIEs in the 1960s, to which their governments responded through different instruments and to different degrees. Indeed the housing sector displays the most pronounced policy differences among the NIEs. In retrospect, some policies have performed remarkably more effectively than others. The central objective of this chapter is to describe the housing-policy measures and assess the outcomes. It will show that deep intervention in Singapore may have worked just as effectively as light intervention in Taiwan. Hong Kong and Korea, on the other hand, intervened extensively – the former through public expenditure and the latter through regulations – but they have little to show for their efforts.

Policy history

Hong Kong

Wartime destruction and immigration from China created appalling housing conditions in the colony: an estimated 15 per cent of the population were living as squatters and twice as many in substandard and inadequate housing. It was in such a context that the government in 1948 promoted the establishment of the Hong Kong Housing Society as a non-profit organization to provide low-cost housing. A few years later, in 1952, it backed the establishment of the Hong Kong Settlers' Housing Corporation to build cottages for a seven-year "hire purchase". Yet the government's general policy attitude towards housing was one of *laissez-faire*, leaving it to the market to determine allocation of housing.

The government's attitude changed in 1953 when a fire in the squatter colony of Shek Kip Mei left 53,000 people homeless and highlighted the gravity of the housing problem (Castells *et al.*, 1990). In the following year, the Resettlement Department was established to provide emergency housing to the fire victims. Resettlement of squatters quickly became the centrepiece of the colony's housing policy for the next three decades. Between 1954 and 1964, the government resettled 250,000 people and the number exceeded one million by 1971 (La Grange and Pretorius, 2002: 725).

At the same time as it was trying to address the housing shortage, the government was taking measures that arguably aggravated the problem. By imposing rent control on pre-war housing, it had essentially encouraged owners to demolish their old stock and build new homes that were exempt from controls: 320,000 people were evicted from pre-war housing between 1962 and 1965 alone (ibid.: 724). The severely limited supply of the land by the government for housing purposes further aggravated the problem.

Between 1965 and 1972, the Housing Board planned to house 220,000 people each year and launched several initiatives to achieve its slum-clearance objective. However, its performance fell significantly short of the target, as an average of only 100,000 people were housed each year. The housing programme received a boost in 1972 when the government launched the Ten Year Housing Plan (1973–1983) with the target of building 1.5 million units, though not even half the target was actually reached (Wong, 1998: 35–36).

The mid 1970s saw the launch of home-ownership schemes that grew in importance in the subsequent decades. The first to be launched was the Home Ownership Scheme (HOS) in 1976, followed by the Private Sector Participation Scheme (PSPS) in 1978. The schemes marked the beginning of the government's effort to concentrate on ownership instead of rental housing (Lee, 1994: 179). The schemes aim to provide apartments for sale at prices well below market value to families with monthly incomes currently not exceeding US$3,333 and to public-housing tenants without means tests. The two are essentially similar programmes, except that under the PSPS scheme the government offers sites for sale by tender to private developers to build apartments for sale at a fixed price to purchasers nominated by the Housing Authority. The objective of PSPS was to improve quality and efficiency, and introduce variety and innovation in home construction, though the results have been disappointing. The price of HOS/PSPS apartments seek to cover building costs, excluding land value: the prices are typically 25–40 per cent below the market price of comparable private apartments (Wong, 1998: 65). There are resale restrictions in place to curb profiting from the subsidized units. Purchasers of HOS and PSPS apartments can borrow up to 90–95 per cent of the purchase price from financial institutions at a reduced interest rate, which is possible because of the loan guarantee offered by the Housing Authority. Approximately 134,000 houses were sold under the HOS/PSPS scheme during the 1978–1996 period, with plans to sell another 175,000 HOS/PSPS over the 1995–2001 period (Hong Kong Government, 1997). The economic crisis of the late 1990s and the collapsing housing prices strained the scheme as potential buyers became increasingly hesitant about housing investment. In the face of declining demand, many HOS units were sold back to the Housing Authority for release as rental apartments in 1998–1999 (Lee and Yip, 2001: 65).

The late 1980s was a time of policy activism in Hong Kong, and in the housing sector this was reflected in the announcement of "Long Term Housing Strategy" (LTHS) in 1987. It set the target of providing adequate and affordable housing to all by 2001 and emphasized the government's commitment to relying on the private sector to expand home ownership. It specifically mentioned a reduction in emphasis on public rental housing in favour of assisted home ownership.

The Home Purchase Loan Scheme (HPLS) was introduced in 1988 with the objective of assisting buyers with the initial down payment towards housing purchases. It provides loans for purchasing housing from private developers to all public-housing tenants and to others whose monthly income is under US$3,333. The reason for exempting public-housing tenants from income limits is to encourage well-off tenants to vacate rental housing and buy their own apartments. The scheme offers an interest-free loan of US$77,000 repayable over a maximum of 20 years, or a monthly subsidy of US$541 for four years. Some 46,000 households took advantage of the scheme over the 1988–2000 period (*Hong Kong Fact Sheet – Housing*, http://www.housingauthority.gov.hk/en/aboutus/resources/).

However, the government's policy of promoting home ownership became increasingly difficult to pursue in the wake of sky-rocketing housing prices. In 1991, just after the Gulf War, housing prices increased by 50 per cent within three months, to which the government responded with a raft of measures to curb speculation: a tax on the sale and purchase of unfinished apartments was introduced, the minimum deposits towards purchase was increased from 1.5 to 10 per cent of the purchase price, and the mortgage ceiling was set at 70 per cent of the price (Lee, 1994: 183). These were drastic measures for a place known for non-intervention.

The Tenant Purchase Scheme (TPS) was first introduced as a pilot scheme (called Sale of Apartments to Sitting Tenants) in 1991, but the take-up rate was disappointing because of the relatively high prices being asked and because of the stringent restrictions on resale. The scheme was relaunched on more attractive terms in 1998, and 67,000 tenants took advantage of the scheme within the first four years. The price for TPS housing in the year 2000 was set at 55 per cent of the market value, with additional discounts for early take-up, bringing down the price to as low as 18 per cent of the market value in some cases (www.info.gov.hk/hd/eng/hd/hos/). The prices are so low that they seem designed to bribe tenants to buy the unit. The government plans to offer 250,000 apartments under the scheme over the 1998–2008 period (Hong Kong Government, 1999).

Government assistance for home ownership for the middle class was further beefed up with the launch of the Sandwich Class Housing Scheme in 1993. It aimed to help middle-income families (with a monthly income of US$4,230–US$7,692 in 1998) living in rented private accommodation with the purchase of their own homes. It offered subsidized public housing of superior quality or a subsidized loan for the purchase of private housing. It was a highly popular scheme, which was oversubscribed by four times. However, the scheme was discontinued in 1998 in line with the government's strategy of reducing its involvement in the production of public housing.

The problem of sky-rocketing housing prices and the stress it imposed on potential buyers led the government to establish a Task Force on Land Supply and Property Prices in March 1994. Among other things, the Task Force recommended an enhanced supply of land and accelerated housing production in both the public and private sectors. The government instead agreed to curb speculation by restricting when and how developers could sell apartments. The measures had the intended impact in the short run, as prices dropped by 10–15 per cent in the following year.

The Long Term Housing Strategy 1998 was even more ambitious than its 1987 predecessor: it sought to produce 85,000 apartments a year – 59 per cent in the public sector and 41 per cent in the private sector – and to raise home ownership to 70 per cent by 2007. It also sought to more than halve the average waiting time for public rental housing to three years by 2005.

In 1998, Home Starter Loan Scheme (HSLS) was launched to assist first-time buyers. It offers a maximum loan amount of US$77,000 to first-time homebuyers with monthly household incomes of under US$8,975; the ceiling is high enough to qualify much of the population. Nearly 46,000 loans were granted under the scheme by the end of 2001 (*Hong Kong Fact Sheet – Housing*, http://www.housingauthority.gov.hk/en/aboutus/resources/). The Buy or Rent Option (BRO) scheme, launched in the same year as HSLS, gives prospective public-housing tenants the option of buying apartments at a discounted price. The government provides a non-repayable mortgage subsidy amounting to US$20,768 to eligible buyers for six years. Over 40,000 families were offered apartments under Phase I of the Scheme, launched in June 1999 (Hong Kong Housing Bureau, 1999: 17).

The home-ownership schemes were augmented by efforts to encourage well-off tenants to move out of public housing: the means test for public housing was made more stringent, public-housing rents were raised by a substantial margin, the ceiling for HPLS loans was raised nine-fold in eight years, and the supply of HOS/PSPS apartments was increased (Yip and Lau, 1997: 47).

The nature of the housing problem in Hong Kong completely changed in late 1997 when the housing market went into a tailspin following the outbreak of the economic crisis. To stabilize prices in the face of the collapsing market, the government imposed a moratorium on land sales between June 1998 and March 1999. It also shelved its target to build 85,000 apartments a year in order not to further depress prices. Indeed, private builders, who include some of the most influential people in Hong Kong, have in recent years been calling on the government to reduce its role in providing housing and instead concentrate on subsidizing home owners, which they hope will lift prices (*Hong Kong Standard*, 8 July 1999). The government seems to have complied, as there has been a discernible policy shift towards providing subsidized loans for the purchase of housing produced by the private sector.

Singapore

The first serious attempt to address housing problems on the island was made by the British Colonial Administration in 1927 when it established the Singapore Improvement Trust (SIT). Lack of funds and government commitment meant the trust could make only modest gains: by 1959, when it was abolished, it had constructed 23,264 units housing 9 per cent of the population (Asher and Yong 1997: 305). The outbreak of World War II aggravated the problem of inadequate housing, compounded further by rent-gouging that had become common as a result of shortage.

Just over a year after coming to power in 1959, the PAP set up the Housing and Development Board (HDB) as a statutory body with comprehensive responsibility for public housing and urban development. The importance the government attributed to the sector was reflected in the large financial allocation and legislative backing it provided to the HDB. Under the first two Five Year Plans (1960–1965 and 1965–1970) the HDB completed 120,669 public-housing units, and another 64,821 in the following four years, all ahead of target. This was the PAP government's most concrete achievement, which paid rich political dividends in the subsequent years and decades. The achievement was possible because the government was willing to experiment with low-cost and high-rise housing on a large scale (Sim, Lim and Tay, 1993: 93–94).

In 1964 the government announced its goal of creating a "home-owning democracy" in which 90 per cent of the population would live in homes they owned. The same year, HDB apartments became available not only for rent but also for purchase, under the newly announced Home Ownership Scheme. To facilitate purchase, the HDB offered mortgage loans at a 6.25 per cent interest rate repayable over 15 years. But the take-up rate was low because of low income and savings at the time. This changed with the announcement of the CPF Approved Housing Scheme in 1968, which allowed CPF members to use their provident fund to make both down payment and repayment of loans; the purchase of private housing using CPF funds was permitted in 1981.

Preventing the emergence of ethnic and socio-economic ghettos, such as those found in many American and some European cities, has been an important objective of the government's housing policy. The HDB deliberately provides all apartment sizes in all estates in order to prevent geographical segregation of income groups and deliberately ensures a balanced racial mix in every public-housing estate through the allocation process.

The housing policy became increasingly ambitious over time, setting ever-higher objectives. Its objective in the 1960s was simply to clear slums by building basic housing, but by the 1970s this had changed to paying attention to quality, design, location, and infrastructure support. By the 1980s the HDB had scaled up to catering for the middle classes, which included superior finish and an emphasis on the general quality of life in the estates (Eng and Kong, 1997). Eligibility for HDB housing was progressively relaxed, so much so that over 90 per cent of the population became eligible for it.

Furthermore, from 1989 onwards the government began to actively promote the resale market for HDB apartments: an income ceiling for the purchase of resale housing was eliminated, the ceiling on HDB mortgage loans was raised to 80 per cent of the market value, and substantial grants (US$15,400–US$25,600) were made available to first-time buyers and to those buying property near their parents. The objective was to expand the market for second-hand HDB housing and to enable the owners to realize gains similar to those enjoyed by private home owners. It was also to enable Singaporeans to buy homes of their choice on the open market if they were unhappy with what they had been allocated through lottery when buying directly from the government. There was a huge increase in the price of second-hand HDB apartments in the mid 1990s, though in 1998 the prices slid back to the 1995 level and continue (in 2003) to be depressed.

The objective of 90 per cent home ownership was finally reached in the late 1980s and the government began to provide various kinds of assistance and subsidies to enable the remaining 10 per cent of the population to purchase their own homes (Chua, 2000: 50). At the same time the government turned to improving the quality of older HDB estates. In 1989 it announced a US$8 billion, 15-year programme for upgrading older estates, which would eventually affect as many as 95 per cent of HDB residents. Instead of demolishing older estates, which would perhaps have been a cheaper option, it decided to refurbish the existing estates, improving the facilities, and creating precincts to promote social interaction (Eng and Kong, 1997: 444–446).

In the mid 1990s, the government was concerned about the rapid price increase of lower-end private housing, which was causing much angst among the middle classes who would rather own private housing for reasons of status and potential investment returns but could not afford it. To satisfy this group, the government began to build executive condominiums, which were priced lower than comparable private condominiums and involved fewer resale and use restrictions than regular HDB apartments. It indicated that executive condominiums would eventually form 10 per cent of the new housing stock. It also believed that they would put downward pressure on private housing prices and make them more affordable to those aspiring to own such apartments (Tan, 1998: 107).

The government also began to promote private housing in the 1990s. The 1991 Revised Concept Plan set the goal of increasing the proportion of private housing from 17.5 per cent of the total stock in 1990 to 20 per cent in 2000, 25 per cent in 2010, and, eventually, to 30 per cent. It began to sell land on 99-year leases to private developers towards this objective. However, such apartments have been less popular with buyers, who continue to prefer freehold property (Chua, 2000: 53). But the government itself began to water down people's expectations in the mid 1990s after realizing that the population's demand for housing was almost insatiable, as people demanded better and bigger housing once their basic needs were met. More significantly, the government did not take kindly to the prospect of losing control over the population that it had enjoyed through public housing (ibid.: 59).

Korea

The origin of South Korea's contemporary housing problem goes back to the Korean War, which saw the destruction of almost a million houses (Ha, 1987: 80). Yet the government rarely intervened in the housing sector, except for in the construction of relief housing. The Five Year Plans for housing that were regularly announced after 1962 made little difference in practice as they persistently failed to achieve what were very modest goals (Kim, 1995: 29). It was not until the late 1980s that the government began to intervene decisively and in a manner that actually improved housing outcomes.

To indicate its commitment to solving the housing problem, in 1962 the government replaced the Korea Housing Administration with the present Korea National Housing Corporation (KNHC) with the responsibility for building, financing, and managing low-cost public housing. It was followed by the passage of the Public Housing Law in 1963 to provide public loans to private firms for housing construction, but little was done to put it into practice. In 1969, a Presidential Order was issued requiring all private construction firms to invest in housing and requiring local governments to direct 10 per cent of their expenditure to housing construction (Lin, 1996: 75). The Korea Housing Bank (KHB) was established in the same year to mobilize private funds for housing, in addition to engaging in regular banking. The KHB raises funds through the sale of housing bonds and various subscription deposit schemes that give various level of preference for housing loans to depositors. The interest on the deposit as well as the loan used to be considerably lower than the market rate, but the difference became negligible in the 1990s as a result of general deregulation of the financial industry in Korea.

The housing problems continued unabated and began to trigger political unrest. In 1971, dissatisfaction with the new town in Gwangju planned to accommodate squatters from Seoul caused a riot. It was in this context that the government in 1972 launched the Housing Construction Ten-Year Plan (1972–1981) to build 2.5 million houses, but the plan was later shelved on the grounds of difficult economic conditions at the time. In the same year, the Public Housing Law was replaced with the Housing

Construction Promotion Law, providing for the issue of housing bonds and lottery to raise funds (Kim, 1997: 109).

The difficulties with locating and developing land, and the windfall profits that private developers were viewed as making, led the government in 1975 to establish the Korea Land Bank as a public agency that would compete with private developers in developing land. It was reorganized as the Korea Land Development Corporation (KLDC) in 1979, later renamed the Korea Land Corporation (KOLAND) in 1996.

In 1977, the Housing Construction Promotion Act was amended once again, this time to give an expanded role to private builders. The government saw housing shortage as a supply problem and, as such, concentrated on helping builders, especially the *chaebols*, which were viewed as possessing the necessary financial capacity and technical skills to build large housing estates (Yoon, 1994). Other supply-side measures included standardization of construction materials, expansion of housing finance, and various tax benefits for builders (Kim, 1997: 110). On the demand side, public and designated private builders were allowed to issue housing exchange bonds (later replaced by the Housing Savings Scheme), which entitled subscribers to new units at a controlled price, which was 50–66 per cent lower than the market price.

Housing demand continued to outstrip supply, however, because of the attractive investment returns it offered and the formation of new households among the 1955–1960 baby-boomers. At the same time, supply was constrained by the government-sponsored Heavy and Chemical Industrialization Plan, which dried out loanable funds for housing. These factors combined with rampant speculation led the government to introduce broad anti-speculation measures in 1978. The introduction of price controls and capital gains tax led to an immediate rise in the demand for housing at the same time as supply was cut back because of reduced profitability. The 1980–1981 economic recession worsened the problem, with 1981 experiencing the lowest housing output since 1974. The government's subsequent pump-priming tactics included the launch of urban-renewal measures, which led to a turnaround and eventually a housing boom.

The Housing Construction Promotion Law was amended yet again in 1981, which, among other things, provided for the establishment of the National Housing Fund (NHF). It was to be a public fund under the Ministry of Construction and Transportation – but managed by the KHB – for financing low-income housing, both ownership and rental. It raises resources through subscription deposits, the issue of housing bonds, and operating a housing lottery. The funds were available as loans at a discounted interest rate to developers and buyers, but they involved numerous restrictions on both purchase and resale.

In the early 1980s, the government also began to provide indirect subsidies such as cheap land, various tax advantages, and low-interest loans to builders for the construction of modest-price housing. The measures were followed by a boom in the housing market, which led the government to impose various taxes on purchase, maintenance, and sale of housing to control speculation by buyers. They were accompanied by regulations of prices at which developers could sell apartments, which had the unintended but predictable effect of reducing supply.

It had become clear by the late 1980s that the housing policy was not reaching low-income families. In 1988, the government announced the Two Million Housing Construction Plan for the 1988–1992 period. To achieve that goal, it began to supply a large amount of residential land through new town developments, expansion of housing credit, and removal of various regulations restricting residential developments. It also decided to promote the building of 190,000 low-rent public rental housing units and allocated US$4.8 billion, amounting to 85 per cent of the construction costs, towards the goal. The decision to directly build rental apartments followed the recognition that the less well-off could be reached only through rental housing.

Unlike the earlier plans, the 1988–1992 plan for two million units actually exceeded its target. The target was achieved with very little additional expenditure on the part of the government and funded largely by the buyers themselves, who were motivated by the prospect of capital gains. The private developers bore 76 per cent of the cost of the road and train infrastructure built in the new towns. By the early 1990s, housing shortage had eased and prices stabilized, leading to calls for the removal of regulations that had accumulated over the years to address the problem of acute shortage and price inflation.

The 1997 economic crisis was followed by a downturn in the housing market. As a part of the package of IMF-imposed reforms, the government removed most of the restrictions that it had introduced over the years and retained them well after they had ceased to be useful. The NHF and KHB began offering market-rate interest on subscription deposits and housing bonds in 1994. The controls on the sale price of new apartments began to be eased in 1995 and were removed entirely in 2000. At the same time, the KHB was privatized in 1997. The "excessive capital gains on land" law was repealed in January 1999, after the court ruled that it was unconstitutional. The bond-bidding requirement for the purchase of the new housing was abolished in July 1999, though the requirement for the purchase of the Housing Bond still continues even though it gives almost the same interest rate as the market rate. The waiting period for the purchase of another housing unit was also abolished in 1999.

The sharp increase in housing rent and prices, especially in Seoul, in 2001 and 2002 prompted the government to increase its regulation of the housing market. It re-introduced the compulsory ratio for small housing units in large development projects and also raised capital gains tax and property taxes. It is too early to comment on the effects of these measures.

Taiwan

Taiwan's housing problems began with a population influx from the mainland after 1949. A typhoon in 1953 caused widespread devastation and drew attention to the housing problems on the island. The government responded by establishing the "Public Housing Committee of Executive Yuan" in 1954 and a statute was passed in 1957 to facilitate loans for public-housing constructions (Construction and Planning Administration, 1993a: 4). Much of the Committee's funds during its existence (1955–1958) was, however, spent on building 8,500 units for government officials. It was finally abolished in 1958 and replaced with a yet weaker agency (Public Housing Construction and Planning Committee) within the Taiwan provincial government (Wen, 1988: 118–120). The Committee made no noticeable impact on the housing conditions on the island.

A series of political and economic events in the 1970s compounded the housing problems and forced the government to act. The problems began when the Taiwanese housing market entered a recession in 1971 following the island's expulsion from the United Nations. This was followed by the oil crisis of 1973 and the subsequent high inflation, which led people to hedge by investing in real estate. To address the problem of high inflation and the speculative behaviour it had generated, in 1974 the government tightened money supply and imposed severe restrictions on who could borrow and on the maximum amount (US$10,000) they could borrow. The death of Chiang Kai Shek in 1975, and the political uncertainty it portended, led to another recession in the housing market, which had the effect of improving affordability, which in turn led the government to ease the restrictions on loans in 1977. The ceiling on the maximum loan amount for buyers was raised to US$20,000 (at a time when the average price of a housing unit in Taipei was US$35,000) and for builders it was raised to 40 per cent of the building cost.

Recognizing the gravity of the problem, in 1979 housing was included as one of the major priorities of the 12-point National Development Plan, which set construction of 25,000 housing units each year as its target. A major breakthrough came about in 1981 when mortgage interest expenses were made tax-deductible to promote home ownership and assist with the recession gripping the real-estate market at the time. Up to US$3,125 in interest-rate payment per year was tax deductible, but the limit was raised to US$9,375 in 1999. This has probably been the single most important measure for promoting home ownership, though it has not yet been adequately studied or even acknowledged in the literature.

Restrictions on housing loans were further relaxed in 1982 and the remainder were rapidly diluted or removed altogether in the following few years. The banks themselves were eager to extend loans for housing – the result was a boom in housing loans and a buoyant housing market. At the same time, the government increased money supply with the purpose of depreciating the currency. The result was a boom in the stock and, later, the property market, which made housing unaffordable to the lower income groups.

Housing affordability became a major political issue following a series of political protests in Taipei just before the general elections in August 1989, which forced the government to act. It announced a tax rebate to first-time homebuyers and set the target of building 34,000 public-housing units annually. The announced measures were later scaled back following protests from real-estate developers and their political allies, who feared a decline in prices and profitability, and only about 5,000 units were ever built (Li, 1998: 150, 167). What made the real difference was the inflow of new housing investments searching for windfall profits that were common at the time. The result was a housing-construction boom and an oversupply, from which the housing industry is yet to recover entirely.

To accommodate the low-income families who could not afford housing despite increased affordability, in 1994 the government decided to support the construction of about 20,000 units a year, or one-sixth of the 140,000 people on the waiting list for public housing at the time (*China Economic News Service*, 23 June 1994). Tax concessions were offered to buyers and private builders towards this objective.

Government policy since the 1980s has focused on increasing home ownership through subsidized loans to homebuyers. In addition to tax deductibility of interest payment, the government guarantees loans for individual homebuyers for the purchase of one home in their lifetime and pays for a portion of the interest charges. The loan schemes are centred on occupation and income groups. As of 2001, private-sector workers and low-income individuals pay a 5 per cent interest rate on amounts up to US$78,125 and 7.6 per cent for loans exceeding that amount, while government employees and military personnel pay 3 per cent. The 2–4 per cent difference between the market rate and what the borrowers pay is covered by the government. The number of households receiving housing loans from the government increased from 9,733 in 1993 to 23,353 in 1999 (*Social Indicators 1999*).

Recently, the government began actively to consider subsidizing renters instead of buyers. This was prompted by the realization that the increased affordability resulting from price depreciation in the 1990s had made little difference to low-income families, which had neither the savings nor the income to buy apartments, even with subsidized loans. Subsidized rental housing offers a better means of reaching such families, with the additional advantage of addressing the problem of the high vacancy rate that has been endemic to the housing market in Taiwan for a decade.

HOUSING

Provision

Hong Kong

The Hong Kong government's ownership of much of the land in the territory has had a large impact on its capacity to intervene in the housing sector, and indeed in the economy generally. Proceeds from sale of raw land to private developers is a major source of revenue for the government. Public ownership of land also allows the government to provide housing to about half the population at a nominal cost.

Hong Kong has one of the largest public-housing programmes in the world for both ownership and rental. Eligibility conditions for public rental housing vary according to the size of the family and are adjusted periodically to reflect changes in income levels and the cost of living. For a family of four, the combined household income limit was US$2,272 per month in 2000, and the total net asset limit was US$60,325. Public-housing tenants are prohibited from owning other residential housing or earning interest in housing, though a survey in 1995 found that 13 per cent of public-rental tenants actually owned private property (Hong Kong Government, 1997).

Public-housing rents, in principle, take into account inflation rates, operating costs, and the relative value of the estate. However, in practice rents are considerably lower than they would be if these criteria were strictly applied. While rents are periodically adjusted, the increase has been generally lower than the improvement in tenants' income. A survey in 1984 revealed that public-housing rents had increased by only 7 per cent in constant price terms over the preceding 10 years, compared to a 97 per cent increase in tenants' household income (Hong Kong Housing Authority, 1985). To put a curb on well-off people living in public housing, in 1990 the government began to charge double rent from those tenants whose income was 50 per cent above the eligibility limit, but even this amounted to less than two-thirds of the market rent. Not surprisingly, only 2 per cent of the households charged with double rent between 1987 and 1993 subsequently vacated (Wong, 1995: 43–44).

Schemes to promote home ownership began in the 1970s and were expanded greatly in the late 1990s. The government has established an array of schemes for the purpose, some involving in-kind subsidy – HOS/PSPS, TPS, BO – while others offer cash subsidy (HPLS and HSLS). There were 88,000 government-sponsored "housing opportunities" – that is to say, the number of ownership units promoted by all government schemes – in 1998, compared to only 18,735 in the preceding year (Chiu, 1999: 336). As a result, ownership in the public-housing sector increased from around 5 per cent in 1983 to 34 per cent in 2000, while the share of rental housing declined correspondingly (La Grange and Pretorius, 2002: 723).

Over the past two decades, more than 1.3 million housing units in total have been built in Hong Kong, peaking during 1985–1990, when 79,326 units on average were built annually, and hitting the bottom during 1995–1999, when only 31,860 units were built annually. The public sector on average contributed around 60 per cent of all housing built in the early 1980s, but this fell to around 55 per cent and stayed at that level until the mid 1990s. However, private construction declined rapidly after the 1997 economic crisis, leading public housing's share to shoot up to 66 per cent. Rental housing formed almost all of public housing built until the late 1970s, but its share fell to 73 per cent on average in the 1980s and by the late 1990s it was only 51 per cent (www.cityu.edu.hk/hkhousing/hs/default.htm).

The majority of the housing stock is still in the private sector, despite massive construction of public housing since the 1970s: it formed 53 per cent of the stock in 1996, compared to 56 per cent in 1982 (La Grange and Pretorius, 1999: 28). Owner-occupied housing is the norm in the private sector and its share of all private housing has increased over the years, from 57 per cent in 1982 to 72 per cent in 1996. In the public sector, in contrast, it is rental housing that is dominant, despite the decline in its share from 97 per cent of the total in 1980 to 69 per cent in 1999 (Hong Kong Census and Statistics Department, 2000).

Singapore

The Singapore government owns more than 85 per cent of the total land on the island, which is more than twice the share it owned in 1960. Much of the land was acquired under the Land Acquisition Act of 1966, which allows the government to compulsorily acquire land at below the market price. Between 1973 and 1987, the compensation it paid was the price prevailing in 1973, but this was gradually increased in the following years and it finally began to pay the market rate in 1995 (Tan, 1998: 18). The government justified the lower payment on the grounds that the acquisition of undeveloped land undermined speculation, thus keeping housing prices affordable. Of course, the government itself sold the land at prevailing market prices, raking in huge sums (Chua, 2000: 51). Be that as it may, extensive ownership of land, and cheap acquisition of land it did not already own, enabled the government to provide affordable housing to much of the population at a modest cost.

There are a variety of housing schemes in Singapore to help all but the very rich buy public housing.[1] The price of HDB apartments is set to recover development and construction costs, which are significantly lower than the market price. Mortgage financing to the maximum of 80–90 per cent of the price for a period of up to 25 years is available to buyers of a HDB apartment. To qualify for the loan, gross family income must be below US$4,460 per month, except for three-room apartments (which are subsidized and targeted at poorer families), for which the limit is US$870 per month. The ceiling is quite high, as 94 per cent of Singaporeans are eligible to purchase public housing. Those owing private property are ineligible, as are those who have already bought public housing twice.

The government policy deliberately discriminates against rental housing in the public sector, in contrast to the many benefits available to promote the purchase of public housing. Restrictions on the rental of public housing include a ceiling of US$470 on monthly income and a prohibition of the use of CPF to pay rent. The restrictions are intended to ensure that renting is resorted to only by those who cannot afford to buy even small and subsidized HDB apartments. The number of public-rental-housing units is small and formed less than 10 per cent of total stock in 1998.

The average annual rate of production of public housing was 11,722 units in the 1960s, 24,134 units during the 1970s, 30,900 units during the 1980s, and 19,799 units in 1991–1995 (www.hdb.gov.sg/isoa031p.nsf/). Almost a million (911,369) public-housing units were built over the 1960–1999 period, with the majority built during the 1970s and 1980s – this is a large number for a country with only 920,000 households (Singapore Department of Statistics, 2001: 58).

The public housing's share of total stock increased rapidly from 38 per cent in 1970 to 70 per cent in 1980, rising to 81 per cent in 1995, when it stabilized and then began gradually to decrease (Singapore Department of Statistics, 2001: 58). The percentage of the population living in public housing increased from 23 in 1965 to 68 in 1980 and 85 in 1990, and remained at around 86 per cent throughout the 1990s. Of all HDB residents, 82 per cent lived in self-owned homes.

Application for public-ownership apartments was, until recently, strong despite near-universal ownership. In 1996, 67,346 applications were received for the purchase of new apartments, but these declined sharply in the subsequent years. It is not yet clear if this is a long-term trend or a temporary dip reflecting the recessionary economic conditions. A large proportion of the applications since the early 1990s have been from those wanting to upgrade from existing self-owned public housing.

The private-housing stock's share of the total began to increase in the late 1990s, after declining continuously, and often rapidly, for three decades. Of all private-housing stock, around two-thirds are apartments and condominiums and one-third are landed properties. Private apartments and condominiums have been the fastest-growing segment of the housing market in recent years, expanding from just over 3 per cent of the total stock in the 1970s and 1980s to 6 per cent in 1990 and 10 per cent in 1999 (Singapore Department of Statistics, 2001: 58). The share of total stock accounted by landed properties, which represent the most prestigious and expensive segment of the market, was 13 per cent in 1970 and 9 per cent in 1980, before stabilizing at 7 per cent in the 1990s.

Korea

The Korean state does not have as complete a dominance over the supply of land as its counterparts in Hong Kong and Singapore. Much of the land suitable for housing is privately held and the government encounters considerable difficulty in acquiring it, despite the passing of the Land Expropriation Act of 1962 and the Housing Estate Development Promotion Act of 1980, empowering it to acquire land after paying the market price (Kim, 1997: 128). This limits the government's capacity to accord priority to public agencies in the allocation of greenfield sites (Yoon, 1994: 57). It offers land for sale at a 20 per cent discount for rental units under 60 sqm and a 10 per cent discount for rental units of 60–85 sqm and ownership units under 90 sqm.

On the supply side, the government introduced the New Apartment Price Ceiling in 1982 to check rampant speculation in the property market. At the same time, many tax incentives were introduced, most notably for the construction of low-income rental housing. The regulations were further strengthened in 1990 when the government set a ceiling of 200 pyong (660 sqm) on the size of the land that a household could own in major urban areas; land held in excess of the limit was subject to an annual holding tax of 7–11 per cent (Park, 1998: 279). It also introduced the Aggregate Land Tax, which imposed an additional 50 per cent tax on capital gains in excess of the national average (Kim, 1997: 95).

The government also instituted a panoply of measures to curtail demand for housing in 1982. At purchase, buyers were required to pay an acquisition tax of 2 per cent of the actual price and a registration tax of 3 per cent of the assessed value. Various property taxes amounting to 1.3 per cent of the assessed value were also imposed. Moreover, a hefty capital-gains tax of 51–76 per cent, depending, among other things, on the length of time for which the property was held, was imposed. The regulation of demand was further strengthened when a "bond-bidding" system was introduced in 1983, whereby buyers in high-demand neighbourhoods were required to bid for National Housing Bonds paying below-market interest rates. The average size of the bond was US$11,000 in 1985 (Yoon, 1994) and had the effect of increasing the housing cost by that amount. Another measure was a waiting period of three years, later increased to five years, before a home owner could purchase another new unit. In addition, a potential buyer had to maintain a subscription deposit account either with NHF or KHB or hold housing bonds issued by them for a period of time before he or she could purchase a new apartment.

On top of these regulations, the government began in the late 1970s to provide housing directly through the KNHC. However, instead of providing additional funds for it, the government gave indirect benefits in the form of tax incentives and priority allocation of land and NHF funds. The KNHC could also develop land for sale, which turned out to be a highly profitable activity. But these were insufficient for carrying out its massive mandate, which led the KNHC to concentrate on housing for sale rather than for rent. To purchase KNHC housing, one must not already own a property and must have maintained a Housing Subscription Savings deposit with the NHF for a set period. In cases of demand exceeding supply, which there invariably were, selection was made according to the total amount of money saved and the length of non-ownership.

There was little emphasis on rental housing – public rental stock formed only 4.4 per cent of all stock in 1990 – but this began to change in the late 1980s (Yoon, 1994: 56). Even when the KNHC built housing for rent, it was only for three to five years, after which the unit was sold. It was only in 1989 that permanent public rental housing began to be built. A public rental programme was launched in 1989 targeting social welfare recipients, those displaced by urban redevelopment activities, and low-income veterans, while home owners and single-member households were excluded. But to secure public rental housing, tenants were required to pay initial deposits of US$1,150–2,300, depending on the size of the unit, and had to pay US$58–80 rent per month.

The government has had five-year plans for housing construction since the early 1960s but most of them have failed to achieve their target by a wide margin. The government put little money towards achieving the target, and instead relied on the private sector responding to government regulations. The plans began to come closer to achieving their target in the late 1970s, when the government increased its participation in housing construction (Kim, 1993: 271–273). A total of 1.8 million housing units were built during the 1972–1981 period, of which 41 per cent were in the public sector, defined loosely as any unit partially or fully funded in some form by the government (Ha, 1987: 88). The massive expansion of state involvement in the late 1980s is reflected in the construction of 6.6 million units during the 1988–1999 period, of which 37 per cent were in the public sector (www.moct.go.kr/EngHome/DataCenter/Statistic/Statistic01.htm). And of all the so-called "public" units built during the 1990s, more than half was accounted by KHB, which operated largely as a private bank.

Just over half a million units were built by the KNHC over the 1962–1989 period, and of these 65 per cent were for ownership (Kim, 1995: 41; Yoon, 1994: 56). Production by the KNHC shifted into high gear in 1990: it built nearly half a million units between 1989 and 1996, raising its total share of housing stock to 11 per cent (Hahn, 1998: 89).

The total housing stock in Korea increased at an average annual rate of 2 per cent during the 1960s and 1970s, 3.3 per cent during the 1980s, and 1.9 per cent during the 1990–1995 period. As a result, the total housing stock increased from 4.4 million in 1960 to 11.1 million in 1995 (http://152.99.129.22/mcte/e_index.htm; Yoon, 1994: 24). However, the share of owner-occupied housing declined from 79 per cent of the housing stock in 1960 to 52 per cent in 1995, despite government policies in support of this form of tenure (Lin, 1996: 87).

Taiwan

The private sector is the dominant supplier of housing in Taiwan. The backbone of the system is small builders – unlike the dominance of the large builders in the other NIEs (Li, 1998: 131) – who respond rapidly to changes in housing conditions. The heavy reliance on pre-sale system similarly facilitates rapid response, as the builders are in direct contact with buyers (Li, 1998: 120–125).

Military personnel, civil servants, teachers, and, to a much lesser extent, private-sector workers are the main beneficiaries of the public-housing programme in Taiwan. The subsidized loans for civil servants and military personnel carry an interest rate of 3.5 per cent, whereas private-sector workers pay 8 per cent. Moreover, senior officials get a larger loan, and, consequently, larger subsidy (Lin, 1996: 121–122). A small number of subsidized public housing is available to low-income households and single females at rents capped at 8 per cent of costs. The government also builds and sells inexpensive housing to low-income families: however, only 240,000 such units were built between 1953 and 1989 and none thereafter.

The government increased its policy attention to housing when it was adopted as a part of the six-year development plans in 1976. Direct government construction of housing was at its high point in 1976–1981 when 67,565 units were constructed, and then again in 1990 and the mid 1990s (Construction and Planning Administration, 1999). After reaching a high point in 1995, construction began to decline, reaching as few as 24 units in 1999, which is hardly surprising given the high vacancy rate in Taiwan (http://www.cpami.gov.tw/english/english.htm).

About two million units were built in Taiwan between 1982 and 1999. Of the total, well over 90 per cent were in the private sector. In 1999 there were only 529,564 units in public housing (including those built privately with loans from the government), of which 45 per cent had been allocated to low-income groups, 27 per cent to private-sector workers, and 24 per cent to government employees (Construction and Planning Administration, 1999).

Comparative

All NIE governments, but especially those in Hong Kong and Singapore, are extensively involved in the provision of housing. The instruments of intervention, however, vary considerably across the NIEs, as is evident in Table 5.1. Evidently, the two city-states rely heavily on direct provision. The Hong Kong government also provides various types of subsidies to buyers. In Singapore, the government does not, for the most part, directly subsidize buyers but rather enables them to borrow at a low rate, which is possible because the government itself borrows cheaply from the CPF. Korea relies mostly on the regulation of demand and supply, though the restrictiveness of the regulations relaxed markedly in the late 1990s. Taiwan has the lowest level of involvement in the provision of housing, and as far as involvement does exist, it largely takes the form of subsidizing buyers through tax deduction of interest payment on housing loans.

The different levels of government involvement in the provision of housing is reflected in the different shares of total housing stock accounted by the public sector, as shown in Table 5.2. The public sector's share varies from 5 per cent in Taiwan to 81 per cent in Singapore, with Korea being closer to Taiwan and Hong Kong to Singapore. The government is a minority provider in all NIEs except Singapore. The definition of the public sector used here is broad: most of the "public housing" in Singapore is privately owned and this is increasingly true in Hong Kong as well. A significant proportion of public housing in Korea is privately owned, actually or potentially. As such, the table only indicates broad trends rather than actual shares.

The housing stocks in the NIEs display different, and changing, tenure trends (see Table 5.3). In Hong Kong, almost three-quarters of the public-housing stock is occupied by tenants, while about the same proportion of the private stock is occupied by owners. However, in both the public and private sectors the share of owner-occupied housing has increased at the expense of rental housing. In Korea, the majority of housing in both the public and private sectors is owner-occupied. More than 90 per cent of the housing stock in both sectors in Singapore is owner-occupied, and

Table 5.1 Key policy instruments in the housing sector

Hong Kong	Direct provision and, increasingly, purchaser subsidy
Singapore	Direct provision and regulation of housing finance
Korea	Regulation of sale and purchase
Taiwan	Tax subsidy for mortgage expenses and some purchaser subsidy

Table 5.2 Public housing stock,[1] percentage of total stock

Hong Kong	44 (1982)	44 (2000)
Singapore	38 (1970)	81 (1995)
Korea	17 (1984)	19 (1990)
Taiwan	5 (1985)	4 (1990)

Notes
Figures within brackets denote the year.
1 Includes all housing units built by the government (either directly or through private contractors) and subsequently rented or sold.

Table 5.3 Ownership and rental housing stock by sector, per cent

	Years	Public				Private			
		Ownership		Rental		Ownership		Rental	
Hong Kong	1982, 1996	5	25	95	75	57	72	43	28
Singapore	1970, 1995	21	91	79	9	33	90	67	10
Korea	1988–1998	–	60	–	40	–	–	–	–
Taiwan	1980, 1990	27	83	73	17	84	78	16	22

Sources: La Grange and Pretorius, 1999; Ministry of Transportation and Construction, http://152.99.129.22/mcte/e_index.htm; Singapore Department of Statistics, 2001; Taiwan Census of Housing 1995.

these shares have increased many times since the 1970s. A similar distribution between owners and tenants obtains in Taiwan.

Financing

Hong Kong

Investment in housing is large in Hong Kong: it formed 15 per cent of the gross fixed capital formation (GFCF) in 1990 and rose to 22 per cent in 1999 (Hong Kong Census and Statistics Department, 2000). The investment amounted to 4 and 6 per cent of the GDP in the respective years.

Rental housing was financed largely from public sources and ownership housing from private sources, until in the 1980s this changed when the government began to promote home ownership and started to offer various incentives – including grants, subsidized land and loans, and loan guarantees – to make ownership more attractive and affordable. The actual government expenditure on promoting home ownership is nearly impossible to estimate because of the complex range of indirect subsidies involved.

All we can know with certainty is that public expenditure on public housing increased almost six-fold in nominal terms between 1987 and 1998, from US$0.9 billion to US$5.3 billion. However, as a percentage of TGE its share rose only slightly, from 13 to 15 per cent (http://www.info.gov.hk/hd/eng/hd/stat_98/). The expenditure data does not, however, include the value of land granted to public housing, no doubt the most significant form of government support for housing in Hong Kong. The value of land provided by the government for public rental housing between 1973 and 1994 is estimated at $10.1 billion (Leong, 1995: 16). The data also excludes various in-kind subsidies that the government provides to home buyers through the HOS/PSPS, TPS, and BO schemes. Nor does it include the cost of housing it provides to government employees: a total of US$436 million was spent on housing for 23,222 civil servants in 1998–1999 (Estimates of Revenue and Expenditure, 2000).

Much of the government's direct expenditure on housing is in the form of grants to cover the Housing Authority's deficit. In addition to government grants, the Housing Authority derives its income from rents on and the sale of residential and commercial properties. It realizes handsome profits from its commercial operations, except in rental housing, which yields deficits. The average loss – which is covered by government subsidy – per rental apartment, excluding the value of land, was estimated to be around US$30 per month in 1997 (Hong Kong Government, 1997). Increasing revenues from its other activities, however, enabled the Housing Authority to amass a surplus of US$8.5 billion over the 1995–1999 period (Hong Kong Census and Statistics Department, 2000).

Singapore

The impressive increase in housing construction and stock in Singapore is reflected in the financial resources devoted to it. Total annual investment in housing increased from US$1.4 billion in 1987 to US$7.7 billion in 1999, amounting to 21 and 28 per cent of the total gross capital formation and 7 and 9 per cent of the GDP in the respective years (Singapore Department of Statistics, 2001). Government-owned institutions – the HDB and Post Office Savings Bank – have accounted for around two-thirds of the outstanding housing loans since 1980 (Phang, 2001: 451).

The government's share of housing is actually smaller than is indicated by its presence in the housing market. Indeed it spends only a modest amount, achieving its objective instead by facilitating conditions for both supply of and demand for housing. This is accomplished through a highly complex financial arrangement, as depicted in Figure 5.1. To facilitate supply, the government provides land (much of which it acquired at below-market price) and concessional loans to HDB to build housing.

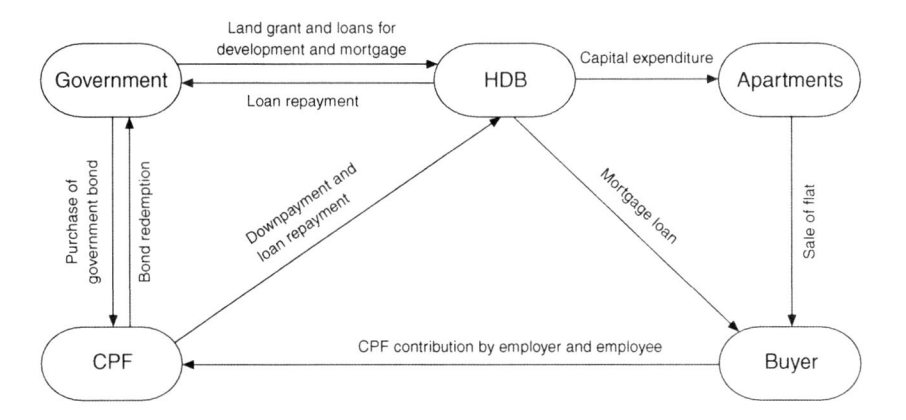

Figure 5.1 Schematic view of finance for public housing in Singapore (adapted from Phang, 2001: 449).

It also provides grants to cover HDB's deficits from renting and, to a lesser extent, selling some units below cost. Such government grants to HDB amounted to S$5.6 billion over the 1960–1996 period (Asher and Yong, 1997: 306). It has also been footing the bulk of the expenditure for renovation of older HDB blocks: it pays for between 79 (executive apartments) and 92 (three-room apartments) per cent of the total costs of "standard" renovation.

On the demand side, the government assists homebuyers by allowing them to use their CPF balance for both making downpayments and servicing the loan, but not for paying rent. Buyers of public-housing apartments are eligible for HDB loans of up to a maximum of 80 per cent (possibly rising to 90 per cent in certain cases) of the selling price for up to 30 years. The interest rate is pegged to the prevailing Post Office Savings Bank's housing-loan interest rate, which was 4 per cent in 2000. The government estimates that 90 per cent of Singaporean households are able to meet their mortgage commitments from monthly savings in their CPF account and do not have to dip into their disposable income to service the loan. Thus, most Singaporean families are able to own apartments without significantly affecting their monthly disposable income (Chua, 2000: 49).

Revenue from the sale of apartments is the main source of HDB's revenue. The price of HDB apartments is set to recover construction costs and takes location into consideration. However, there is some cross-subsidization in favour of smaller units, which are expected to be taken up only by low-income families. The concessions on smaller units include waiver of down payment, 100 per cent mortgage loan, and extended repayment period.

Since sales of HDB apartments recover almost all the associated costs of selling, there is virtually no direct government expenditure towards subsidy for ownership housing, which is nearly 90 per cent of the housing stock. The only subsidy available to buyers is for those purchasing smaller units, but these are cross-subsidized by buyers of larger apartments rather than from government coffers. To the extent that there is any direct government subsidy, it is targeted at HDB rental housing, which is primarily intended for low-income households. Accordingly, HDB rents are about two-thirds lower than the market rate for comparable private apartments. But this affects only a small share of the housing stock, which is unlikely to involve significant financial commitment on the part of the government.

Government subsidy for housing would, however, appear significant if the current market value of land on which HDB housing is built is taken into consideration. It may be recalled that much of the land in Singapore is owned by the government, which it acquired at below the market price. If the current market value of land is taken into consideration, then nearly all HDB apartments are subsidized to some extent, in the sense that buyers pay less than they would otherwise pay. When land costs are excluded, only 40 per cent of the HDB apartments would be deemed to have been subsidized to any extent (Tan, 1998: 18).

Korea

Housing investment in Korea was relatively high in the 1970s, somewhat lower in the 1980s, and high again in the 1990s. It formed, on average, 20 per cent of the GFCF in the 1970s, 16 per cent in the 1980s, and 21 per cent in the 1990s. Housing investments accordingly amounted to 5.4 per cent of the GDP in 1970s, 4.8 per cent in the 1980s, and 7.3 per cent in the 1990s.

However, housing in Korea until the 1980s was bought largely from equity rather than loan because of the various government regulations intended to channel loans to economic development projects. During the 1970s, on average 88 per cent of the housing price was financed from equity, with another 6 per cent borrowed from the curb market. Not surprisingly, housing loans formed only 18 per cent of total housing investment as recently as 1996, though the share jumped to 37 per cent in 1997, only to crash to 5 per cent in the following year amidst the banking crisis (interview with Dr Yoon, 16 January 2001). Informal loans from family and kerb market formed around three-quarters of the housing loans as recently as 1988, but declined to one-half by 1994 and no doubt declined yet further in the subsequent years (Choei, 1996: 61). The controls on housing loans were finally relaxed in the late 1980s amidst general relaxation of the financial industry in Korea. The relaxation is reflected in the fact that the total outstanding loans for housing amounted to only 3 per cent of GNP in 1981, but rose to 9 per cent in 1991, and further to 12 per cent in 1997 (Lee and Yoon, undated; interview with Dr Yoon, 16 January 2001). This is still, of course, nowhere near the 55 per cent of GNP that housing loans form in the USA, the 45 per cent in the UK, and the 33 per cent in Japan (Lin, 1996: 102).

The government's expenditure on housing has fluctuated over the years but has never exceeded 1 per cent of TGE. In fact, only 5.6 per cent of the total spending on housing during the 1988–1992 period came directly from the government (Ha, 1987: 88; Yoon, 1994: 72), but its share had fallen to under 0.1 per cent by the late 1990s (interview with Dr Yoon, 16 January 2001).

The low public expenditure in Korea is partially explained by the fact that subsidies are delivered indirectly and therefore do not appear in spending data. All firms in Korea until recently were required to buy housing bonds at below-market interest rate (3–5 per cent per annum) at the time of registering their business. Construction firms and entertainment establishments were required to buy additional bonds at the time of being awarded a new contract or renewing their licences. In addition to maintaining a subscription deposit at NHF or KHB, potential homebuyers have also had to buy housing bonds. The Housing Bonds (Type 1) issued by the NHF raised US$6.7 billion over the 1997–2000 period. The money raised from the sale of housing bonds was channelled into public housing but is not considered public expenditure.

The significance of NHF as a source of housing finance began to increase in the late 1980s. Of the total housing loans taken out in 1988, the NHF contributed 40 per cent, but by 1994 its share had risen to 52 per cent. The increasing participation of private financial institutions in the home-loan market has meant a declining role for the KHB, from 47 per cent of total housing loans in 1988 to 26 per cent in 1994 and yet further in the subsequent years (Lee and Yoon, undated).

Taiwan

Annual investment in residential building increased from NT$19 billion in 1975 to a high of NT$251 billion in 1993, but consistently declined thereafter, reaching a low of NT$155 in 1999 (DGBAS, 2000a). These formed 10, 17, and 7 per cent respectively of the total gross domestic capital formation (GDCF). The declining investment in housing since the early 1990s may well be a correction of what in retrospect appears to be an over-investment in the late 1980s and early 1990s. Indeed the apparent over-investment in housing during the period is believed to be a significant source of the Taiwan financial industry's malaise in the late 1990s, as around one-quarter of the domestic banks' outstanding loans are to the housing sector and much of the remainder is collateralized by real estate.

Until the mid 1990s, much of the investment in housing in Taiwan was from buyers' own equity rather than from loans because of the strict controls on housing loans directed at channelling savings to economic development projects. The effects of the controls are clearly evident in the fact that housing accounted for only 4 per cent of all outstanding bank loans until 1972.

The restriction on bank loans began to be lifted in the 1980s and this is reflected in the declining importance of equity and informal loans as sources of housing finance. Approximately 64 per cent of the purchase price on average came from equity in 1980, compared to only 30–40 per cent during the 1990s (Lin, 1996: 113). The restrictions on formal loans for housing also meant a booming informal market, which provided around one-quarter of all housing credit until the 1980s despite interest rates of two to three times that charged by formal financial institutions (Chang, 1997: 70–72).

By the late 1980s, the government began to realize that the easing of restrictions on housing loans was in itself insufficient to make housing affordable to the lower income groups, especially in Taipei. It accordingly announced the Six Year Housing Plan (1992–1997), which earmarked an expenditure of NT$176 billion for the construction of public housing, plus NT$10 billion to subsidize interest payments on housing loans (Construction and Planning Administration, 1993a: 9). Much of the plan was never carried out in the face of the housing glut that had emerged as a result of a massive flow of private funds into housing in search of capital gains.

Comparative

The NIEs devote different shares of their economic resources to housing, as is shown in Table 5.4. As one would expect, capital formation in housing as a percentage of GFCF is highest in Singapore and Hong Kong, followed by Korea and, distantly, Taiwan. Indeed, for all except Taiwan the share is higher than the 7–18 per cent of GFCF found in international comparisons. Actual housing investments in Hong Kong are, in fact, considerably larger than they appear in the table because it excludes the value of land provided almost free of charge towards public housing. Not only is the housing investment in Singapore large, it has also gone through the least fluctuations, reflecting the government's commitment to maintaining its large presence in the housing sector. The housing's share of GFCF used to be low in Korea but rose rapidly in the late 1980s following a shift in government policy to emphasize housing, but it began to decline in 1994 and the trend has persisted. Similarly, housing investment in Taiwan increased in the late 1980s and early 1990s, and then entered a period of sustained decline in 1993. Nevertheless, the small share in Taiwan is remarkable, especially considering that it is one of the better performers in terms of outcomes.

Housing is traditionally financed from equity but formal loans' share tends to increase in tandem with economic development – this general pattern is evident in the NIEs as well, albeit starting at different times and at a different pace. The change occurred first in Singapore when in the late 1960s HDB began to provide loans exceeding 80 per cent of the purchase of public housing. In Hong Kong, the growth of the lending market was stymied by the dominance of public housing, which concentrated

Table 5.4 Residential housing's share of total gross fixed capital formation, per cent

	1993	1999
Hong Kong	15	21
Singapore	25	28
Korea	23	18
Taiwan	17	7

Source: Various national data.

mainly on rental apartments. The lending market emerged only after the government began to encourage the purchase of both public and private housing and the buyers took up the opportunity for the handsome investment returns that real estate offered. In Korea and Taiwan, on the other hand, the government maintained severe restrictions on housing investments until the 1980s in order to channel scarce funds into economic development. It was only after the relaxation of the controls starting in the late 1980s that housing loans were able to gain significance and reached levels similar to those in the city-states by the early 1990s.

Public expenditure on housing, unlike many other policy sectors, says little about the nature of the policy or its impact. As we shall see in the next section, a great deal can be achieved by spending little, as is the case in Singapore and Taiwan. Conversely, a lot can be spent, as in Hong Kong, without making much dent into resolving the problem. Of course, it is possible to spend little and impose inefficient regulations that worsen the problem, as seems to have been the case in Korea until the late 1980s. Be that as it may, government spending on housing both as a percentage of GDP as well as TGE is the highest in Hong Kong, followed by Singapore, and, distantly, by Korea and Taiwan. There is probably no other place in the world where housing accounts for one-quarter of the total government expenditure, as is the case in Hong Kong.

Table 5.5 shows that the governments in Hong Kong and Singapore spend vastly more than their counterparts in Korea and Taiwan. Although it is nearly impossible to estimate accurately, there is no doubt that the table would look quite different if all housing-related expenditures and their substitutes were included. Thus the figures for Hong Kong would be yet higher if the value of land provided free of charge to public housing were counted as public expenditure. Although not of the same magnitude as those for Hong Kong, the figures for Singapore too would be higher if the market value of the land on which public housing is built were

Table 5.5 Public expenditure on housing as percentage of GDP and total government expenditure

	% of GDP				% of TGE			
	1975	1985	1995	1999	1975	1985	1995	1999
Hong Kong	2.4	3.4	3.2	5.4	16.0	21.0	18.2	24.6
Singapore	1.3	1.1	1.3	2.5	7.1	4.2	8.1	13.5
Korea	0.2	0.9	0.5	0.4^1	1.1	1.0	2.4	1.9^1
Taiwan	–	0.6^2	0.9	1.0	–	2.5^2	3.1	4.1

Sources: IMF, *Government Finance Statistics*, various years; *Statistical Yearbook of the Republic of China, 2000*.

Notes
1 1997.
2 Includes "community development" and "environment protection".

included rather than the amount the government actually paid. The data also exclude the implied expenditures on tax incentives, which are substantial in the case of Taiwan. The Ministry of Finance in Taiwan estimates that NT$5.2 billion was allowed in tax exemption for housing-interest payment in 1999 alone. The costs of the various restrictions on buyers and sellers and the various tax incentives in Korea are also substantial but are, again, not included in the table.

Outcomes

Hong Kong

Hong Kong has come a long way from being, until the 1970s, a place known for its poor housing conditions, although it is still some way from eradicating the problem. Nearly 30 per cent of all households lived in squatter housing in 1986, but the share had fallen to 9 per cent by 1999 (www.cityu.edu.hk/hkhousing/hs/). While this is a major achievement, it does not reflect well on a place as wealthy as Hong Kong.

The home-ownership rate in Hong Kong has improved impressively since the 1970s though it is still below the rates in Singapore and Taiwan. Overall home ownership increased from 33 per cent in 1982 to 48 per cent in 1990 to 53 per cent in 2000 (La Grange and Pretorius, 1999: 28; Housing Statistics, http://www.housingauthority.gov.hk/eng/hd). The increase was particularly pronounced in the public sector, where it rose from 5 to 18 to 33 per cent of the total public-housing stock over the same period. In the private sector, it increased from 57 to 74 per cent of the stock between 1982 and 1990, but then dipped slightly to 72 per cent by 2000. Thus, 47 per cent of all households continue to live in rental housing – 67 per cent in the public sector and 28 per cent in the private sector – in Hong Kong despite government efforts to increase the ownership rate.

Housing conditions in Hong Kong have also improved over the years. The mean floor area per person in Housing Authority rental apartments increased from 6.2 sqm in 1988 to 9.0 sqm in 1999, a vast improvement over the 2.2 sqm of the 1960s. Private housing is of very divergent quality, ranging from plush to decrepit, much worse than in public-housing estates. Indeed 73 per cent of private residences are smaller than 60 sqm and only 10 per cent are larger than 90 sqm (Chou and Shih, 1995: 8).

Sky-rocketing house prices, especially for private housing, used to be a constant feature in Hong Kong until the economic crisis of 1997. Average private-housing prices on the Hong Kong Island rose by 192 per cent between 1987 and 1997, from US$3,450 per sqm to US$10,157 per sqm. In comparison, average public-housing prices rose by only 36 per cent over the same period, from US$1,026 per sqm to US$1,409 per sqm (http://www.cityu.edu.hk/hkhousing/hs/others/). However, private-housing prices experienced almost a 40 per cent decline over the

1997–1999 period, unlike public-housing prices, which remained largely unchanged. Rents for private housing have been more stable, increasing by 76 per cent over the 1990–1997 period, followed by a decline of 26 per cent over the next two years (Hong Kong Census and Statistics Department, 2000).

A study by Kalra *et al.* (2000) showed that in mid 1997, when housing prices were at a peak, Hong Kong property prices were 40–45 per cent above what the "fundamentals" suggested. They found empirical evidence confirming the widely held belief that prices are driven by speculative demand rather than market fundamentals.

The huge difference in the price of public and private housing explains the continued high demand for the former, despite the government's efforts to promote private housing. There were still 108,000 households on the waiting list for public rental housing in 1999, though this was considerably fewer than the 159,000 waiting for it in 1988. The average waiting time was 5.2 years in 1999, which was only slightly short of the LTHS 1998's target of 5 years (Hong Kong Government, 1997).

Housing prices increased considerably faster than did income between the late 1980s and the mid 1990s. As a result, the price-to-income ratio rose from about 8 to more than 12 between 1984 and 1997 (La Grange and Pretorius, 1999: 54). Servicing housing loans puts enormous burden on households: the average mortgage repayment was 70 to 120 per cent of the average household income throughout the 1988–1998 period (Lee and Yip, 2001: 74). A median-income household in 1997 needed three years' earnings for downpayment on an average small apartment (40 sqm) and would have had to devote 88 per cent of its household income to service the loan (Yip and Lau, 1997: 45).

The rent-to-income ratio has been rather stable in comparison, rising from 6.5 in 1985 to 11.0 in 1998 (www.cityu.edu.hk/hkhousing/hs/default.htm). However, there is a large difference between rents for public and private housing, as the latter was almost three times more expensive and the gap was widening until the collapse of the private-housing market in late 1997 (Wong, 1998: 59). The rent-to-income ratio for public housing increased from 7.4 to 8.8 over the 1988–1998 period, whereas it increased from 17.5 to 25.8 for private housing. However, a review commissioned by the government in 1990 found that the average masked the fact that the ratio for public housing actually ranged from 5.2 to 10.6 per cent, being higher when tenants moved in and declining thereafter because rents increased less slowly than the tenants' incomes. LTHS 1998 recommended that rents be raised to a level equal to 15–18.5 per cent of the median income, depending on the size of the apartment (Hong Kong Government, 1997), but the recommendations are yet to be implemented.

On the supply side, it is arguable that both the government and builders, not to mention owners, have an interest in maintaining high prices. The government is believed to deliberately keep prices high because revenue from land sales form almost one-third of its total revenues (Liu, 1994: 69–70). The sale of public land by auction favours large developers, which is a key reason for the high degree of concentration in the housing industry in Hong Kong. Between 1991 and 1994, the five largest developers produced 60 per cent of all new housing units. During the same period, profits were as high as 364 per cent on land purchased through tender and 109 per cent on land purchased through auction (Chan, 2000: 35).

There is considerable debate on the efficiency of the government's subsidy for public housing. Wong (1998) estimates that the gross monthly subsidy provided to a typical public-housing household amounted to US$102 in 1981 and US$225 in 1991, while the average net monthly benefits it received were only US$56 and US$161 respectively. The benefits-to-subsidy ratio was thus only 59 and 72 per cent, representing a large loss for the society as a whole, though this loss has declined because of a reduction in subsidy (Wong, 1998: 85).

Critics have argued that public housing only marginally reduces income inequality in Hong Kong despite the government's preoccupation with it. Lui (1997: 98) argues that the mean income of public-housing residents was substantially higher than that of residents in private housing throughout the 1976–1991 period. Similarly, Wong (1998: 48) argues that except for the top income decile, proportionately more low-income households live in private rather than public housing. The data should be treated with caution, however, because private housing includes a lot of temporary housing and bedspace, while the middle class lives mainly in public housing. Otherwise, according to the 1996 census, the median household income of dwellers of Housing Authority rental apartments was less than half of that of households living in their own private house or apartment.

Singapore

Within a decade of the launch of the Home Ownership Scheme in 1964, Singapore had solved the worst of its housing shortage. Indeed by 1990 housing stock began to exceed households by 4 per cent. However, there continues to be unmet demand for public housing as a result of new household formation and from among those upgrading from an older or smaller apartment. The waiting period for the purchase of a new HDB apartment in 2000 was 12–18 months, depending on the locality, for first-time buyers and 36 months for those buying their second HDB apartment (each adult couple may buy up to two in their lifetime).

More remarkably, the increase in supply was not of rental but of ownership housing. Thus, the housing-ownership rate rose at about the same pace as housing supply (Singapore Department of Statistics, 2001: 58). By the 1990s, about 90 per cent of households in both public and private housing were living in accommodation owned by themselves, compared to only 30 per cent in 1970. Such a high level of private ownership of public housing has no parallel in the capitalist world, as countries where public housing is significant tend to be characterized by rental rather than ownership housing.

The increase in housing supply and ownership has been accompanied by an improvement in living conditions and general amenities. Long gone are the days when three-quarters of the population was living in overcrowded conditions (Goh, 1956) and housing conditions were described as primitive. Of a population of only 1.6 million in 1960, about 15 per cent were estimated to be living in slums and another 18 per cent in squatter areas (Eng and Kong, 1997: 441).

The public-housing programme was originally launched to cater for the lower-income groups but was later extended to middle-income groups – it now reaches all but the very top income brackets and this is reflected in the quality of the stock. Although private apartments continue to enjoy significantly higher prestige than public apartments, the former have been rapidly closing the quality gap. Approximately 63 per cent of all HDB apartments in 1999 consisted of four rooms or more, compared to only 44 per cent a decade earlier. During the same period, the proportion of three-room apartments declined from 41 to 29 per cent, and of one- and two-room HDB apartments from 14 to 7 per cent (Statistical Highlights, *Housing*, 2000: 59). Housing density has accordingly decreased from 5.1 persons per unit in 1980 to 4.4 in 1990 and remained unchanged a decade later (Sim, Lim and Tay, 1993: 85; Singapore Department of Statistics, 2001). The median living space in Singapore is 24 sqm, which is more than twice the size of that in Hong Kong (*Straits Times*, 28 October 2002).

However, the price of private housing has appreciated far more rapidly than HDB apartments: the average price of the former increased four times between 1990 and 1997, whereas for HDB apartments it increased only three times (Phang, 2001: 454). HDB apartment prices increased on average by 3 to 4 per cent a year during the 1981–1987 period and by 12–15 per cent a year during the 1992–1995 period (Tan, 1998: 19). The higher increase in the 1990s was partially a reflection of the better and larger apartments that HDB had begun to build.

Because of the huge political and economic stakes, the government is conscious of the need to keep housing affordable while allowing a healthy return on investment (Vasoo and Lee, 2001: 279). Indeed the price of HDB apartments changed little in real terms until the end of the 1980s, with the increase largely reflecting the rise in construction costs. In the mid 1990s, when prices rose more rapidly, the government shielded low-income households from the increase by pegging the price of three- and four-room HDB apartments to income levels (Tan, 1998: 20). The government claims that three-room apartments are affordable to 90 per cent of Singaporean households, and that 70 per cent can afford a four-room apartment. The average monthly mortgage repayments form approximately 18 per cent of the average household income for four-room HDB apartments and 19 per cent for five-room apartments. Most HDB residents are able to service their mortgage loans entirely from their CPF contributions (*Business Times*, 13 March 2000).

The price-to-income ratio for public housing has been stable, ranging from one to four, depending on the size of the unit (Asher and Yong, 1997: 306). The average rent-to-income ratio is not a meaningful indicator in Singapore because rented housing is occupied largely by foreign workers, who tend to be concentrated in the lowest and the highest income brackets, living in either the least or the most expensive housing.

Korea

Korea had a worsening housing supply until the 1980s because of the faster rate of household formation than of housing construction. Between 1960 and 1990, the number of households expanded by 242 per cent but the number of housing units increased by only 207 per cent. As a result, the housing-shortage rate increased from 18 per cent in 1960 to 28 per cent in 1990. The trend eventually reversed in the 1990s, and by 2000 the housing shortage had declined to 8 per cent. However, the shortage remains acute in urban areas, especially in Seoul, where there was a shortage of 18 per cent in 2000 and is likely to have worsened in the subsequent years (Ha, 2002: 196; OECD, 2003: 121).

Home ownership declined in the 1970s and 1980s before rising in the 1990s, though still only 54 per cent of the Korean households lived in self-owned housing in 1999. The nearly half of the population that lives in rental housing does so in private rather than public housing, as public rental housing formed only 6 per cent of the total housing stock in the late 1990s. Despite its declining popularity, the Chonsei[2] system is the most popular rental form, accommodating 30 per cent of all households in 1995, compared to 12 per cent who lived in monthly rental housing.

The average floor space per dwelling in Korea increased from 41.4 sqm in 1975 to 58.6 sqm in 1995, while the per capita floor space increased from 8.2 sqm to 17.2 sqm (Korea National Statistical Office, 1999). The average number of rooms per household correspondingly increased from 2.2 to 3.1, while the average number of persons per room declined from 2.3 to 1.1 over the same period. By 1995, 84 per cent of housing units had modern kitchens and 75 per cent had flush toilets, compared to 18 and 18 per cent respectively in 1980 (Korea National Statistical Office, 1999; Kang, 1993: 258). However, improvement in room-occupancy density and floor space has been attributable primarily to the decrease in household size rather than to the improvement in housing size *per se* (Lee and Yoon, undated).

Housing prices have fluctuated widely since the late 1980s. Prices almost doubled between 1988 and 1991 and then declined continuously, at first gradually and then sharply in 1997. While monthly rents also fell during much of the 1990s, the amount required for the Chonsei deposit increased steadily – it tripled between 1987 and 1997 – except for a short decline in 1997. But in 2000 housing rents began to climb up again, followed by an increase in housing prices as tenants took advantage of the low interest rate to buy their own home. As a result, between January 2001 and December 2002 housing rent increased on average by 40 per cent and prices by 55 per cent (OECD, 2003: 120). The increases have been particularly sharp in Seoul.

The price fluctuations have been reflected in the price-to-income ratio, which increased from 6.5 in 1989 to 9.2 in 1991 but then declined to 5.3 in 1995 and yet further in the subsequent years. The ratio is higher in Seoul, where it was 6.3 in 1997, and the rent-to-income ratio was 22.6. The monthly rent equivalent of Chonsei housing is hard to establish, but it is estimated to be approximately 38 per cent of the tenants' gross income (Choei, 1996: 52).

The regulation of private providers, which was the main instrument of housing policy in Korea until the 1980s, is widely believed to have been inefficient and a major reason for housing unaffordability in the country. High capital-gains tax and a minimum waiting period for the purchase of subsequent housing restricted mobility and hindered filtration whereby occupants move on to more expensive housing, leaving the vacated unit for lower-income families (Hahn, 1998: 101). Similarly, the price ceiling discouraged housing investment at the same time that it encouraged demand – resulting in acute shortage (ibid.: 104). The bond-bidding system and the requirement to purchase housing bonds by businesses increased the cost of purchase and made housing yet more unaffordable. Quantitative assessments of the impact of government-sponsored financing schemes, especially KHB, have found them to be highly inefficient (Choei, 1996).

The government's housing policy and its emphasis on home ownership helped only the middle classes. Passing all or much of the cost of housing on to buyers minimized the burden on the state exchequer, but it also did little to improve affordability for low-income households (Kim, 1995: 39–42). The comparatively heavier burden on lower-income groups is reflected in the fact that while an average Korean family spent 17.4 per cent of its family income on housing, the lowest decile family spent 29.4 per cent and the highest decile spent 12.4 per cent (Choei, 1996: 52). It was only in the late 1990s that the government's policy began to improve affordability for low-income households (Kim, 1995: 33; Ha, 1994; Yoon, 1994: 148).

Taiwan

Similar to the other NIEs, Taiwan had abysmal housing conditions in the 1950s, but the worst of its problem had been overcome by the 1960s.

Indeed Taiwan has had an over-supply, with a vacancy rate in the 13–19 per cent range continuously since 1970 (Construction and Planning Administration, 1999). The high vacancy rate is the result of a regulatory and financial environment enabling small-scale developers who dominate the Taiwan economy to put units on the market with relative ease, leading to over-supply during price booms.

Taiwan's home-ownership rate is one of the highest in the world, only slightly below Singapore's. The rate of home ownership increased from 67 per cent in 1965 to 78 per cent in 1985, to 85 per cent in 1997, and is still rising. As is to be expected, it is lower in Taipei, at about 70 per cent, which is still a sharp improvement from 63 per cent in 1979 (Lin, 1993: 28).

Housing conditions too have improved remarkably: the average size of dwelling in Taiwan increased from 62 sqm in 1962 to 114 sqm in 1995, though it was only 88.5 sqm in Taipei (Li, 1998: 36; *The China News*, 24 June 1994: 3). Rental units are on average one-third smaller than ownership units. The number of households per housing unit fell from 1.2 in 1980 to 1.0 in 1990, while the average dwelling space per person increased from 14 sqm in 1976 to 31 sqm in 1995.

Housing prices in Taipei have experienced significant fluctuations over the decades, but nevertheless increased by 13 per cent during the 1970s and 153 per cent during the 1980s. However, they declined by 7 per cent over the 1990–1998 period (Construction and Planning Administration, 1999). In 1998, prices in nominal terms were lower than they were in 1989; in real terms they were a lot lower. However, there are sharper fluctuations in Taiwan than in other countries in the region: on an annual basis, Taipei housing prices increased by 26 per cent in 1988 and by 56 per cent in 1989 and declined by 22 per cent in 1974 and 15 per cent in 1995.

The average price-to-income ratio was 7.2 in 1975, declining to 3.4 in 1985, but then it rose to 7.6 in 1990. The ratio was as high as 12 in Taipei in 1990, but is likely to have fallen by a wide margin since (Lin, 1996: 99). The rent-to-income ratio has also fluctuated: it rose from 7.3 in 1979 to 9.5 in 1985, but then declined to 8.5 per cent in 1989 and yet further in the following decade (Lin, 1993: 28). Rental expenses tend to be lower than ownership expenses because rental houses are smaller, older, and of lower quality – the high vacancy rate also keeps rents down.

The minimal government intervention in housing in Taiwan since the 1980s has been highly efficient in promoting supply and improving affordability. The almost free market in housing that exists there has promoted widespread investment in housing for speculative purposes, leading to excess supply. While in the short run it increased inequality (Li, 1998: 97–98), the long-term effect of it was over-supply and, eventually, increased affordability.

Comparative

All four NIEs started the 1950s with chronic housing shortage but by the 1980s they all had an over-supply, except for Korea, which continues to experience shortage (see Table 5.6). In actual fact, however, housing shortage in the NIEs is larger than suggested in the table. Despite the apparent 100 per cent supply in Hong Kong, 2 per cent of all households (in 2000) live in some sort of temporary housing. The shortage is particularly acute in Seoul, where housing supply is short by around 18 per cent. In Singapore, the shortage is confined to single-person households and low-paid foreign workers. In Taiwan, a housing glut co-exists with a housing shortage among families who cannot afford to buy despite historically low prices in real terms.

Although the public's expectation of home ownership in the NIEs is as strong as, if not stronger than, anywhere in the world, the expectation has been largely fulfilled only in Singapore and Taiwan (see Table 5.7). But even in Hong Kong and Korea, home ownership has increased tremendously since the 1970s. Only in Korea has ownership declined, though even there it increased in the 1990s.

Both housing prices and rent in the NIEs are generally higher relative to income than in developed and developing countries. As Table 5.8 shows, only Singapore compares favourably with the median price-to-income ratio of 4 in the developed countries and 6 in the developing countries (World Bank, 1993: 26). Hong Kong has the heaviest housing burden, with a price ratio of 12 and a rent ratio of 11. There is a vast

Table 5.6 Housing stock as percentage of households

	1970	Late 1990s
Hong Kong	77	100
Singapore	91 (1980)	104
Korea	78	92
Taiwan	100	103

Sources: Kim and Kim, 1998; Hong Kong Housing in Figures, 2000; Statistics Singapore, 2001; Wen, 1988: 27.

Table 5.7 Home ownership, percentage of population

	1970	1990s
Hong Kong	18	53 (2000)
Singapore	22 (1966)	90 (1995)
Korea	69	54 (1999)
Taiwan	66	84 (1996)

Sources: Lin, 1996: 91–92; *Hong Kong Social and Economic Trends 1997*; Chen and Wu, 1997; Singapore Statistical Highlights, 2000; Wen, 1988: 37.

Table 5.8 Price and rent-to-income ratio[1]

	Price[1]	Rent[2]
Hong Kong	12 (1997)	11 (1998)[1]
Singapore	4 (1990)	–
Korea[3]	6 (1997)	23 (1998)
Taiwan	8 (1990)	9 (1989)

Sources: Lin, 1996: 91–92; La Grange and Pretorius, 1999: 54.

Notes
1 Average housing price as multiple of average annual income.
2 Average rent as percentage of average monthly income.
3 Data for Seoul only.

difference between public and private housing (each of which forms half of the housing stock) in Hong Kong: the rent ratio for private housing (26) is almost three times the ratio for public housing (9). While the price ratio of 6 in Korea appears unexceptional, the rent ratio of 23 is extraordinary. While no recent data are available for Taiwan, both price- and rent-to-income ratios are considerably lower than the 8 and 9 respectively shown in the table because of the steep decline in housing prices during the 1990s.

Conclusion

All the four NIEs were dragged into dealing with the housing problem in the 1950s, but no government responded as extensively or enthusiastically as Singapore's and, to a lesser extent, Hong Kong's. The Taiwanese government undertook only limited intervention, which allowed market forces to determine the outcomes. In contrast, Korea intervened heavily, albeit reluctantly and haphazardly, through regulations that worsened the situation until it began to change tack in the late 1980s.

Provision of housing is dominant by the public sector in Singapore, while in Hong Kong housing supply is almost evenly split between the private and public sectors. In contrast, it is private housing that is dominant in Korea and Taiwan. The large government involvement in the provision of housing in the two city-states is to a large extent a result of the near monopoly that the two governments enjoy over land supply, which allows them to provide public housing at a modest cost. Were they to pay the market price for land, the cost of public housing would have been enormous and it is inconceivable that they would have been able to undertake the task given their limited taxation base. The predominance of private ownership of land in Korea and Taiwan makes it difficult, and expensive, for the governments to provide housing directly.

The Hong Kong government is the largest spender on housing in the region, and has been so since the 1970s. The Taiwan government, in contrast, is the smallest spender, which is consistent with its *laissez-faire* attitude towards housing. The Korean government similarly spends little on housing but, unlike Taiwan, it controls the market through extensive regulations, though many of the regulations were removed or relaxed in the late 1980s. The Singapore government has ambitious goals, but achieves them through tight control over all aspects of the housing market without supplanting it or spending a great deal. It has set up elaborate regulatory and financing arrangements in order to keep costs low for producers (the government itself is the largest producer) and prices affordable for buyers. On the financing side, it enables buyers to borrow inexpensively from their own retirement fund.

The Asian NIEs would seem to fit Kemeny's (1981) category of "home owning" rather than "cost renting" housing systems. All four governments have established or promoted financial arrangements to provide loans to the middle classes for housing purchase on a preferential basis. Hong Kong used to be an exception in that the government policy was targeted at providing rental housing to low-income families, but this began to change in the 1970s when the government started to promote ownership and the shift became particularly pronounced in the 1990s. In all NIEs, the governments actively or implicitly discourage the rental market by reserving it for the poor, thereby stigmatizing it. Of the four, Singapore has for a long time had the most elaborate arrangement for promoting home ownership and discouraging rented housing.

While promoting home ownership has been the key focus of housing policy in all the four NIEs, as indeed in other parts of the world, only Singapore and Taiwan in the region have largely succeeded in achieving their objective. However, they accomplished the goal through entirely different strategies: Singapore through extensive state involvement and planning and Taiwan through reliance on the market mechanism. Without directly regulating prices, the Singapore government has used its dominant position as the largest landlord and real-estate developer to ensure that housing prices are broadly consistent with the government's objectives. In Taiwan, in contrast, tax incentives for home loans, coupled with borrowers chasing windfall profits, caused over-supply of housing which was eventually reflected in declining prices and improved affordability. Hong Kong, in comparison, has pursued a contradictory strategy of making housing affordable while allowing developers to realise handsome profits. The contradiction is reflected in modest outcomes despite massive expenditures.

We find, again, two broad patterns in the NIEs' housing policy. On the one hand are Hong Kong and Singapore, which emphasize private housing. There are, of course, significant in-group differences. Singapore, unlike Hong Kong, spends little on housing, whereas Korea contrasts sharply with Taiwan in the heavy regulation it imposes on the housing sector.

6
EDUCATION

Unlike many social policies that are often attacked for stifling economic well-being, there is a broad consensus that a well designed education policy is essential for promoting economic development. There is ample empirical evidence confirming that the education level of the labour-force is a significant determinant of economic growth (see Lockheed and Verspoor, 1989: 3; Patrinos, undated; Tilak, 1989; World Bank, 1995). A recent large-scale UNESCO–OECD study further confirmed that there was a strong positive relationship between investment in education and economic growth in both developed and developing countries (OECD, 2003). Technological advances and economic globalization in recent decades are believed to have heightened education's contribution to international economic competitiveness (UNESCO, 1993: 16). There are social benefits to be derived from investment in education as well: in addition to slowing down population growth, the education of women has a positive impact on their children's, and eventually the entire population's, health.

Even mainstream economists admit the case for state intervention in education on the grounds of various market failures that lead to its insufficient or inefficient provision (Colclough, 1996: 589–590). But they tend to prefer targeted intervention, directed at specific market failures and instances where the potential benefits of intervention are the greatest. They especially favour government support for education confined to primary and women's education because these are deemed to yield maximum benefits for the society as a whole (Psacharopoulos, 1994: 1325). Unlike the strong evidence on the positive economic effects of education, studies have found conflicting evidence regarding the effects of public spending on education (for review, see Gupta *et al.*, 1999).

Regardless of the conflicting evidence regarding the effects of the state's support for education, there have been increasing calls for reducing its role so as to allow the market to play a larger role in allocating educational resources (see Lockheed and Jimenez, 1994; West, 1995). It is argued that governments often do not have sufficient resources to invest adequately in education and, when they do, they are frequently misdirected because of political and informational constraints. By concentrating only on the priority areas and leaving the rest to the market, it is held that governments would promote an efficient allocation of resources while still acquitting essential social responsibilities. Following from this line of argument, it is proposed that governments should concentrate on primary education; public educational institutions should levy higher tuition fees,[1] with provision for scholarship for poorer students and easier access to educational loans; and there should be an expansion of private schools (Colclough, 1996: 590–591).

While there is considerable merit in the proposed market-oriented solutions, their proponents often exaggerate and misrepresent the shortcomings of the state and the benefits of the market (see Cummings and Riddell, 1994; Puiggros, 1997). Reviews of empirical evidence show no firm conclusion in favour of private schools, as a lot depends on the context. In some countries government schools are regarded as exclusive and others it is the private schools that are exclusive – the efficiency of the two sectors therefore depends on the types of schools being considered. Moreover, while in some countries private schools may be more efficient in an economic sense, this may be at the expense of quality. Recent research also shows that the returns on investment in secondary and higher education are greater than was previously thought (OECD, 2003), thus undermining the case for policy emphasis only on primary education. The proponents of private education make much of the fact that public education, especially at higher levels, is disproportionately availed by the rich. While this is no doubt true, the distribution is not as lopsided as is often presented. Moreover, the argument that there is "excess demand" for education because of government subsidy must be tempered by the fact that demand elasticity is higher for poor people and, consequently, reduction in subsidy will reduce the poor's demand more than it will that of the rich.

Education policy in East Asia and the vital role it purportedly played in promoting economic development has received considerable attention in the literature. It is argued that the region's economic dynamism was to a significant extent a result of the governments' heavy emphasis on education, especially primary education (see Appelbaum and Henderson, 1992; Kuznets, 1988; Lewin, 1998; McMahon, 1999; Morris, 1996; Ogawa and Jones, 1993; World Bank, 1993). The supporting evidence is, however, less conclusive than it is often made out to be. Behrman and Schneider (1994) show that the rapidly growing Asian economies did not invest more in education before economic growth took off than their slower-growing counterparts, suggesting that other factors may be at work. It is time we advance the debate by first laying out the essential features of the NIE governments' education policy.

In this chapter we will see that the education policy varies considerably across the NIEs. While the state has been by far the largest provider and financier of education in all four economies, the role of private providers and payments exhibits vast differences. However, in recent years all four governments have emphasized efforts to promote devolution, diversity, innovation, cost efficiency, and greater public support for private institutions. These would be familiar to observers of education policy elsewhere as nearly all Western and many non-Western countries mention the same objectives (Walford, 2001). At a deeper level, we notice two education-policy clusters among the NIEs, with Hong Kong and Singapore in one group and Korea and Taiwan in the other. The chapter will show that the first group is characterized by large state involvement in the provision and financing of education, while private provision and financing play a significant role in the second group.

Policy history

Hong Kong

The colonial government had almost no involvement in education in Hong Kong until the mid nineteenth century. For instance, in 1854 the government was providing grants to only five schools, which together enrolled 150 students, out of the total school-age population of 8,800. Similarly, it spent just $125 on education that year, compared to $8,620 on policing (Tse, 1998: 92). The situation changed with the influx of refugees from China following the Taiping Rebellion, which led the government to establish the Board of Education in 1860, subsequently upgraded to the Department of Education in 1865. The increasing government role was a part of its effort to mollify the disaffection among the population against the colonial rule and to prepare the local population for junior administrative positions (ibid.). Yet the government gave only cursory attention to education, except for small grants to schools. The first Head of the Department of Education, F. Stewart, in 1865 noted the problems of high drop-out rates in primary schools, rote learning, and the grim socio-economic conditions that stymied learning, and so argued for increased government funding for education (Yee, 1995: 39).

Initially government grants were available to all schools regardless of their language of instruction or religious affiliation, but this changed in 1873 when the government decided to give grants only to schools that taught a minimum of four consecutive hours of non-religious education. In 1895, the grants were further restricted to schools that taught in English. A side effect of the policy not to fund religious or non-English schools was that the government lost regulatory control over Chinese schools. To regain control, the government finally reversed its policy in 1904. The overthrow of the Ching dynasty in 1911 and the nationalist government's resolve to reach out to overseas Chinese galvanized the British colonial government to further strengthen its control over Chinese schools, which eventuated in an ordinance in 1913 requiring all schools to register with the government and to meet specified minimum standards (Post, 1993: 244; Tse, 1998: 95).

The population of Hong Kong was growing rapidly in the inter-war years with no corresponding increase in educational opportunities. Private schools mushroomed in the 1920s and 1930s to meet the increasing demand for education: all but 22 of the 1,300 schools in Hong Kong in 1939 were private (ibid.: 96).

The government's attitude towards education changed rapidly after the Civil War in China led to an influx of refugees and heightened political tension in the colony. It responded by tightening control over education through the Education Ordinance of 1953, which brought all schools under strict control of the Department of Education and banned all political activities in schools. It also began to subsidize all private schools that met minimum standards and increased the number of public schools. Between 1951 and 1966 the number of schools doubled, enrolment almost tripled, and public expenditure on education increased five-fold. Nevertheless, only 3.5 per cent of all schools in 1966 were in the public sector.

Reforms picked up speed following the establishment of the Education Commission and its subsequent White Paper released in 1965 recommending free and compulsory primary schooling. The Education Department was, as a part of the effort to implement the report, directed to expand the number of public schools and increase subsidized places in private schools. The legislation providing for six free and compulsory years of education was enacted in 1971. However, secondary education continued to remain exclusive, admitting only 50 per cent of primary-school graduates in 1975.

The 1970s saw the start of active government involvement in education (Cheng and Wong, 1997), evident in the large number of consultation documents issued during the period: "Secondary Education in Hong Kong Over the Next Decade" in 1974, "Development of Senior Secondary and Tertiary Education" in 1978, the "Primary Education and Pre-Primary Services" in 1981, and, arguably the most significant of all, "A Perspective on Education in Hong Kong" in 1992, also known as the Llewellyn Report. The 1974 document recommended increasing compulsory education to nine years, enhanced subsidy for lower-secondary schools (Forms 1–3), a new entrance examination for admission to upper-secondary schools, and a greater emphasis on vocational and technical education. The government followed up on the report by announcing free and compulsory junior secondary education in 1978. In 1981, the Education Department was put under the Education and Manpower Branch, further subjugating education to the manpower needs of the economy (Tse, 1998: 110).

Expanding education opportunities was the main focus of government policy throughout the 1980s (Post, 1996: 157). But the focus changed somewhat in the early 1990s when the government began to promote education quality, and in particular elite schools in both the public and private sectors (Lee and Cheung, 1992). At the same time, it began to promote private schools (Tan, 1993: 84). In 1988, the Education Commission noted the need to recognize "the educational benefits of a strong, independent private sector" and called for the provision of Direct Subsidy (DSS) to private and aided schools to improve their educational standards while maintaining their autonomy.

The DSS schools were finally established and given a high degree of autonomy in selecting students, determining curriculum, and charging fees. However, to encourage such schools to keep their fees low, the government subsidy is inversely related to their fees (ibid.: 87–88). Furthermore, to allay public fears that the support for DSS was going to be at the expense of public and aided schools, the government promised to not allow more than one-third of the secondary schools to join the scheme (ibid.: 89). Most of the schools that joined the DSS were either "international" schools or "Leftist" schools associated with PRC that had previously remained outside the mainstream and did not receive public funds. Aided and non-international private schools have largely avoided DSS, despite government encouragement, because they do not see significant advantage in it.

Higher education had an early start in Hong Kong with the establishment of the Hong Kong College of Medicine in 1887. However, it was not until 1911 that a fully fledged institution, the University of Hong Kong, was established. The move was partly inspired by a desire to counter the perceived growing Japanese influence in China and the region generally. No new university was established until 1963, when the Chinese University of Hong Kong was founded. While the number of university places increased in the following years, less than 4 per cent of those completing senior secondary school were enrolled in universities in 1990, though this was still a large increase from the 1.6 per cent in 1960 (Tse, 1998: 100).

The expansion of higher education picked up pace in the early 1990s when the existing colleges and polytechnics were converted into universities and a new Open University of Hong Kong was established. By the end of the 1990s, 8 per cent of the age cohort were going to university and the government set a target of 18 per cent for the near future (Chan and Leung, 1997: 67). The expansion of higher education was accompanied by efforts to introduce modern management techniques and make the institutions more responsive to market forces. In its 1996 report, the University Grants Committee recommended that higher-educational institutions recover 18 per cent of their costs through tuition fees, and that government funding for universities be more closely tied to teaching and research performance (Mok, 1997). In his 2000 Policy Address, Tung Chee Hwa announced a target of enrolling 60 per cent of high-school graduates in tertiary institutions within ten years.

Language of instruction has been a controversial issue for more than a century in Hong Kong. On the one hand, an overwhelming majority of official reports and academic studies since the 1860s have called for Chinese as the medium of instruction (Tsui *et al.*, 1999). But the demand was largely ignored and instruction continued to be offered in English because of the exigencies of colonial rule and the need to maintain Hong Kong's international economic competitiveness. This changed somewhat in 1974 when schools were allowed the choice between English and Chinese, though in practice an overwhelming majority continued to teach in English. More drastic change came about in 1998 when all schools, except those explicitly exempted, were required to teach in Chinese: eventually, 307 schools were designated as Chinese-medium schools and 114 as English-medium schools. The public, however, views Chinese schools as inferior and resents the denial of English-language teaching to its children. Businesses too are opposed to the change because they fear that a downgrading of English would reduce Hong Kong's international economic competitiveness. There is no indication that the government is considering a reversal of the policy.

In the context of increasing efforts to promote private schools and the changes wrought by globalization and the colony's return to China, the Education Commission launched a major review of the education system in 1998. The report (Hong Kong Education Commission, 2000) is full of the buzz-words found in similar documents elsewhere. It sets out the education policy's goals as seeking to "build a lifelong learning society" and "inject diversity in education ideologies, modes of financing and focus of curriculum". The report places considerable emphasis on a flexible assessment of students, teacher training, and quality-assurance measures.

The structure of education in Hong Kong consists of kindergarten, six years of primary schooling, three years of junior secondary, and three or four years of senior secondary. Primary and junior secondary schooling is compulsory. Academic Aptitude Test (AAT) results were used for admission to junior secondary, but the test was abolished in 2000 on the belief that it was promoting rote learning. Most students take the Hong Kong Certificate of Education Examination (HKCEE) at the end of junior secondary and the Hong Kong Advanced Level Examination (HKALE) at the end of senior secondary. The government is in the process of completely overhauling the current examination and school-placement system at the secondary level with the objective of giving greater autonomy to schools, broader choice for students, and reduced emphasis on examination.

Singapore

Throughout the nineteenth century, the colonial government's involvement in education was confined to providing a few years of free primary education to the ethnic Malays. Schools was generally established and run by missionaries, wealthy individuals, and clan associations. There were a wide variety of schools in terms of curriculum, medium of instruction, sources of financing, and staff quality (Tan, 1997). Substantial changes came about in 1946 when the government announced a ten-year plan for providing free but voluntary primary education. While the parents were free to choose any of the four official languages for the education of their children, the funding formula favoured "regional" schools, which were non-ethnic and used English as the medium of instruction.

In 1955 the All Party Committee was established to look into the problems faced by Chinese schools. The Committee recommended that all four main languages – English, Chinese, Malay, and Tamil – be given equal treatment and all schools use a common curriculum, regardless of their language of instruction. It also recommended bilingual education at the primary level and trilingual education – English, Malay, and the mother tongue – at the secondary level. The report was subsequently published as a White Paper and a few months later formalized in the Education Ordinance of 1957.

The Ordinance marked a turning point in the regulation of schools and the development of a national education system in Singapore (Tan, 1997). It set up a highly centralized system requiring compulsory registration of all schools and close supervision of their operation. Accompanying regulations applied uniform funding formula to government and aided schools. The next major overhaul of primary and secondary education was undertaken following the publication of the Goh Report in 1978, which recommended that students be "streamed" into different courses according to their ability. The recommendation was implemented and fine-tuned over the 1980s. At the same time, English gradually became the first language of instruction at every level of education, although study of a second language remained compulsory for most students.

The first higher-education institution, King Edward College, was established in 1905, followed by the Raffles College in 1929. The two colleges were combined to form the University of Malaya in 1949. With funds donated by the Chinese business community, Nanyang University was established as a private Chinese-language institution in 1953, though it was not granted university status until 1959. However, the government viewed the new university as a hotbed of communism and merged it with the University of Singapore in 1980 to form the National University of Singapore. In 1990 the old Nanyang University was re-established as the Nanyang Technological University. The Singapore Management University commenced operation as the island's third university in 2000. It is a private university but is funded largely by the government. In addition, the Singapore Institute of Management operates the Open University Degree Programme (OUDP) in conjunction with Britain's Open University. There are also four polytechnics in Singapore teaching a range of business, technical, and arts courses.

Although the provision and financing of education in Singapore is more dominated by the state than in the other NIEs, the government began to withdraw somewhat in the mid 1980s. Following the government's vision statement in 1984 to turn Singapore into a "City of excellence" and "an innovative society", the First Deputy Prime Minister argued that centralization had stifled initiative and innovation among schools and led the prestigious schools to lose their individual character. He proposed devolution and greater competition among schools as solutions to the problem. Similar statements by other senior government officials became routine in subsequent months and years. American studies showing the superiority of private schools because of the competition among them were presented to support the case for promoting devolution and competition (Tan, 1993: 82).

The first batch of "independent" schools – all elite schools with a strong reputation and excellent results in competitive examinations – was established in 1989. Such schools enjoy a high degree of autonomy in setting fees, selecting pupils and teachers, and determining the curriculum, though within the parameters established by the government. They receive additional funds from the government, on top of the higher tuition fees they charge. In response to the criticism that independent schools cater to the rich, the government began to establish "autonomous" schools from among the better managed neighbourhood public schools in 1994. These schools are less independent, and receive less government subsidy and charge lower fees, than the "independent" schools but more than the regular schools. A means-tested financial-assistance scheme is in place for children from less well-off families attending independent and autonomous schools. In 2000, the government announced that the number of autonomous schools would be increased gradually and that they would eventually enrol 25 per cent of all students at the secondary level. Thus Singapore has, in effect, a three-tier school system consisting of independent, autonomous, and regular schools. In addition, there is a Gifted Education Programme (GEP) – launched in 1994 – to cater for about 1 per cent of all children deemed to be exceptionally gifted with academic skills. The identification of pupils for GEP is carried out through series of tests at Years 3 and 6 of primary school.

Singaporean leaders are sensitive to allegations of educational inequities and go to great lengths to ensure the appearance of fairness. In recent years the government has launched measures it claims are designed to help children from groups that do not perform well in schools. In 1990 it announced the Edusave scheme for all students between the ages of 6 and 16 years. The scheme provides a set amount of money that can be used for any school-related activity: educational trips, tuition classes in schools, music and computer classes, and textbooks, for example. The scheme is being financed with income from a US$3.5 billion fund set up by the government. Launching the scheme, the Prime Minster said: "I want to temper our meritocratic, free market system with compassion and more equal opportunities . . . . With Edusave, all children, rich or poor, are brought to the same starting line, properly equipped to run" (*Straits Times*, 16 August 1993: 26). Edusave was refined in 1995 when Edusave Merit bursaries were launched for outstanding students in the top 25 per cent of the school cohort from households with a family income of less than US$1,740 per month.

Another move intended to improve the educational performance of groups whose children have not traditionally performed well is the establishment of ethnic associations to provide tuition classes to children belonging to their ethnic groups. Referred to as "self-help groups", Mendaki, Chinese Development Assistance Council (CDAC), and Sinda are intended to assist Malay, Chinese, and Indian children with learning difficulties. They are expected to raise funds from members of their own ethnic community, and whatever amount they raise is matched by the government.

International economic competitiveness has been a major concern of the Singapore government. In 1997 the government published a position paper – "Thinking Schools, Learning Nation" – outlining its vision for the future. The document places a lot of emphasis on developing national culture and identity, emphasizing rights and responsibilities as well as the need to embrace information technology and promote creativity. Accordingly, recent reforms have concentrated on the introduction of information technology in education, reducing learning content in the school curriculum, expanding opportunities for thinking and creativity, devolving decision-making authority to schools, and assessing school performance against objective indicators (Gopinathan and Ho, 2000).

The education system in Singapore consists of six years of primary education and four years of secondary education. Singapore was one of the few countries in the region with no compulsory education, but this changed in 2003 when its six years of primary schooling became compulsory. At the end of the sixth year of primary school, pupils sit the Primary School Leaving Examination (PSLE), which forms the basis for "streaming" into Special, Express, or Normal tracks at the secondary-school level. The examination is academically oriented and the laggards are regarded as unsuited for academic study. The majority of students are admitted to the Express stream, while the Special stream is for a select group of top students who are taught both English and the mother tongue at an advanced level. The Normal stream is further subdivided into academic and technical streams, and includes students who have been assessed as lacking academic potential and are accordingly put through a less demanding curriculum. The Normal secondary students proceed to apprenticeships or Institutes of Technical Education after five years of study. Special and Express students sit O Level examinations at the end of their fourth year. The top 20 per cent of the cohort proceed to two-year junior college, the following 40 per cent to three-year polytechnic, and the remainder to vocational institutions. The A Level examination at the end of junior college determines eligibility for admission to universities. While some movement across streams is possible, the system of streaming of students according to their perceived academic aptitude is strictly and often rigidly applied.

Korea

Many features of the contemporary education system in Korea go back to the Chosun dynasty (1332–1910), when the main purpose of education was the selection of political and social elites and the promotion of loyalty to the king (Chung, 1998: 84). The Japanese rulers (1910–1945) continued the legacy, buttressed by enhanced state control over education (Synott, 1995). They also made serious efforts to promote primary education, evident in the fact that primary-school enrolments stood at nearly 45 per cent in 1945 (McGinn, 1980: 82). However, very few Koreans had the opportunity to continue to secondary- or higher-education level (Lee, undated). The legacy of employing education as a mechanism for selecting elites, strong state control over education, and concentration on primary education continues to this day, albeit in a diluted form since the early 1990s.

Japanese imperial education was replaced with a system inspired by liberal-democratic values during American military rule (1945–1948) and efforts were made to allow greater administrative freedom at the local level. However, the conservative and anti-democratic credentials of some of the people associated with the reforms discredited and stymied the reform efforts. In any event, the American rule was for too short a period to make a significant difference to the system that had developed over centuries. The war with North Korea and the anti-communist fervour it generated further weakened the democratic impulses.

The Park government viewed education as an integral part of its economic development policy and subjected it to rigorous manpower planning and strict control over curriculum and administration of schools (Kim, 2000). The Economic Planning Board produced five-year plans for education in which manpower needs were a vital consideration. The subjugation of education to economic development objectives was evident in the importance attributed to vocational education. All education-policy statements after the early 1960s called for increasing enrolment in vocational institutions to 70 per cent of all enrolment but this goal was never achieved and indeed stayed under 50 per cent, which is still high by international standards (Adams and Gottlieb, 1993: 137).

To expand educational opportunities, the entrance examination for admission to junior secondary schools was abolished in 1968 and to senior secondary schools in 1974 and children were assigned to a school in their residential district through lottery. To reduce pressure on children, private tutoring at the school level was abolished in 1980. The ban had little effect, as the ratio of students in private tutoring actually tripled between 1980 and 2000, while private expenditure on it increased 22 times (Chung, 2002: 4–5). Tutoring to prepare for entrance to prestigious universities has particularly exacerbated over the years. It was no great loss, therefore, when in 2000 the Supreme Court ruled that the ban on tutoring was unconstitutional and struck it down.

The state's main role in education has, however, been one of regulator rather than provider or financier. Indeed Korea is unmatched in the extent to which it relies on private provision and financing of education (OECD, 1999a: 185). It all started in the aftermath of the war when private providers moved in to fill a gap left by public institutions that were starved of resources. It was further accelerated by the suspension of the Financial Subsidy for Local Education Law – which earmarked 13 per cent of government revenues for education – between 1972 and 1981 and the proliferation of private institutions that followed. Even after funding was restored, the perceived poor conditions in public schools coupled with rise in income levels led families to continue to send their children to private schools (Chung, 1998).

Comprehensive education reform began with the establishment of the Presidential Commission for Education Reform in 1985, but not much was done to implement it until the 1990s. The Presidential Commission – which was abolished in 1987 but revived in a stronger form in 1993 – released four reports between 1995 and 1997. A common feature of the reports was a commitment to efficiency via competition and choice and to equality of opportunity (OECD, 1999a: 191). While the Commission did not promote privatization as such, it did recommend greater autonomy for school administrators and local authorities, and greater public support for private schools. Other notable recommendations were free preschool education and greater diversity in the school curriculum at all levels.

The reports were followed up by devolution of the education system, with the government establishing only broad guidelines, leaving it to the local authorities and individual schools to manage their staffing and financial matters, and even their curriculum. The central government's funding for education is increasingly disbursed as a lump sum to local authorities, which have considerable autonomy in allocating the funds to schools, which in turn have broad discretion in how the money is spent (Paik, 1995: 11). In 2000 the government decided to establish a limited number of schools for gifted children at the secondary level (*Korea Herald*, 16 January 2001).

The school system consists of six years of primary school and three years each of junior and senior secondary school, followed by four years of college or university. Primary education is compulsory and been free since 1979. Junior secondary education has been compulsory – but not free, except in rural areas – since 1985. Children are assigned junior secondary places within their residential area through lottery. Senior secondary schools are divided into academic and vocational institutions, with the former enrolling around three-fifths of the students at this level. Education at this level is voluntary and subject to tuition fees. Higher-education institutions in Korea fall into five categories – four-year colleges and universities; teachers' colleges; vocational junior colleges; polytechnics; and miscellaneous schools – and all charge varying levels of fees.

Taiwan

The Japanese colonial government (1895–1945) established an education system in Taiwan that was, as in Korea, modern with relatively high enrolment. The colonial government believed that education was the best way of ensuring imperial control over the local population (Yang, 2001). The end of the colonial rule in 1945 was followed by efforts to systematically eradicate Japanese influence in education and make it more "Chinese". The education system that existed in China before the Civil War – adopted in 1922 and loosely patterned after the American system – was introduced following the KMT's arrival in Taiwan (Cheng, 1995: 6).

The 1947 Constitution (Articles 159 and 160) guarantees basic education for all children. It also specifies the minimum proportion of total public expenditure that each level of government must spend on education, science, and culture: 15 per cent for the central, 25 per cent for the provincial, and 35 per cent for the local government (ibid.: 8). The KMT was preoccupied with other concerns in the early years of its rule and its first major educational-policy initiative was not launched until 1968, when it introduced nine years of compulsory education.

The education system in Taiwan until the mid 1980s was, reflecting the authoritarian character of the KMT regime, highly centralized and subject to rigorous planning of economic development objectives. Manpower Development Plans (MDP) were formulated in the context of the Four Year Economic Development Plan (Sun, 1998: 32). The objective of the earlier MPDs was to expand technical education to support its export drive and strict control was exercised over what was taught at the secondary and tertiary levels and how many could enrol in them. The entrance examination for admission to universities and junior colleges was the key mechanism for implementing manpower goals.

The government recognized the need for education reform in the early 1980s, indicated in the establishment of the Research Group for Education Reform in 1983. The group recommended a range of institutional reforms, but very few of its recommendations were actually implemented (Yang, 2001). Reform efforts became more genuine and deeper only after the end of martial law in 1987. The period saw measures to broaden access to education, end the rigid distinction between technical and general education, give greater choice of subjects to students, and more emphasis on local than mainland Chinese issues (Law, 1997). In 1987 the government began to provide a subsidy of US$157 per semester to each child enrolled in primary and kindergarten school. It was followed by the "Medium Term Plan for Developing and Improving Infant Education" in 1993, which promised pre-primary education to all five year olds. The entrance examination for senior secondary schools was eliminated in 1990 and compulsory education was extended by one year to ten in 1993. The University Law was amended in 1993 to reinstate and expand institutional autonomy, which had been lost under Martial Law.

By the early 1990s, there was growing public perception that the education system was not meeting the society's economic, political, and social expectations (Yang, 2001). An *ad hoc* cabinet-level Council on Education Reform was established in September 1994 to chart out a new course, which published its report ("Consultation Report on Educational Reform") in 1996. An inter-ministerial agency (Commission for Promoting Education Reform) was established in the following year to implement the proposed reforms. The Commission recommended greater autonomy for schools and teachers, an expanded choice for children and their parents, improvements in teaching standards at all levels, and a reduced emphasis on examination. The government accepted the recommendations and allocated US$5.5 billion over five years to implement them. A range of legislations – including University Law, Teachers Education Act, and Law of Teachers' Union and Teachers Selection – were enacted to put the proposals into effect. Mok (2000: 644) summarizes the 1990s reforms as being imbued by ideas of "denationalization, decentralization and autonomization, and marketization".

The 1990s reforms included a new curriculum that will eventually establish a fully articulated system of nine years of education with uniform basic subjects for all pupils while allowing flexibility with respect to elective subjects (Ou, 1999). Entrance examination at the senior-secondary level was abolished in 2001 and at the tertiary level in 2002. In 1998 the government decided to increase the ratio of general high-school places from 36 to 50 per cent, while correspondingly reducing the places in vocational schools (Shan and Chang, 2000: 203). In the same year, a new curriculum promoting "core competence" including creativity, technology, and "higher-order thinking" was adopted in junior and senior secondary schools.

Since 1945, the education system has been divided into $6+3+3+$ tertiary. The six years of primary education and three years of junior education are compulsory and free. Students at these levels are assigned to schools within their neighbourhood. After completing nine years of compulsory education, students enter three-year general or vocational schools or five-year junior colleges. Entrance to senior-secondary level is determined by performance in the Basic Competency Test, which assesses generic skills. In addition to colleges and universities, the higher-education system in Taiwan includes two- and three-year junior colleges (the former admits only graduates of senior vocational high schools while the latter admits only senior-high graduates), the last two years of five-year junior colleges, and colleges and universities.

Provision

Hong Kong

Only a small proportion of educational institutions in Hong Kong are in the public sector in the strict sense of the term: in 2000, only 5 per cent of primary schools and 8 per cent of secondary schools were owned and operated by the government, while another 83 and 74 per cent respectively were aided schools. The latter are, however, government schools in all respects but ownership, as the state provides almost all the funds and controls who they admit and what they teach. Government and aided schools considered together form more than four-fifths of all schools in Hong Kong.

At the kindergarten level, the government's involvement is limited to advising on curriculum and providing modest finance for operation and fee remission for needy children. Non-profit schools form 58 per cent of kindergarten institutions, accounting for 62 per cent of enrolment, while the rest are in commercial institutions (Chan and Leung, 1997: 57–68).

At the primary-school level, government and aided schools account for 88 per cent of all schools as well as enrolment. Similarly, at the secondary level they form 82 per cent of all schools and over 88 per cent of enrolment. However, even private schools receive substantial funds from the government under the "bought places" and "caput" arrangement whereby teaching is contracted out to private institutions (ibid.: 58). There were 34 DSS schools in 2001: 32 at the secondary level and two at primary level. All higher-education institutions in Hong Kong are either public or aided.

Under the Secondary School Places Allocation (SSPA) system, students are admitted to schools in their neighbourhood, although schools are allowed to pick up to 20 per cent of their intake from outside the neighbourhood. Prestigious schools, however, are for the most part located in prosperous neighbourhoods, which filters out children from less well-off neighbourhoods (ibid.: 66).

Singapore

The government has been the main provider of education in Singapore since the 1960s. Around three-quarters of all schools and enrolment have been in government schools and most of the remainder in aided schools, which are for all practical purposes government schools. In 2000, only two schools (out of a total of 377) enrolling 0.2 per cent of all students were in truly private schools (Singapore Ministry of Education, 2001). Of all secondary schools, 18 are designated as "Autonomous" and 8 as "Independent" schools. Excluded from the education system are the "international" schools, which follow the curriculum of another country, cater to expatriate children, and recover the full cost of education through fees: there were 29 such schools enrolling 17,734 students in 2000.

Pre-primary education in Singapore is provided by the private sector and the government's role consists largely of registering institutions and exercising general supervision. Although primary education became compulsory only in 2003, almost all children of the relevant age have been attending school since the 1980s. Secondary schooling is still voluntary, but most children in the age group attend school. Of all secondary-school pupils, 14 per cent were attending autonomous schools and 7 per cent were attending independent schools in 2000, while the rest were in regular public or aided schools.

Enrolment at university more than doubled between 1985 and 1999, and tripled for polytechnics. Nevertheless, the universities together accept less than half of all applicants for admission, and the polytechnics too decline a large proportion of applicants. The only institution open to all is the Open University, which does not seem popular with Singaporeans given its small enrolment. A large number of school-leavers must, as a result, go abroad for further studies. In 1990 there were 15,300 students studying overseas, about three-quarters of whom were registered in undergraduate programmes (Selvaratnam, 1994: 47). The public resents the limited places at local tertiary institutions, but the government is adamant that admission must remain selective to maintain high standards.

The late 1990s saw the emergence of a new trend towards enrolment in post-secondary programmes offered by foreign institutions either directly or in conjunction with local institutions, but these do not usually award degrees. Enrolment in such programmes reached 21,010 in 2000, compared to 37,650 who were enrolled in local higher-education institutions (Yeo, 2001).

Korea

Preschool education has traditionally been provided by private firms and religious organizations, but the government has gradually brought such schools under greater control. The Pre-Education Promotion Law of 1977 and 1982 accelerated their expansion as well as government control over them. Enrolment at this level increased twenty times between 1965 and 1990, with the expansion particularly strong between 1980 and 1985 (Adams and Gottlieb, 1993: 45).

The public sector is the dominant provider of education only at the primary- and junior-secondary-school levels: almost all schools at the primary level and over 70 per cent at the junior-secondary level are in the public sector, but, its share amounts to only 49 per cent at the senior-secondary level and a meagre 21 per cent at the tertiary levels (ibid.: 45). However, public schools tend to be larger and to enrol a larger percentage of students. In 1999, 99 per cent of the students at primary level, 75 per cent at the junior-secondary level, and 86 per cent at the senior-secondary level were attending public institutions. At the tertiary level, only 10 per cent of enrolment in junior colleges and 17 per cent in universities and colleges were in public institutions (KEDI, 2000).

Almost all private schools in Korea have been subsidized since 1990. However, increased subsidy has been accompanied by greater government regulation and, as such, private schools have little control over admission, curriculum, tuition fees, and management (Paik, 1995: 20). The large private-education sector in Korea does not therefore make for greater competition among providers. It is only at the higher-education level that private institutions enjoy some autonomy in their operation and there is competition among institutions.

Korea has an extensive public vocational-training system. Admission to tertiary institutions is on the basis of a common entrance examination: only 34.5 per cent of the applicants for places in junior colleges were admitted in 1990 (Adams and Gottlieb, 1993: 63), but the proportion has steadily increased and now almost everyone seeking higher education finds admission somewhere. The lack of tertiary-education opportunities in the past partially explains the existence of the large vocational sector in Korea.

Higher-education enrolment has undergone enormous growth, increasing from 0.2 million in 1970 to 3.2 million in 1999. However, the proportion attending regular four- and three-year institutions has declined, offset by the increasing proportion attending open universities. Of all tertiary students, the percentage enrolled in public four-year institutions declined from 20 in 1980 to 14 in 1993, from 48 to 42 in private four-year colleges, and from 27 to 23 in junior vocational colleges. At the same time, the share enrolled in open universities increased from 5 to 21 per cent over the period in question (OECD, 1999a: 188). However, competition at prestigious universities continues to be as intense as before.

Taiwan

The total number of educational institutions at all levels in Taiwan almost doubled between 1970 and 1999. Private institutions accounted for the increase, as the share of institutions in the public sector declined modestly. The decline in the public sector's share was concentrated at the tertiary level, as its share increased at other levels (ROC, Ministry of Education, 2002). The private sector is now the dominant provider of education in Taiwan, containing 81 per cent of all educational institutions and 74 per cent of all pupils in 1995. Nevertheless, the public sector is still the dominant provider, in terms of share of total enrolment, at the primary (99 per cent in 1995), junior secondary schools (95 per cent), and senior secondary schools (72 per cent). The private sector, on the other hand, is the dominant provider in kindergartens (74 per cent), senior vocational schools (37 per cent), junior colleges (85 per cent), and colleges and universities (58 per cent).

Enrolment at the primary level increased dramatically in the 1950s and 1960s and at the junior-secondary level in the 1970s and 1980s, following the introduction of nine years of compulsory education in 1968, but tapered off subsequently as a result of declining birth rates. The introduction of the five-year junior college system in 1965 opened up new opportunities, which led to a massive increase in enrolment in such institutions but then slowed down in the 1970s. The most spectacular increase in enrolment in the 1980s and 1990s was at the higher-education level (Cheng, 1995: 12). These episodic patterns of educational expansion partially reflect shifts in government policy, which started by emphasizing primary education but then gradually moved upwards, but they also reflect the demographic structure characterized by the steep drop in birth rate in the 1960s. In line with the government's industrial-policy objectives, the proportion of students enrolled in the vocational stream increased from 37 per cent in 1965 to 50 per cent in the 1980s and 54 per cent in the 1990s (Sun, 1998: 40).

The Ministry of Education used to set strict quotas on the number of students admitted in each discipline in tertiary institutions, but the restrictions have been gradually weakened. The share of applicants admitted to tertiary institutions is still restricted, however, despite improvements in recent years. The share of applicants who were admitted to universities following joint entrance examination ranged between 27 and 30 per cent during the 1978–1987 period, but then began to rise, climbing to 37 per cent by 1993. For junior colleges, the admission rate was 24–27 per cent of applicants between 1978 and 1987, increased to 31 per cent in 1989, but declined steadily thereafter, hovering between 13 and 18 per cent between 1990 and 1993 (ibid.: 64). The percentage of students who sat for junior college, college, and university entrance examination and were offered admission increased from 44 per cent in 1994 to 60 per cent in 1997 (ROC, Ministry of Education, 2002).

Comparative

The distinction between private and public educational institutions, straightforward as it seems, is difficult to maintain in practice. Some private schools receive large public funding and are heavily regulated by the government, while some public institutions derive considerable revenues from private payments and enjoy a high degree of operational autonomy from the government. The distribution of enrolment in public and private institutions is shown in Table 6.1. Aided schools in Hong Kong and Singapore are classified as public in this table because there is little that is private about them. The table shows that with the exception of kindergarten, the government's role in the provision of education declines with each successive level. Between 72 and 100 per cent of all pre-primary enrolment in all four NIEs is in private institutions. The opposite is the case at the primary level, where the state is the dominant provider of education in all the NIEs. At the secondary-school level, Hong Kong and Singapore have the smallest private sector while private institutions account for almost two-fifths of enrolment in Korea and Taiwan. The greatest difference among the NIEs is at the higher-education level, where an overwhelming majority of students in Korea and Taiwan are in private institutions while the opposite is the case in Hong Kong and Singapore. Overall, the public sector is largest in Singapore, followed by Hong Kong, Korea, and Taiwan.

While all four NIEs are committed to vocational education because of the crucial role it purportedly plays in economic development, especially at the early stages of industrialization, the actual level of emphasis on it varies considerably among them. As shown in Table 6.2, the emphasis on technical education is highest in Taiwan, followed by Korea, and is lowest in Hong Kong. Although no hard evidence is available, only 9 per cent of the relevant age cohort at the secondary level in Hong Kong are estimated to be enrolled in vocational institutions. There is an observed tendency for the emphasis on vocational education to increase at the initial stages

Table 6.1 Enrolment in private educational institutions as percentage of total enrolment, 1996

	Pre-primary	Primary	Secondary	Higher education (1993)
Hong Kong	100	10	12	0
Singapore	72 (1990)	1	1	0
Korea	79	2	38	81
Taiwan	74	1	40	70

Sources: Bray, 1998; UNESCO, 2001.

Table 6.2 Enrolment in vocational secondary education, per cent

	1960	1993
Hong Kong	–	10
Singapore	21	38
Korea	40	40
Taiwan	45 (1965)	70

Sources: Mingat and Tan, 1998; Tilak, 2001: 26.

Table 6.3 Pupil–teacher ratio

	Primary		Secondary		Tertiary	
	1970	Late 1990s	1970	Late 1990s	1970	Late 1990s
Hong Kong	33.0	23.7	21.9	19.1	15.2	–
Singapore	29.7	25.0	19.9	19.3	11.9	13.8
Korea	56.9	32.2	36.5	24.2	19.3	25.8
Taiwan	41.1	12.8	23.1	17.8	16.6	17.9
OECD	17.5	16.9	–	13.8	–	–

Sources: World Development Indicators, 2002; ROC, Ministry of Education, 2002.

of economic development and then to reach a plateau, before declining at the higher stages (Mingat and Tan, 1998). Korea and Taiwan confirm the expected trend, as by the late 1990s both were experiencing a decline in enrolment in vocational institutions. However, enrolment in vocational institutions continues to increase in Hong Kong and Singapore, albeit from a low base in the case of the former, despite the fact that the two city-states are the most industrialized in the region.

Traditional educational literature makes much of the ratio of students to teachers as an indicator of an education system's quality, but this has been challenged recently by those who argue that there is only a weak relationship between large class sizes and inferior educational outcomes (Hanushek, 1995; Mingat and Tan, 1998). Be that as it may, Table 6.3 shows that the NIEs have had large class sizes compared to the industrialized OECD countries, but these have declined in recent years. Of the four NIEs, the students-to-teacher ratio is highest in Korea, probably because of the preponderance of private schools in Korea and their tendency to utilize resources more intensively. The lower ratio in Singapore and Hong Kong similarly reflects the smaller role the private sector plays in their education systems.

Financing

Hong Kong

At the primary and junior-secondary levels, there are no fees in government or aided schools. Fees may be charged by public senior secondary schools, and while they are as high as US$1,123 per annum at some schools, most schools have only small fees. Fees at private schools outside the DSS are high, though they vary a great deal: the annual tuition fee at the Hong Kong International School, for example, is US$16,564 for the final year of high school. Fees are more modest at DSS schools: usually US$257–US$1,283 per annum at the junior-secondary level.

In 1973 the government decided to recover 12 per cent of the cost of higher education through fees and in 1991 raised the target to 18 per cent, but the target was never achieved in practice. In 1989, revenues from tuition fees formed 6.5–10.8 per cent of the universities' recurrent expenditures (Bray, 1993). The government has described higher tuition fees as acceptable because of the availability of educational loans, which began to be offered in 1969. The loans were interest-free until 1987, but have since charged a 2.5 per cent interest, which applies from the date of graduation and is repayable over five years. The share of students receiving loans has declined consistently, falling from 63 per cent in 1980 to 31 per cent in 1992 (ibid.: 39).

Education has received the second-largest, after housing, proportion of total government spending since the 1970s, receiving on average 17–18 per cent of the total. Unfortunately, data on private education are not available to enable calculation of total education expenditures in Hong Kong. However, the level of private expenditure is likely to be small given the predominance of the public sector in the provision of education.

Singapore

In Singapore, students at primary level do not pay tuition fees, while those in secondary and pre-university institutions pay only nominal fees. Fees are significant only in "independent" schools, which are free to set their own fees. Compared to fees of US$7 per month charged at government schools, independent schools charge US$94–US$200 per month. Each independent school also receives a subsidy similar to those received by government schools. Undergraduate tuition fees for non-medical courses at the National University of Singapore are US$3,190 per year for Singaporean students and slightly higher for foreigners.

Education has alternated with defence as the most expensive item in the government's budget in Singapore. It attracted US$2.6 billion in government funding in 1997, which was a huge increase from the US$0.8 billion a decade earlier (Singapore Government, MOE, 2000). The proportion of the government's expenditures devoted to various levels has changed, declining at the primary and secondary levels and increasing at higher education, partly as a result of changing enrolment patterns resulting from demographic changes. Between 1982 and 1997, the share of the government's education expenditure allocated to primary education declined from 34 to 25 per cent, to secondary education from 38 to 34 per cent, but increased for higher education from 23 to 34 per cent.

Although the rate of participation in higher education is low in Singapore, the resources devoted to it are high. In 1999, government subsidy amounted to US$15,988 for each university student and US$7,552 for each polytechnic student. However, per-student spending on polytechnics grew four times faster than that on universities over the preceding decade, showing the increased prominence given to technical education

(Singapore Government, MOE, 2000). The subsidies form about four-fifths of the recurrent costs and all of the capital costs of providing higher education in Singapore. The government has repeatedly expressed its intention to reduce the subsidies to only 60 per cent of the operating costs (Selvaratnam, 1994: 80). The institutions are being encouraged to raise tuition fees to cover 25 per cent of their operating costs.

Private-consumption expenditure data for education in Singapore includes "recreation", which makes them unusable for estimating total education expenditures. However, it would be reasonable to say that they are significant but not large, reflecting the widespread practice of private tutoring at all levels.

Korea

Except for primary schools, all institutions at all levels in both public and private sectors in Korea levy varying levels of fees. The tuition fees charged by public and private institutions up to the secondary level are broadly similar, but they are considerably higher in private institutions at the tertiary level. Moreover, the fees at both public and private institutions have risen tremendously over the years, increasing almost eight-fold during 1975–1995 at the junior-secondary level, around ten times at the senior-secondary level, and around twelve times at the tertiary level (www.moe.go.kr/english/edukorea/edukorea2/). At the higher-education level, the government accounts for 68 per cent of public institutions' expenditures but only 28 per cent of expenditures at private institutions, which, as will be recalled, enrol two-fifths of the students at this level (Lee, 2002: 5).

Total (public and private) educational expenditures have formed around 10 per cent of the GNP for the last two decades. Education expenditures, however, are mostly accounted for by out-of-school, and largely out-of-pocket, private expenditures (Paik, 1995: 12). When both in-school and out-of-school expenditures are considered together, the government has accounted for only around 29 per cent of the total over the three decades.

Education has been the second-largest item in the government budget in Korea, just after economic development. Public expenditure on education as a percentage of GDP increased from 2.2 in 1975 to 3.8 in 1997. Of the total government expenditure, education's share similarly increased from 14 to 17.5 per cent during the same period. The largest share of government education expenditure is directed at the primary and junior-secondary levels: around 50 per cent in the 1990s, compared to 40 per cent in the 1960s (ibid.: 12).

What is most remarkable about Korea is the large proportion of educational expenditures accounted for by private payments towards private tuition, books, school uniforms, transportation, and extra-curricular activities. These out-of-school expenditures have formed 48–50 per cent of total educational expenditures since the 1960s (ibid.: 16). The notable feature of out-of-school expenditures is the large share accounted for by private tutoring, which rose from 16 to 37 per cent between 1977 and 1994 (ibid.: 23). Thus, despite the increase in government expenditure on education, much of the total educational expenditures is accounted for by private sources. Education imposes a significant and increasing financial burden on Koreans: its share of the urban household's total consumption expenditure increased from 5.9 per cent in 1978 to 7.2 in 1988 to 11.2 in 1998 (Korea National Statistical Office, 1999).

Taiwan

There are no tuition fees for the first nine years of education in Taiwan. But at other levels, private expenditures are involved in studying at public institutions, and public expenditures at private schools. In 1993, the government accounted for 96 per cent of the public schools' expenditures and 8 per cent of the private schools'. However, unlike the trend in most other countries, tuition fees' share of education expenditures in Taiwan has declined at every level, in both public and private institutions. Nevertheless, fees are still significant in private vocational schools and colleges: in 1993 they formed 92 per cent of private senior vocational schools' revenues, 78 per cent of private junior colleges' revenues, and 75 per cent of private universities' revenues (Cheng, 1995: 31–32). The government has decided that in future it will provide only 80 per cent of the higher-education sector's expenditures and that public institutions will have to raise the remainder on their own (Mok, 2000).

Educational expenditures, both public and private, have increased at a phenomenal rate in Taiwan: between 1971 and 1997 they increased at an average annual rate of 180 per cent overall in nominal terms and by 21 per cent on a per-student basis. As a result, total education expenditures' share of GDP increased from 4 to over 6 per cent over the period, despite the very rapid expansion of the GDP itself (ROC, Ministry of Education, 2002). The government accounts for the majority of education expenditure in Taiwan, though its share declined during the 1990s, from approximately 81 per cent in the 1970s and 1980s to around 77 per cent in recent years (ibid.). However, it must be noted that the pre-1990 data for public expenditure on education are unreliable and exaggerated (Ku, 1997: 58).

Public expenditure on education as a percentage of GNP grew consistently for decades before declining somewhat in the late 1990s: it stood at 4 per cent in the 1970s and 1980s and 5 per cent in the 1990s (ROC, Ministry of Education, 2002). Private expenditure on education grew at a slower rate, from under 1 per cent of GNP until the 1980s to slightly over 1 per cent in the following decade.

Contrary to what is commonly claimed in the literature, it is not primary but secondary education that receives the largest share of public expenditure in Taiwan. For three decades until the 1990s, approximately 24 per cent of public-education expenditures on average was devoted to primary education while 32 per cent was devoted to secondary education (ibid.). The massive increase in tertiary education in the 1990s was not accompanied by an increase in the share of public expenditure devoted to it, as it remained within the 21–23 per cent range as before. It was only for pre-primary and special education that there was a slight increase in the 1990s compared to the previous decades.

Comparative

Total (both private and public) expenditure on education forms 11 per cent of the GDP in Korea and 7 per cent in Taiwan, compared to 6 per cent in OECD countries (World Development Indicators, 2002; ROC, Ministry of Education, 2002). Although no usable data is available for Hong Kong and Singapore, their total education expenditure is likely to be lower. Korea, in all likelihood, spends the largest share of the GDP on education in the world. Its total education expenditure is higher than would be predicted for its level of economic development, while its public expenditure is lower (Lee, 2002: 10). But even Taiwan spends a large share of GDP on education than most OECD countries.

The majority of expenditure on education in all NIEs except Korea comes from the government. Public expenditures form 73 per cent of total education expenditures in Taiwan but only 36 per cent in Korea. The government's share is likely to be the highest in the two city-states because of the overwhelming state dominance in the provision of education and the relatively low tuition fees at public institutions.

Public expenditure on education as a percentage of GDP in the NIEs increased in the 1970s and 1980s and then the pace slowed down or reversed somewhat in the 1990s. Table 6.4 shows that the largest public

Table 6.4 Public expenditure on education, percentage of GDP and total government expenditure

	% of GDP			% of TGE		
	1975	1985	1999	1975	1985	1999
Hong Kong	2.9	2.8	4.1	19.2	16.7	18.7
Singapore	3.6	5.9	3.8	20.2	21.6	20.0
Korea	2.2	3.0	3.8	14.0	18.4	15.9
Taiwan	3.6	4.1	4.9	16.6	17.8	20.4
OECD	5.8	5.0	5.4	–	–	14.0

Sources: IMF, *Government Financial Statistics 2000*; ADB, 2002; ROC, Ministry of Education, 2002.

spending on education is in Taiwan and Hong Kong, followed by Korea and Singapore. Remarkably, they all spend considerably less than the OECD average.

Education is one of the three largest items of public expenditure in all four NIEs, attracting between 16 and 20 per cent of total public expenditures. Table 6.4 shows that Taiwan devotes the largest share of public expenditure to education, followed closely by Singapore and Hong Kong, and distantly by Korea. All four devote a greater share of total government expenditure to education than the OECD countries.

It has been observed that a vital reason for the region's economic dynamism is the fiscal priority given there to primary education (Mingat and Tan, 1998: 41). While this may have been the case until the 1980s, it is only in Korea that this continues to be the case. As shown in Table 6.5, it is secondary education that attracts the largest share of public funds in Taiwan, while it is higher education in Hong Kong and Singapore that receives the largest share. The declining share devoted to primary education and the increasing share for other levels are a function of declining birth rate as well as changing industrial structure and the concomitant need for a more skilled workforce. The case of Korea is significant for the small share of public expenditures that flows to higher education because of the heavy reliance on private payments.

Public spending on vocational education is not particularly large in the NIEs: it comprises 3 per cent of total public spending on education in Hong Kong, 6 per cent in Korea, 5 per cent in Singapore, and 8 per cent in Taiwan (Tilak: 2001: 26). These proportions are larger than in the developing countries, but considerably lower than in the OECD countries, which tend to spend between 11 and 18 per cent. However, there are indications that the private sector in the NIEs spends more on vocational training than is the case in the OECD (ibid.).

Public spending is, of course, only a part of total spending because of the funds raised from private sources, especially at the higher levels of

Table 6.5 Distribution of current public expenditure on education by level, 1996, per cent

	Kindergarten and primary	*Secondary*	*Higher*
Hong Kong	22	35	37
Korea	45	37	8
Singapore	26	35	35
Taiwan	27	32	21
OECD	31	39	21

Sources: UNESCO, 2001; ROC, Ministry of Education, 2002; World Bank, 1995.

Note
The rows do not add to 100 because they exclude overhead items not attributable to educational institutions.

education. Table 6.6 shows private expenditures' share of total education expenditure at the senior-secondary and tertiary levels, as primary education is compulsory and most of the cost is borne by governments. The prominence of private institutions at post-primary levels of education in Korea and, to a lesser extent, Taiwan is evident in the table. Nearly half of all expenditures on senior-secondary education is accounted for by private sources in both Korea and Taiwan. It is worth remembering that even public secondary schools in Korea have significant tuition fees, accounting for nearly 29 per cent of their revenues. At the higher-education level, however, a massive 64 per cent is accounted for by private sources in Korea (rising to 78 per cent by 2001 (OECD, 2003: 82)) and a more modest 47 per cent in Taiwan. Private payments form a much smaller share of education expenditures in the two city states at every level of education. However, considering that nearly all higher-education institutions in Hong Kong and Singapore are in the public sector, the share of private expenditures is not insignificant.

The education system in the NIEs is generally low-cost by international standards. Since costs vary with the standard of living, recording unit costs as a percentage of per capita GDP is a simple but effective way of comparing costs. Table 6.7 shows no consistent pattern across the levels of

Table 6.6 Private expenditure as percentage of total expenditure on education

	Senior secondary		Tertiary	
	1980	1993	1980	1993
Singapore	24 (1970)	4	–	25
Korea	69	43	59	64
Taiwan	44	45	62	47

Source: Mingat and Tan, 1998.

Table 6.7 Government education expenditure per student, public institutions, percentage of GNP per capita

	Primary		Secondary		Higher	
	1965	1995	1965	1995	1965	1995
Hong Kong	5.2	7.8	8.2	12.5	61.7	52.0[2]
Singapore	10.2	7.8	13.3	12.0	59.4	28.2
Korea	6.2	18.8	8.6	12.9	36.7	6.0
Taiwan	10.8[1]	18.7	18.6[1]	24.6	60.9[1]	42.1
High income OECD	11.0	20.5	–	23.2	52.6	37.6

Sources: World Development Indicators, 2002; ROC, Ministry of Education, 2002.

Notes
1 1983.
2 1991.

education, as costs vary enormously at different levels in every country. At the primary level, in every NIE the costs are lower than in OECD countries, and among the four, they are the lowest in Hong Kong and Singapore. At the secondary level, the cost in the NIEs is nearly half the level in the OECD, except for Taiwan where it is slightly higher. The greatest diversity is at the higher-education level, where unit costs range from 51 per cent of per capita GDP in Hong Kong to only 6 per cent in Korea, whereas the OECD average is 38 per cent. Singapore is the only country in the group where the unit cost of education as a percentage of GDP has declined, whereas in the others per capita GDP grew fast but per capita education expenditures grew yet faster.

Education costs are to a large extent a function of teachers' salary, which typically forms 50–75 per cent of schools' operating costs. There are interesting variations across the NIEs in this regard, as shown in Table 6.8. In Korea and, especially, Hong Kong, the teachers seem to be very handsomely paid compared to much of the population, while in Singapore they are paid slightly less.

Outcomes

Hong Kong

Enrolment at the primary and junior-secondary levels in Hong Kong is universal and indeed compulsory. However, only three-quarters of the relevant age groups attend senior secondary schools, which is lower than in the other NIEs. In comparison, it has very high enrolment, 83 per cent, at the pre-primary level. The situation is less sanguine at the higher-education level, which enrols only 27 per cent of the relevant age cohort, though this was four times higher than during the early 1970s. This is low for a place with one of the highest income levels in the world.

The improvement in the population's educational qualifications as a result of expanding school enrolment is noticeable. The proportion of the population with no or only kindergarten or primary education declined from 44 per cent in 1986 to 29 per cent in 2001. At the same time, the percentage of those with secondary education increased from 43 to 54 per cent and those with some post-secondary education from 9 to 16 per cent (Hong Kong Census and Statistics Department, 2001).

Table 6.8 Average public primary school teachers' salary as multiple of per capita GDP

Hong Kong	2.5
Singapore	0.9
Korea	1.9

Source: Acedo and Uemura, 2001: 51.

The primary and secondary education system is relatively equitable in that there is little difference between boys and girls in terms of admission and completion at the primary and secondary levels. More significantly, the system has become increasingly equal in terms of the opportunities it affords. Mother's education and family income used to be an important determinant of completion of primary and junior-secondary education, but began to play a rather minor role by the 1980s (Post, 1996). However, family background continues to affect educational achievement, as children from educated and prosperous families continue to perform better in schools (cited in Comparative Education Policy Research Group, 1998: 39).

The education system at the tertiary level continues to be unequal, despite improvements. Thus, while the probability of the children of blue-collar workers receiving post-secondary education doubled during the 1980s, they were still only half as likely to receive it as their white-collar-worker counterparts (Post, 1996: 163). More importantly, the limited access to tertiary education increases income inequality because it allows those with higher degrees to command substantially higher income upon employment and the income premium has increased over the years. University graduates earned 2.9 times the earnings of high-school graduates in 1991, compared to 2.8 in 1976 (Lui, 1997: 82).

Singapore

Although there is no compulsory education in Singapore – primary education became compulsory only in 2003 – there has been nearly universal enrolment at the primary and secondary levels. At the higher-education level, on the other hand, enrolment is still low by international standards despite significant improvements in recent years. Compared to only 6 per cent in 1970, it was higher than before but still only 44 per cent of the relevant age group was attending tertiary institutions in the late 1990s.

Expanding enrolment is reflected in the population's educational qualifications. The share of the population with no education declined from 40 per cent in 1965 to 7 per cent in 1997, while the share of those with a university degree increased from almost nil to 9 per cent. The mean years of schooling increased similarly from 4.7 in 1980 to 7.8 in 1997.

Improvements in the completion rate have raised the system's internal efficiency by reducing the failure rate in schools. The share of primary-school students successfully completing the national examination (PSLE) increased from 69 per cent in 1980 to 96 per cent in 1999. Similarly, the proportion of students passing the junior-secondary-school leaving examination (with at least five O Level passes) increased from 40 to 76 per cent, while the proportion passing the senior-secondary-school leaving examination (A Level) increased from 67 to 86 per cent over the same period (Singapore Ministry of Education, various years).

As in other countries, educational performance in Singapore depends a great deal on parents' education. Children of graduate parents are 16 times more likely to make it to the top 10 per cent of performers in the PSLE examination (which determines a host of opportunities, including education stream, school, and scholarships) compared to those whose fathers were non-graduates and mothers had only primary education (Mukhopadhaya, 2000: 63). Performance also depends on family income and the "independent" school system may well be perpetuating this: 38 per cent of independent-school students come from families in the top income quintile (ibid.). Children from less well-off families, living in small public-housing flats, are correspondingly under-represented in such schools. Other researchers too have found socio-economic class and ethnicity as significant determinants of school performance (Chang and Mani, 1995; Quah *et al.*, 1995; Zhang, 1993).

Limited higher-education opportunities have probably increased inequality in Singapore, just as they have in Hong Kong. The per capita income of those with higher education is usually many times higher than that of those with only secondary education. While data on income distribution by level of education is not available, the average income of the top five occupations in 1999 was 16 times that of the bottom five occupations (Singapore Department of Statistics, 2000). Unsurprisingly, most well-paying occupations involve higher-education qualifications.

The large public subsidy for education shows up in disproportionately high private returns on education. The private return in 1980 was 20 per cent for primary education and 19 per cent for secondary education, while the social rates of returns were only 9 and 14 per cent respectively (Eng, 1990: 23). At higher-education level, limited opportunities coupled with high subsidy cause personal returns to exceed social returns to an even greater extent. The average return on university education was 32 per cent for the individual and 21 per cent for the society (cited in Eng, 1990: 23). The lopsided return structure is not only inefficient but may well be contributing to income inequality in Singapore.

Korea

The expansion of enrolment in Korea has been impressive at every level, but particularly at the kindergarten and higher-education levels. Between 1965 and 1996, gross enrolment in kindergartens increased from 1 to 88 per cent, whereas post-secondary enrolment increased from 9 to 68 per cent. As mentioned earlier, primary-school enrolment was already high during Japanese rule and had reached 100 per cent by the 1960s.

Almost all primary- and junior-secondary-school students advanced to the next level in 1999, a huge increase from only 54 per cent and 69 per cent respectively in 1965. The improvement in the transition from secondary to higher education has been equally impressive: 32 per cent in 1965 and 85 per cent in 1999. Even 38 per cent of vocational secondary school graduates were going on to tertiary education in 1999, compared to just 8 per cent as recently as 1990 (OECD, 2003).

As a result of increasing enrolment, the percentage of the adult population with no or only primary education declined from 80 per cent in the 1960s to 24 per cent in the 1990s. At the same time, the share of the population with secondary education increased from 17 to 62 per cent, and of those with higher-education from 3 to 14 per cent.

The education system in Korea is largely egalitarian despite the dominance of private provision and financing. There is now negligible difference in the enrolment ratios for males and females, except at the higher-education level, where female enrolment is 30 percentage points below male enroment. The abolition of the entrance examination at junior- and senior-secondary levels was a key reason for the achievement of universal secondary education. The assignment of students to schools by lottery is intended to inhibit the emergence of elite schools. However, since the students are assigned schools within the locality in which they live, neighbourhoods with a higher proportion of educated professionals (such as those south of the Han river in Seoul) tend to have better prepared pupils and hence better schools, though this cannot be confirmed because of lack of official data (Sorensen, 1994: 20). Private schools in some prosperous urban neighbourhoods have emerged as a new breed of elite schools because parents in such neighbourhoods can afford to pay for what they believe is higher-quality education (Chung, 1998: 96).

Unlike in Hong Kong and Singapore, education has reduced inequality in Korea, even though wage differentials by educational attainment continue to be substantial. The average wage of male workers with a college education peaked in a relative term at 2.1 times the average wage of those with only a high-school education in 1976 and then gradually declined to 1.4 in 1993 (Lee, undated).

Taiwan

In Taiwan, enrolment is nearly universal at the primary and secondary levels but it has a relatively low rate at the kindergarten level. Higher-education enrolments used to be low, but as a result of continuous improvement over the years – gross enrolment rose from 7 per cent in 1970 to 64 per cent in 1999 – it is now comparable to that of other countries at similar levels of socio-economic development.

Completion of education at one level and transition to the next has improved at every level. In 1971, only 81 per cent of primary-school graduates, 70 per cent of junior-secondary graduates, and 44 per cent of secondary-school graduates went on to the next level of education (ROC, Ministry of Education, 2002). By the late 1990s, nearly all primary and junior-secondary graduates, 67 per cent of senior-secondary graduates, and even 30 per cent of vocational-school graduates were going to the next level of education. The improving enrolment rate is reflected in the educational level of the workforce whereby the percentage of employed persons with only primary education or lower declined from 74 per cent in 1968 to 19 per cent in 1999, while those with tertiary qualifications increased from 5 to 11 per cent (Cheng, 1995: 34; DGBAS, 2000).

Enrolment patterns exhibit some gender bias, however. While females form the majority of enrolment at primary and secondary levels, it is men who form the majority in higher-education institutions (http://www.edu.tw/statistics/english/c1.htm). Females form 57 per cent of enrolment in senior secondary schools and 53 per cent in senior vocational schools, but only 43 per cent at colleges and universities (Cheng, 1995: 10–11).

As in Korea, and in contrast to Hong Kong and Singapore, wage differentials related to education have eroded in Taiwan. In 1968, the wage of university graduates was more than three times that of primary-school graduates, but this had reduced to only twice the amount by 1992 (ibid.: 34). For university and junior college graduates, relative wages increased until 1989 and then declined continuously (Sun, 1998: 189–190). The erosion of wage premiums for university degrees has had the side effect of reducing the wage differentials between university graduates and non-graduates, which has improved the pattern of income distribution (ibid.: 194).

However, opportunities for higher education still vary considerably according to family household income. Children from families in the wealthiest quintile continue disproportionately to go to colleges and universities, though there have been significant improvements in this regard because of the expansion of tertiary-education opportunities. Nearly one-half of all students at this level came from households in the richest quintile in the 1950s, but their share had declined to one-third by the early 1990s (Cheng, 1995: 43) and yet further in subsequent years. However, only 5 per cent of college and university students came from the lowest quintile in 1993, which was only a slight improvement over the 4 per cent in 1953. Thus what the expansion of higher-education opportunities seems to have done is to make higher-education more accessible to the middle rather than the lower classes.

Comparative

The educational outcomes in the NIEs vary by a wide margin, especially at the pre-primary and tertiary levels. Starting with enrolment, Table 6.9 shows large differences among the four NIEs at every level of education except primary. Kindergarten enrolment in Hong Kong and Korea significantly exceeds the level in Singapore and Taiwan as well as in the OECD. Nearly all children in all four NIEs were attending primary schools by as early as 1970 and the trend continues. At the secondary-school level,

EDUCATION

Table 6.9 Gross enrolment,[1] per cent

	Pre-primary		Primary		Secondary		Higher	
	1970	Late 1990s	1970	Late 1990s	1970	Late 1990s	1970	Late 1990s
Hong Kong	48	83	117	94	36	72	7	27
Singapore	5	19	106	97	46	99	6	44
Korea	3	88	103	94	42	97	7	72
Taiwan	–	24	100	101	52	96	7	64
OECD	40	75	100	103	76	106	26	60

Sources: Singapore Ministry of Education, 2001; World Development Indicators, 2002; UNESCO, 2001.

Note
1 Excludes those studying overseas.

Korea, Singapore, and Taiwan have universal enrolment, whereas almost one-quarter of the relevant age cohort in Hong Kong do not attend senior secondary schools. It is in enrolment at the higher-education level that we see the greatest variations and the difference has widened over the years. While the NIEs all had similar levels of enrolment in 1970, by the late 1990s the enrolment rate in Korea and Taiwan was significantly higher than in the two city-states. Indeed tertiary enrolment in Korea and Taiwan is now higher than in the OECD while in Hong Kong it is nearly one-half of the OECD level.

There is little difference among boys and girls in terms of educational enrolment in the NIEs, except at the higher-education level (see Table 6.10). The gender imbalance in favour of males at the higher-education level in the NIEs except Taiwan is particularly noticeable because of the higher female enrolment at the secondary level. It speaks volumes on the glass ceiling that continues to prevent women from pursuing higher education and, later, higher-paying jobs.

The increasing enrolment at every level is reflected in the NIE

Table 6.10 Male and female gross enrolment ratios, late 1990s

	Pre-primary		Primary		Secondary		Higher	
	Male	Female	Male	Female	Male	Female	Male	Female
Hong Kong	82	83	93	96	70	75	24	20 (1993)
Singapore	–	–	95	93	75	74	37	31
Korea	87	89	98	99	98	97	82	52
Taiwan	–	–	103	100	94	98	45	48
OECD	–	–	102	102	105	108	–	–

Sources: ROC, Ministry of Education, 2002; UNESCO, 2001.

population's average years of education. Table 6.11 shows that in 1990 Korea had the most educated population and Singapore the least. Korea's achievement is remarkable: between 1960 and 1990, its population's average years of education more than doubled and now its population is more educated than the OECD average. Taiwan's achievement is only slightly behind Korea's. The lack-lustre improvement in Singapore is noticeable, especially considering the high profile of education in policy debates on the island and the vast sum spent on it. That Singapore does not have compulsory education, while the other NIEs do, coupled with limited higher-education opportunities perhaps explains the difference.

As one would expect, illiteracy in the NIEs has declined rapidly along with expansion of education (see Table 6.12). The illiterate are usually the older people, though their share will gradually decline in the future. Women are also disproportionately represented among the illiterate population, but the difference will atrophy as primary education has been nearly universal for both boys and girls for several decades now.

There has been a proliferation of standardized cross-national tests evaluating the educational achievement of students despite the difficulties involved in establishing questions that are uniform across nations (UNESCO, 1993: 84–85). Moreover, performance at test may reflect the

Table 6.11 Average years of school of the population aged 15 and over, 1960 and 1990

	1960	1990
Hong Kong	5.2	9.2
Singapore	4.3	6.1
Korea	4.3	9.9
Taiwan	3.9	8.0
OECD	7.1	9.0

Source: Barro and Lee, 2000.

Note
Average years of schooling is the sum of the percentage of the population at each level of schooling weighted by the duration at each school.

Table 6.12 Illiteracy rate, percentage of population aged 15 and over

	Total		Female	
	1970	1999	1970	1999
Hong Kong	22	7	35	10
Korea	13	2	20	4
Singapore	27	8	40	12
Taiwan	27 (1978)	9	39 (1978)	13

Sources: World Development Indicators, 2002; DGBAS, 2000.

students' background rather than the quality of their education: in other words, these tests may be evaluating their opportunity to learn rather than the learning itself. Be that as it may, the results of recent tests for science and mathematics skills of 8th Grade students are summarized in Table 6.13. The results show that children in all the NIEs performed significantly better than the international average. Indeed all of the top four ranks in the mathematics test went to the NIEs in 1999. In the science test, Taiwanese and Singaporean children came first and second, Korea stood fifth, while Hong Kong came a distant but still respectable fifteenth.

The NIEs' experience contradicts the widely observed pattern that children in richer countries, generally speaking, perform better than those in poorer countries (Mingat and Tan, 1998). While Singapore's top performance is broadly consistent with its income level, both Korea and Taiwan perform much better than one would expect for their income level. The case of Singapore shows that while its enrolment rates may be lower than in the other NIEs, its highly selective system produces excellent students.

Return on educational investment is a commonly used criterion for evaluating the efficiency of public expenditure, suggesting that public expenditure is warranted only when social returns exceed private returns. Table 6.14 shows returns on investment at the secondary and tertiary levels in the NIEs. As can be seen, private returns are higher than social returns at every level, except for higher education in Taiwan in the early 1970s. The private returns are particularly high at the higher-education level, especially in Hong Kong and Singapore.

Education is often presented as an equalizing force that opens up opportunity for the lower classes that would otherwise be denied them. This is certainly confirmed in Korea and Taiwan, where educational expansion reduced the scarcity rents of the educated (Lewin, 1998: 99). Conversely, the restricted higher-education opportunities in Hong Kong and Singapore have probably aggravated income inequality.

Table 6.13 Average mathematics and science achievement of 8th grade students

	Mathematics		*Science*	
	1995	*1999*	*1995*	*1999*
Hong Kong	588	582 (4)	522	530 (15)
Singapore	643	604 (1)	607	568 (2)
Korea	607	587 (2)	565	549 (5)
Taiwan	–	585 (3)	–	569 (1)
International average	513	487	516	488

Source: Third International Mathematics and Science Study – Report, 1995 and 1999.

Note
Figures in brackets indicate rank among the countries included in the test.

Table 6.14 Social and private returns to investment in education by level, per cent

	Year	Secondary		Higher	
		Social	Private	Social	Private
Hong Kong	1976	15.0	18.5	12.4	25.2
Singapore	1966	17.6	20.0	14.1	25.4
Korea	1986	8.8	10.1	15.5	17.9
Taiwan	1972	12.3	12.7	17.7	15.8
Taiwan[1]	1996	–	3.0	–	12.2
OECD	1970s	10.2	12.4	8.7	12.3

Source: Psacharopoulos, 1994.

Note
1 Chuang and Cao, 2001.

Conclusion

Education receives a great deal of attention from policy-makers in the NIEs, which is reflected in the policy priority accorded it. But, as we have seen in this chapter, the objectives they sought and the way they went about achieving them vary considerably, especially at the pre-primary and tertiary levels.

While economic development was the education system's key goal in all the NIEs, in Korea and Taiwan alone was education subjected to explicit manpower planning, which was reflected in their heavy emphasis on vocational and technical education (Morris, 1996). This was significantly less the case in Singapore and almost negligible in Hong Kong. Similarly, promoting national unity through the education system has been an important objective for the NIE governments. Hong Kong used to be an exception in this regard but this changed with the introduction of Chinese subjects and language of instruction as a means of integrating more closely with mainland China.

There are significant differences in the respective roles of the public and private sectors with respect to provision and financing of education across the NIEs. The provision of education is entirely dominated by the state at all levels in Hong Kong and Singapore, whereas in Korea and Taiwan the state is dominant only in primary and secondary education. With respect to financing, too, the government is the dominant source in the two city-states whereas private contributions form the bulk of education funding in Korea and, to a lesser extent, Taiwan.

The NIEs do not necessarily spend more money on education than other countries – rather it is concentrated at the primary and secondary levels. However, even this is changing as the governments have increased their funding for higher education. The widely held belief that the NIE governments place an exceptionally high emphasis on education is not confirmed by public expenditure data and indeed they devote a smaller percentage of the GDP to it than do OECD countries.

The educational outcomes at the primary and secondary levels in the NIEs are as good as anywhere in the world, but the same cannot be said about higher education. There are insufficient higher-education opportunities in Hong Kong and Singapore, which is also reflected in the shortage of skilled and technical personnel. At the same time, demand for such workers has been high because of rapid industrialization. As a result, those with tertiary qualifications are able to command wage premiums, which aggravates disparities between the wages of university graduates and non-graduates and contributes to income inequality. The two city-states certainly have a lot to learn from their Northeast Asian counterparts with respect to higher education.

While the NIEs' overall performance in the education sphere ranges from very good to excellent, education remains a top concern of the policy-makers and the public alike. The chief recent concern seems to be the apparent lack of creativity and thinking skills among school and university graduates. All governments in the region, as elsewhere, are ostensibly taking measures to address the problem. It is not yet clear if this is just another international fad that will pass or a serious problem whose successful resolution will determine the development success stories of tomorrow.

The clustering of Hong Kong and Singapore in one group, and Korea and Taiwan in the other, is more pronounced in education than in other social policies. The state is dominant in both provision and financing of education at all levels in the two city-states. In comparison, the state is the dominant provider and source of financing only at the primary and secondary levels in Korea and Taiwan. However, tertiary education opportunities are limited in the city states compared to their Northeast Asian counterparts.

7
CONCLUSION

The central objectives of this book have been to understand the nature of income maintenance, health, housing, and education policies in Hong Kong, Korea, Singapore, and Taiwan and to identify patterns of similarities and differences among them. Notwithstanding the vast political, social, and economic similarities among them, the preceding chapters show significant similarities as well as variations in their social policies. At the same time, the degree of similarities is higher between Hong Kong and Singapore on the one hand and between Korea and Taiwan on the other. But before we delineate the salient features of the two groups, let us recapitulate the key findings of the preceding chapters.

Income-maintenance programmes in the NIEs are more developed than is often realized by commentators. Indeed the NIEs have the complete range of programmes found in Western welfare states, except for unemployment benefits, which in a substantial sense exist only in Korea and, to a lesser extent, Taiwan. However, the instruments they rely on for providing income maintenance vary considerably: Hong Kong relies primarily on public assistance, Singapore on provident funds, whereas Korea and Taiwan rely on social insurance. Contribution from employers and employees is the main source of financing the schemes in all the NIEs except Hong Kong, which currently relies mainly on general tax revenues though this will change as the newly established MPF matures. In Singapore and Hong Kong, employees and their employers contribute to an individual provident fund, whereas in Korea and Taiwan they contribute to social insurance. The cost of pensions for civil servants and military personnel is, however, borne largely by governments and, ultimately, the taxpayer in all NIEs. The benefits offered by the main schemes are tied closely to contribution in Korea, Taiwan, and, especially, Singapore, whereas Hong Kong offers flat benefits based on an eligibility test to all except the aged and disabled.

All the known advantages and disadvantages of tax-financed arrangements are evident in Hong Kong, just as those of the contributory arrangements are evident in the other NIEs. The availability of flat benefits to all meeting income and residence criteria makes public assistance a comprehensive safety net, but it involves rapid growth in expenditures in times of economic down-turn, as has been the case in Hong Kong since 1997. Moreover, the widespread perception of abuse undermines public support for it and aggravates the stigma attached to claiming benefits. Contributory programmes are more popular with the government, because they impose little or no burden on the public exchequer, as well as with voters, who view the beneficiaries as having paid for the benefit. On the flip side, contributory schemes leave out the unemployed and those outside formal employment while their earning-related benefits provide little help to low-income earners who need support the most. The availability of public assistance to those outside the social insurance net or inadequately served by it mitigates the problems inherent to contributory schemes, as is the case in Korea and Taiwan. The lack of a robust public-assistance scheme in Singapore coupled with the fact that the provident fund allows for no redistribution across income groups and to people with different lifespans makes for an inadequate income-maintenance system.

In health care, the level of government involvement in provision is higher in Hong Kong and Singapore than in Korea and Taiwan, contrary to the Northeast Asian states' popular image of being more interventionist. In Korea and Taiwan, health care is provided by the private sector but is funded from compulsory contributions to social insurance. Health-care financing in Hong Kong and Singapore is more diverse, with out-patient care funded largely out-of-pocket while in-patient care is heavily subsidized, especially in Hong Kong. The difference between the two groups partially reflects their different colonial legacies: Hong Kong and Singapore were British colonies and were influenced by its tax-funded health-care system, whereas Korea and Taiwan were ruled by Japan, which has had social insurance à la Germany.

Notwithstanding the differences, the NIEs spend a relatively small percentage of their GDP on health care compared to both developed and developing countries. But among them, Taiwan and, especially, Korea spend the most while Hong Kong and, especially, Singapore spend extraordinarily less. The two countries that have the best health-care outcomes are also those that spend the least: Hong Kong and Singapore. What the two city-states have in common is that provision of in-patient health care is largely by the public sector. The case of Singapore is particularly interesting because the public sector's domination does not significantly compromise individual choice, which is regarded as important by middle- and upper-income groups. Korea and Taiwan are examples of how private provision and competition among providers does not lead to lower costs, nor do co-payments and user charges restrain overall demand. Indeed competition in the health-care sector may actually increase costs by promoting over-supply, while user charges limit access for the poor without affecting the rich.

Housing displays the sharpest policy differences among the NIEs in terms of the emphasis they place on it and the instruments they employ. It has attracted the most policy attention in the two city-states, no doubt reflecting their land scarcity and the correspondingly high potential for price inflation, which would adversely affect their international economic competitiveness. The Korean government too intervened in housing, but it did so reluctantly and haphazardly and through indirect measures that worsened housing supply and affordability. The situation in Korea began to improve only in the late 1980s when it dismantled many of the regulations and increased its spending on public housing. The Taiwanese government, in contrast to those of the other NIEs, has had only passive involvement in the housing sector, providing generous tax incentives for interest payments on home loans while leaving the supply and purchase decisions to the market forces.

The public sector dominates housing provision in Hong Kong and Singapore, while the private sector is overwhelmingly dominant in Korea and Taiwan. However, the two city-states differ in that rental housing has traditionally been the main policy focus in Hong Kong while Singapore has emphasized ownership housing, but in recent years Hong Kong too has emphasized ownership. The arrangements for housing finance display even more diverse patterns. Hong Kong relies on expenditure from its general revenues and granting of public land at a nominal price as the main form of financial support for public housing. In Singapore too the granting of public land at below-market price has been a key form of support, but it also has a complex system of housing finance linked to its provident fund, which enables the government to provide cheap loans at no or negligible cost to itself. Korea and Taiwan, in contrast, play a small role in housing finance and, to the extent they do, it takes the form of indirect subsidy.

If home ownership is the chief objective of the NIE governments, then only Singapore and Taiwan in the region have largely succeeded. However, they accomplished the goal through entirely different strategies: Singapore through extensive state planning and regulation and Taiwan through reliance on the market mechanism facilitated by tax subsidy. The Hong Kong government is the largest spender on housing in the region, yet it has only modest results to show for this because of its inability to control the market behaviour of builders. The Korean government, in contrast, spends little on housing, but unlike Taiwan it regulates the market through extensive regulations, which are believed to have aggravated the problem until they were relaxed in the late 1980s.

In contrast to its perception by many social-policy scholars, who do not view education as a part of the welfare state and indeed regard it as a substitute for the latter, education has been a key component of the welfare mix in the Asian NIEs. Policy-makers in the region see it as a catalyst for economic development, which, in turn, they believe is the best guarantee for promoting social welfare. This view is hardly unique to the region, however, as the low social security expenditures in the USA are partly explained by its historically high expenditures on education (Castles, 1989; Heclo, 1981; Heidenheimer, 1981).

While policy-makers in all four NIEs emphasize the importance of education in economic development, only Korea and Taiwan, and, to a lesser extent, Singapore, explicitly subjected it to manpower planning. As with health and housing, the provision of education is dominated by the state in Hong Kong and Singapore, whereas in Korea and Taiwan the state is dominant only in the provision of primary and secondary education. With respect to financing, too, the government is the dominant source in the two city-states whereas private contributions form the bulk of education funding in Korea and, to a lesser extent, Taiwan. Notwithstanding their reputation for emphasizing education, the NIE governments do not spend more money on it than do other countries. Yet it is true that they have traditionally concentrated more on the primary and secondary levels than is typically the case in developing countries, but even this has changed in recent years.

The educational outcomes at the primary and secondary levels in the NIEs are as good as anywhere in the world, but not so for higher education. There are insufficient higher-education opportunities in Hong Kong and Singapore which may have caused the shortage of skilled and technical personnel in the labour-market and contributed to the income inequality. Beyond these differences, all four NIEs are currently engaged in promoting choice, flexibility, and competition in education with the purpose of readying their citizens for facing the challenges of globalization.

The study of social policies in the NIEs shows that there are two national clusters: Hong Kong and Singapore in one group and Korea and Taiwan in the other. In the area of income maintenance, both Hong Kong and Singapore rely on a combination of provident funds and public assistance, whereas Korea and Taiwan rely on social insurance. Similarly, in health care the city-states rely heavily on public provision, especially of in-patient care, and private financing whereas Korea and Taiwan have private provision and public financing. In housing too we find extensive state involvement in Hong Kong and Singapore but not in the two Northeast Asian states, which leave both provision and financing to the private sectors. Education policy, yet again, is characterized by state domination in both provision and financing at all education levels in Hong Kong and Singapore whereas private provision and financing play a significant role in Korea and Taiwan, especially at the tertiary level.

But before we conclude that Hong Kong and Singapore are more statist in their social policies than Korea and Taiwan, we need to understand the nature of the state involvement in the NIEs and purpose. The task may best be addressed in the context of the overall social-policy regimes that obtain in each country. We will not get bogged down here in discussion of what constitutes a regime and its usefulness in understanding policies, but a brief sketch is necessary (for reviews of the literature, see Abrahamson,

1999; Bonoli, 1997; Powell and Barrientos, 2002). Although many authors – including Wilensky and Lebeaux (1958) and Titmuss (1958; 1974) – as far back as the 1950s commented on what later came to be known as regimes, the concept took off in social-policy studies only after the publication of Esping-Andersen's (1990) *Three Worlds of Welfare Capitalism*. The book and its 1999 sequel highlight how study of the role of the state, market. and family in providing welfare and its overall effects reveals features that would go unnoticed looking at the details of individual programmes. His classification of welfare regimes as Liberal, Conservative, and Social democratic based on the primacy of market, family, and state respectively is one of the most widely used taxonomies in contemporary social sciences.

However, his three-fold schema is difficult to sustain in practice because of considerable overlaps among the regimes. Social democracy is particularly problematic because the high level of universal and egalitarian state intervention is not unique to it and is found in Liberal and Conservative regimes as well (Wildeboer Schut *et al.*, 2001). Moreover, Social democratic regimes may be liberal or conservative in orientation in the extent of emphasis they place on the market or family respectively (Powell and Barrientos, 2002; Hicks and Kenworthy, 2003). The problem would be overcome to a large extent by classifying social policies along Liberal and Conservative dimensions based on the primacy they attribute to the market or the family (Kitschelt *et al.*, 1999; Hicks and Kenworthy, 2003).

Liberal regimes emphasize the market whereas their Conservative counterparts emphasize the family. Each dimension in this two-fold classification comprises a progressive end in which state intervention is extensive, benefits are universal and redistributive, and welfare is available as a right. At an extreme, a truly progressive regime would allow total "decommodification" whereby people have access to income independent of market forces (Esping-Andersen, 1990: 3). In this formulation the Social democratic regime is a sub-type of the Liberal regime, albeit one that is more universal and redistributive than classic liberal regimes – we call it a Progressive Liberal. Correspondingly, some Conservative regimes – Germany and Austria, for example – are more universal and redistributive than would be expected from Conservative states, and we may call them Progressive Conservative to distinguish them from their traditional conservative counterparts found in southern Europe.

Liberal[1] welfare regimes are market-based with a substantial role for private provision and funding. Individualism lies at the heart of this regime whereby individuals must fail or succeed on the basis of their own choice and efforts. The market, in so far as it functions through interaction between individual buyer and seller, is viewed as the most efficient means of rewarding effort and the state must stay out of it beyond providing a legal framework for its functioning. Thus Liberalism, in its essence, has limited space for government intervention in social-policy matters, but the position has been relaxed gradually over the decades in recognition of particular circumstances warranting deviation. Thus state involvement in education and health is justified on public goods and positive externality grounds and as an investment in human capital. Income maintenance is similarly justified on grounds of failure in the insurance market and on ethical grounds. However, to ensure that income support does not undermine work incentive, benefits are suggested to be confined to the truly needy and those benefits that are offered are close to subsistence level, and certainly below the lowest paying job. While Liberals do not see a role for the state in housing beyond accommodating the indigent vagrant, Liberal states in export-oriented economies may see it as an issue affecting wages, and hence international competitiveness, which may warrant state involvement in the provision of affordable housing. Thus a high level of state intervention is consistent with Liberal values, so long as it is employed to further individuals' potential for self-realization and does not seriously undermine the market.

The salient features of the Conservative welfare system are a heavy reliance on family for support and services, a right to social protection tied to employment, social insurance funded by private contribution, and a close relationship between contribution and benefits (Kersbergen, 1995). While the role of the state is subsidiary to that of the family, the Conservative state is not reluctant to intervene in order to look after those without support from family, friends, or community and those inadequately served by contributory schemes (Zeylmans, undated). Replacement rates for those in employment are quite generous but those without a strong employment record receive minimal means-tested benefits, which has the effect of reinforcing the existing class, status, and family structures. Western Conservative regimes are also characterized by corporatism whereby trade unions bargain generous benefits for the formally employed sector, thus aggravating and perpetuating their differences with those in informal employment or outside the labour market. In Asia, however, the corporatist element is limited to civil and military employees of the state.

Thus both the Liberal and Conservative regimes are built on the notion of limited state involvement, but at the same time both allow for significant state involvement. To the extent that intervention is universal and redistributive, we call it "progressive". Universalism of state programmes and their redistributive effects are indicators of progressivity. Means testing and social insurance (which are financed from private contribution and pay benefits tied to contribution) are apt examples of the advantages of viewing Liberal and Conservative regimes as a distinct continuum on a progressive scale. The test may be highly selective, in which case it will be Liberal in the traditional sense, or very relaxed, which will make it Progressive Liberal, otherwise called Social democratic in the literature.

Similarly, the inclusion of a redistributive mechanism in contributory social insurance and its universal availability adds a progressive dimension to it, making it Progressive Conservative. "Progressive" as understood here is not a discrete, much less an absolute, category but a continuum on the Liberal and Conservative scales.

It is tempting to brand all four NIEs as what is variously described as Southern, Mediterranean or Rudimentary Conservative welfare states (see Castles, 1996, 1998; Ferrera, 1996; Flaquer, 2000; Guillen and Alvarez, 2001) because of the many similarities between them. In both regions public expenditure on social security is low and the family plays a significant role in providing financial and other support and services. Similarly, a higher proportion of the aged live with their children than is the case in the rest of Europe and both regions are characterized by extensive home ownership, possibly to compensate for inadequate social services and pension (Flaquer, 2000). However, the city-states' heavy reliance on the market for providing and financing social policies and the high importance they attribute to education and housing is at odds with the Conservative tradition.

Study of social policies in the NIEs indicates that Hong Kong and Singapore arguably have Liberal social-policy regimes whereas Korea and Taiwan have Conservative regimes. Alternatively, the two groups may be said to belong respectively to English-speaking and Southern European "families of nations" (Castles, 1998). Each group even has a common political history: the former was ruled by Great Britain and the latter by Japan, which in turn was heavily influenced by Germany. It is hardly surprising that social policies in the two city-states share many crucial features with Britain whereas those in Korea and Taiwan resemble Japan's and Germany's. On virtually all welfare-state measures the NIEs rank lower than their Western counterparts, but the differences are more quantitative than qualitative.

Hong Kong has perhaps the most Liberal political-economic system anywhere. While not a democracy, its political system is thoroughly liberal in the traditional sense, including respect for individual and property rights. Its economic system, although not *laissez-faire*, is perhaps the freest of government intervention. But in social-policy matters, Hong Kong has extensive intervention in the form of government-provided and tax-financed public assistance, in-patient hospital care, public housing, and public schooling. These do not, however, negate its liberal character but rather reinforce it because they support rather than undermine the market. Public assistance for those whose income is below the recognized subsistence level does not necessarily undermine the work incentive while it does enhance political support for a market-based distribution of income. State provision of health care does not only alleviate individual suffering but it also improves labour productivity and mollifies public discontent among those unable to pay for health care. Similarly, public support for housing does not only provide a roof over people's head but also dampens pressures for wages to reflect rising house prices, which will undermine the producers' international economic competitiveness. Government support for education, again, improves the quality of human capital and is therefore not inconsistent with market principles.

Singapore's social policies, but not its political-economic system, are even more Liberal than Hong Kong's. Its main income-maintenance programme is entirely tied to contribution and its public assistance is only for the extremely destitute with no family able to support them. It has extensive state provision of hospital care but everyone except the very poor is expected to pay all or part of the costs. Its housing policy is hard to classify – because on the one hand it involves the state in ways that have few parallels in the capitalist world but on the other hand this has been done without imposing significant costs on the government or supplanting the market. Education is provided by the state and is generously funded from public coffers, but the opportunities for higher education are, as in Hong Kong, limited. The heavy emphasis on education only confirms the government's Liberal orientation à la USA. The President of Singapore in his opening address to the Parliament summed up the government's position very well: "The Government will subsidise investments like education and infrastructure, it will not subsidise consumption expenditure. To do so is to undermine the traditional virtues of thrift, personal responsibility and the will to achieve, and to weaken our economy" (*The Straits Times*, 7 January 1992).

Social policies in Korea have all the hallmarks of a Conservative regime. Korea's pension programme has nearly complete coverage of the employed but is financed from private contributions, and benefits are related to earnings, with particularly high benefits for state employees. Health insurance is also nearly universal in coverage and is based on social insurance with equal benefits across membership. Social insurance is supplemented by public-assistance-type programmes based on stringent means testing for those outside the insurance net. Primary and junior secondary education are universally available and free of charge but families are expected to contribute significantly for pre-school and post-secondary education. State intervention in housing is low and its allocation is left to the market – families are expected to support those without adequate housing. Overall, social policies in Korea provide comprehensive and generous benefits to the population but are biased towards the employed and certainly do not undermine the market and the family as the key providers of social welfare.

Social policies in Taiwan are, at an aggregate level, the most fragmented and at times the most ill-conceived in the region. But beyond the surface of the plethora of social programmes is a common conservative edifice intended to support the role of the market and the family. As in Korea, social insurance based on private contribution is the policy instrument of choice in Taiwan, which offers pension and health-care benefits as a right but also ties them to employment and earning. The notion of the right to public assistance by those not covered by social insurance is even less pronounced than in Korea. State employees, in contrast, enjoy perhaps the most generous pension benefits in the world. The Taiwanese government intervenes little in housing, largely through tax incentives. However, persistent housing oversupply, which has made prices and rents affordable to all but a small segment of the population. The state is more active in education than is the case in Korea but recent efforts to expand the role of private providers may change that.

Social policies in the NIEs have been shaped largely by their colonial legacy and domestic political circumstances. The colonial government in Hong Kong was acutely conscious of its tenuous legitimacy after the mid 1960s and worked hard to accommodate popular preferences without expanding opportunities for democratic participation. The propensity to expand social programmes was particularly high in times of political strife or uncertainty, as in the late 1960s, mid 1980s, and early 1990s. The fear of mass emigration following the agreement to hand the colony back to China in 1984 and the uncertainties promoted by the Tiananmen crackdown in 1989 led the government to take broad-ranging measures involving large expenditures in economic and social spheres to allay public fears about Hong Kong's future.

The Liberal orientation of Singapore's social policies reflects British legacy and the ruling party's comfortable political position in recent decades. After going through turbulent economic and political times in the 1950s and 1960s, Singapore has had stable and generally prosperous conditions since the 1970s. It is not surprising that major social-policy advances were made in the 1960s, as in the subsequent years the government had no political need to resort to expanded social policies (Ramesh, 2000). The economic crises of the mid 1980s and the late 1990s were as difficult times as the PAP government has had to face since the mid 1960s and neither was of sufficient magnitude to threaten the regime. Nevertheless, the government has been mindful of the need to, in the words of the Deputy Prime Minister Lee Hsien Loong, "to temper the hard edge of economic rationality with concern for those less able to look after themselves in a free market system". At the same time he insisted that this must be carried out "without undermining the incentive to work and to achieve, and without incurring the heavy costs which developed welfare states have been unable to avoid" (*The Straits Times*, 24 September 1991). His government believes it has found the solution in highly selective support for income maintenance and health care and broad support for education and housing.

Social policies in Korea have emerged in an entirely different political context than in Hong Kong or Singapore. President Park came to power through a coup amidst economic stagnation and political upheaval and his immediate objective was to solidify his rule. Gaining the support of civil servants and the military by improving pension and health-care benefits for them was a vital part of his political strategy. His government embarked on a state-led export-oriented industrialization whose long-term success depended on an educated labour-force and the government gave top priority to primary and secondary education with a heavy emphasis on vocational schools. Yet the government lacked popular support, as ruling-party candidates struggled to win a majority of votes in successive elections despite tremendous improvement in people's living standards and restrictions on opposition candidates. The establishment of health insurance in 1977 was a sop to urban voters, who were particularly unsupportive of the government. Democratization after 1987 accentuated the pressures on the government, to which it responded through improved pension benefits. Housing did not figure high on the government's economic policy agenda or political strategy, and this was reflected in the meagre resources devoted to it.

Taiwan's social policies reflect the political conditions of the 1940s and 1950s and the period following the end of Martial Law in 1987. While the KMT was still fighting the Communists on the mainland, it adopted a range of education, health, and income-maintenance programmes with the purpose of building popular support for the regime. Its eventual defeat in the Civil War and retreat to Taiwan convinced it all the more of the necessity of policies that appeal to the population, but it sought to achieve these through rapid economic growth rather than populist social policies. After a spurt of expansion in the 1950s and early 1960s, social-policy reform remained at a standstill until the end of martial law in 1987 and the beginning of genuine political competition. The first sector to benefit from the new reality was health care, followed a few years later by income maintenance. Constantly badgered by the DPP on its social-policy record, the KMT hurriedly began to unfurl its proposals in the early 1990s and government officials began to speak of establishing a welfare state.

The international policy climate since the 1980s has not been conducive to the expansion of social policy. Critics of the welfare state have badgered governments to roll back involvement in social-policy matters and have counselled developing countries to ensure they do not take the path followed by Western countries. The critics, who enjoy broad support from international financial institutions and within finance ministries, would prefer arrangements that promote choice and competition among private providers and allow individuals and their families to assume more responsibility for paying for the goods and services they need. Accordingly, they promote individual retirement-savings accounts as the preferred mechanism for maintaining income during retirement. In health care, they suggest reforms in the direction of competition among providers and user charges on consumers. Similarly, in housing they call for a deregulation of the industry and cash grants for tenants and buyers, subject to means tests, rather than public provision of rental or ownership housing. In the same vein, they propose tuition fees at the secondary level and above, coupled with the widespread availability of student loans. The recommended line of reforms is projected as involving the smallest number of adverse effects in terms of distorting the market or undermining work incentive while providing the necessary support to those in need.

What is perhaps not realized by these critics is that many of the suggested reforms were actually practised until they were replaced some decades ago in the industrialized countries and are still practised widely in the developing countries. They forget that states stepped into social-policy matters often reluctantly, because the existing situation was unacceptable to the population. Greater international economic openness may well have made it necessary for social policies to be more flexible and less burdensome on the public exchequer, but this calls for a thoughtful response rather than a retreat to the past.

Singapore offers instructive policy lessons for the critics of the welfare state who call for less state intervention and greater room for market and family in social policies. Its defined contribution scheme based on a savings principle, the CPF, is unable to provide adequate income protection to the majority of the aged despite a contribution rate of around 40 per cent of income. On the other hand, centralized provision and financing of hospital care by the public sector backed by regulated competition among providers has been a great success in delivering quality service at modest cost. Heavy state intervention in the provision of education at the primary- and secondary-school levels, complemented by competition among schools, has been a similar success. Housing is the area in which the state has intervened the most comprehensively and it has good outcomes to show for this.

Lower costs to the government as a result of a greater role of the market and family in the provision of social goods and services do not necessarily mean lower costs to society as a whole. Social expenditure data for Sweden and the USA show that while taxes may be lower in the USA, for families the advantage is offset by greater expenditure on private health, education, pension, and children's day care. Systems that rely on privately-provided benefits (as in the USA) have total costs that are similar to those based on schemes provided and funded by the state, with the additional disadvantage that large chunks of the population are left uncovered or under-serviced under the former (Esping-Andersen, 1997: 72). If indeed our main concern is the cost of welfare to society as a whole, then the role of the state cannot be dismissed as readily as it sometimes is.

Regardless of the governments' policy choices, expenditure on social policies will increase over the coming decades in all Asian NIEs even if no new programmes are established (Heller, 1999). Over the following decades, expenditure on education and housing will decline as a result of falling birth rates, but this will be more than offset by the rising expenditure on income maintenance and health care for the aged. The actual expenditures may be yet higher because of political pressures not just to maintain the existing programmes but to expand them further to enhance citizens' capacity to participate in the global economy and protect them from its adverse effects. In fact one veteran observer of both Western and Asian welfare systems is of the opinion that at least Korea is on its way to becoming a social democratic welfare state of the Nordic kind, combining state-based welfare with active labour-market policies (Kuhnle, 2002). This is perhaps too optimistic but still closer to the mark than a ruling out of the welfare state for East Asia on cultural grounds.

NOTES

1 INTRODUCTION

1 Indicator for Taiwan not included in the UNDP report because of its non-membership. Results calculated by DGBAS using UNDP criteria. HDI value for Taiwan in 1997 was 0.874, which ranked 23rd among 145 economies (*United Daily News*, 14 August 2002).

3 INCOME MAINTENANCE

1 The distinction is not clear-cut in practice, however, as the recently established Mandatory Provident Fund (MPF) in Hong Kong is privately managed and should more appropriately be called an IRA.
2 The amount is calculated by doubling the base salary on the day of retirement, and then multiplying it by service units, which is derived by multiplying years of service by 1.5, to a maximum of 53 units (or 35 years). Thus, someone on the final salary of NT$22,097 per month after 35 years of service will receive a lump-sum amount of NT$1,988,775 <(22,097*2)*30*1.5>. If the same person chooses a monthly pension, s/he receives NT$26,517 per month for the rest of his or her life <(22,097*2)*30*2 (per cent)>.
3 Two units are awarded for each year of service during the first 15 years of employment, after which only one unit is awarded, to the maximum of 45 units. Thus a private-sector worker after 30–35 years of service retiring at a salary level of NT$22,097 per month will receive a lump-sum amount of NT$994,365.
4 "The functions carried out under this programme include the provision of services for child welfare, child care, senior citizens, the disabled and destitute persons, residential institutions, probation and aftercare, voluntary development and coordination, and family welfare as well as the administration of the various financial assistance schemes for the destitute and the needy" (1997/1998: 169). Family Support Services Division was previously called Welfare Services Division. (Singapore, *Budget for the Financial Year*, Singapore: Singapore National Printers, various years.)
5 Includes direct government and social-insurance expenditure on: old-age cash benefits, disability cash benefits, occupational injury and disease, sickness benefits, services for the elderly and disabled people, survivors, family cash benefits, family services, unemployment, and other contingencies. Data for pre-1990 period excludes expenditure from social-insurance funds and, as a result, seriously underestimates total expenditure.
6 Includes social insurance and direct government expenditure on pension, social assistance, social relief, social-welfare services, employment service, medical care

NOTES

and public health. Excludes expenditures from employer-liability schemes. Note that health expenditures are impossible to separate from other welfare expenditures for the pre-1992 period.

7 In 1995, the premium for all social-insurance schemes was reduced in conjunction with the launch of the National Health Insurance and the separation of health insurance from income security functions.

4 HEALTH

1 According to the widely used conventional statistics, however, it is the private sector that is the source of the majority of funds, accounting for 56 per cent of the total 1995–1996 (Liu and Yue, 1998).
2 According to conventional statistics, it actually declined from 16.2 per cent to 13.5 during the same period (ibid.).
3 Includes, as is the normal practice for OECD and recommended by the IMF, both the health component of the Ministry of Health and Welfare's expenditures and expenditures of health insurance funds. Data published by the Korean government, the ADB and IMF (which are based on national data) as well as most commentaries on the subject report much lower figures because they exclude social insurance from public expenditures.

5 HOUSING

1 The term "ownership" of housing in Singapore includes a 99-year lease on the property as well as freehold ownership.
2 Under the *Chonsei* system, the tenant pays a large cash deposit (usually one-third or one-half of the value of the house) at the outset but pays no monthly rent. The principal sum is returned to the tenant at the end of the tenancy; the landlord takes the interest. The Chonsei system carries a higher status than monthly rental housing, but disadvantages those without the necessary saving to pay upfront.

6 EDUCATION

1 For an evaluation of the case for and against cost recovery in education, see King and Tilak, 1997.

7 CONCLUSION

1 Liberalism is understood here in the individualist tradition espoused by David Hume, Adam Smith, Alexis de Tocqueville, and Friedrich Hayek, and not in the perverted sense in which it is used in the USA to describe state intervention.

REFERENCES

Aaron, Henry J. (1967) "Social Security: International Comparisons", O. Eckstein (ed.), *Studies in the Economics of Income Maintenance*, Washington, DC: Brookings Institute, pp. 13–48.

Abel-Smith, Brian (1992) *Cost Containment and New Priorities in Health Care*, Aldershot: Ashgate.

Abrahamson, Peter (1999) "The Welfare Modelling Business", *Social Policy and Administration*, 33: pp. 394–415.

Acedo, Clementina and Mitsue Uemura (2001) *Education Indicators For East Asia and Pacific*, Working Paper No. 23023, Washington, DC: World Bank.

Adams, Don and Esther E. Gottlieb (1993) *Education and Social Change in Korea*, New York: Garland Publishing.

ADB (2002) *Key Indicators of Developing Asian and Pacific Countries 2001*, Manila: Author.

Amenta, Edwin and Bruce G. Carruthers (1988) "The Formative Years of US Social Spending Policies: Theories of the Welfare State and the American States During the Great Depression", *American Sociological Review*, 53: pp. 661–678.

An, C. B. and K. Kim (1994). "Tax and Related Issues in Introducing The Individual Pension System in Korea", *Asian Economies*, 23: pp. 36–65.

Anantaraman, Venkataraman (1990) *Singapore Industrial Relations System*, Singapore: McGraw-Hill.

Appelbaum, Richard P. and Jeffrey Henderson (eds) (1992) *States and Development in the Asian Pacific Region*, Newbury Park: Sage.

Asher, Mukul G. (2002) "Pension Reform in an Affluent and Rapidly Ageing Society: The Singapore's Case", paper presented at international symposium on *Pension Reforms in Asian Countries*, organized by Hitosubashi University, Tokyo, 1–2 February 2002.

Asher, Mukul and Phang Sock Yong (1997) "Public Housing, and Social Protection", Ake E. Andersson, Bjorn Harsman, and John M. Quigley (eds), *Government For The Future: Unification, Fragmentation, and Regionalism*, New York: Elsevier, pp. 287–316.

Asher, Mukul and David Newman (2002) "Private Pensions in Asia: An Assessment of Eight Systems", OECD (ed.), *Regulating Private Pension Schemes: Trends and Challenges*, International Network of Pensions Regulators and Supervisors Conference, 2001, Sofia, Bulgaria, Paris: Organisation for Economic Co-operation and Development, pp. 51–104.

Aspalter, Christian (2002) *Democratization and Welfare State Development in Taiwan*, Aldershot: Ashgate.

REFERENCES

Aw, Tar Choon and Linda Low (1997) "Health Care Provisions in Singapore", Tan Teck Meng and Chew Soon Beng (eds), *Affordable Health Care: Issues and Prospects*, Singapore: Prentice-Hall, pp. 50–71.

Barr, M. D. (2001) "Medical Savings Accounts in Singapore: A Critical Inquiry", *Journal of Health Politics Policy and Law*, 26: 4, pp. 709–726.

Barr, N. (2002) "Reforming Pensions: Myths, Truths, and Policy Choices", *International Social Security Review*, 55: 2, pp. 3–36.

Barro, Robert J. and Jong-Wha Lee (2000) "International Measures of Schooling Years and Schooling Quality", *American Economic Review, Papers and Proceeding*, 86: May, pp. 218–223.

Behrman, J. and R. Schneider (1994) "An International Perspective On Schooling Investments in the Last Quarter Century in Some Fast-Growing East and South East Asian Countries", *Asian Development Review*, 12: 2, pp. 1–50.

Bennett, Sara (1997) "Private Health Care and Public Policy Objectives", Christopher Colclough (ed.), *Marketizing Education and Health in Developing Countries: Miracle Or Mirage?*, Oxford: Clarendon Press, pp. 93–123.

Berman, Peter (1997) "Supply-Side Approaches to Optimizing Private Health Sector Growth", William Newbrander (ed.), *Private Health Sector Growth in Asia: Issues and Implications*, Chichester: John Wiley and Sons, pp. 111–133.

Bonoli, Giuliano (1997) "Classifying Welfare States: A Two-Dimension Approach", *Journal of Social Policy*, 26: 3, pp. 351–372.

Bray, Mark (1993) "Financing Higher Education: A Comparison of Government Strategies in Hong Kong and Macao", Mark Bray (ed.), *The Economics and Financing of Education: Hong Kong and Comparative Perspectives*, Hong Kong: Faculty of Education, University of Hong Kong, pp. 32–50.

Bray, Mark (1998) "Financing Education in Developing Asia: Themes, Tensions, and Policies", *International Journal of Education Research*, 29, pp. 627–642.

Brewer, B. (1993) "An Analysis of Hong Kong's Health Policy", *Journal of Health and Social Policy*, 4: 3, pp. 93–114.

Brewer, Brian and Stewart Macpherson (1997) "Poverty and Social Security", Paul Wilding, Ahmed Shafiqul Huque, and Julia Tao Lai-Po Wah (eds), *Social Policy in Hong Kong*, Cheltenham: Edward Elgar, pp. 72–94.

Brittan, Samuel (1975) "The Economic Contradictions of Democracy", *British Journal of Political Science*, 5, pp. 129–159.

Button, Michael (1995) "Retirement: Providing Income in Old Age", *Benefits and Compensation International*, January/February, 24: 6, pp. 5–10.

Cardarelli, R. (2000) *Singapore: Selected Issues*, IMF Staff Country Report No. 00/83, Washington, DC: IMF.

Castells, M., L. Goh, and R. Y. W. Kwok (1990) *The Shek Kip Mei Syndrome: Economic Development and Public Housing in Hong Kong and Singapore*, London: Pion.

Castles, Francis G. (1989) "Explaining Public Education Expenditure in OECD Nations", *European Journal of Political Research*, 17: 4, pp. 431–448.

Castles, Francis G. (1996) "Welfare State Development in Southern Europe", *West European Politics*, 18: 2, pp. 291–331.

Castles, Francis G. (1998) *Comparative Public Policy: Patterns of Post-War Transformation*, Cheltenham: Edward Elgar.

Castles, Frank and Robert D. McKinlay (1979) "Does Politics Matter? An Analysis of the Public Welfare Commitment in Advanced Democratic States", *European Journal of Political Research*, 7: pp. 169–186.

REFERENCES

Chan, Ho-Mun and Joan Y. H. Leung (1997) "Education", Paul Wilding, Ahmed Shafiqul Huque, and Julia Tao Lai-Po Wah (eds), *Social Policy in Hong Kong*, Cheltenham: Edward Elgar, pp. 55–71.

Chan, Kam Wah (2000) "Prosperity Or Inequality: Deconstructing The Myth of Home Ownership in Hong Kong", *Housing Studies*, 15: 1, pp. 29–44.

Chan, Raymond (1996) Welfare in Newly-Industrialised Society – the Construction of the Welfare State in Hong Kong, Aldershot: Avebury.

Chan, Steve, Cal Clark, and Danny Lam (eds) (1998) *Beyond The Developmental State: East Asia's Political Economies Reconsidered*, New York: St Martin's Press.

Chang, Guangdi (1997) *The Feasibility of Establishing A Secondary Mortgage Market to Improve The Liquidity and Availability of Housing Finance Funds in Taiwan*, PhD Thesis, Texas A&M University.

Chang, Johannes Han Yin and A. Mani (1995) "Higher Education in Singapore: Dual Constraints of Less Competitive Groups", *Southeast Asian Journal of Social Science*, 23: 2, pp. 42–61.

Chang, Kuang-Wen (2000) *A Risk Management Perspective on Public Pension Reform*, DBA Thesis, Boston University.

Chen, Hsiu-Li and Couochen Wu (1997) "Testing Taiwan's High Homeownership Rates in the 1980s", *The Singapore Economic Review*, 42: 1, pp. 73–93.

Cheng, K. M. and S. Y. Wong (1997) "Empowerment of the Powerless through the Politics of the Apolitical: Teacher Professionalisation in Hong Kong", B. J. Biddle *et al.* (eds), *International Handbook of Teachers and Teaching*, Dordrecht: Kluwer, pp. 411–436.

Cheng, Peter Wen Hui (1995) "Education Finance in Taipei, China", paper presented at *Workshop On Financing Human Resource Development in Asia*, organized by the Asian Development Bank Project, Manila, 11–14 July 1995.

Cheng, Shou-Sia and Tung-Liang Chiang (1997) "The Effect of Universal Health Insurance on Health Care Utilisation in Taiwan", *JAMA*, 278: 2, pp. 89–93.

Chiang, T. L. (1997) "Taiwan's 1995 Health Care Reform", *Health Policy*, 39, pp. 225–240.

Ching, Yuan Lin and Yun Peng Chu (1998) "Changes in Earnings Inequality in Taiwan: 1976–1996", paper presented at international conference on *Economic Growth, Poverty and Income Inequality in The Asia Pacific Region*, 19–20 March 1998.

Chiu, Rebecca L. H. (1999) "The Swing of The Pendulum in Housing", Larry Chuen-Ho Chow and Yiu-Kwan Fan (eds), *The Other Hong Kong Report 1998*, Hong Kong: Chinese University Press, pp. 329–351.

Cho, Woo-Hyun (1999) *The Asian Crisis and Addressing Unemployment in Korea*, paper presented at Manila Social Forum, 8–12 November 1999.

Choei, Naue-Young (1996) *A Study On The Distributional and Efficiency Consequences of the Housing Finance Subsidy Programs*, PhD Thesis, University of Pennsylvania.

Choi, Sung Jae (1996) "Aging and Social Policy in Korea", *Korea Journal of Population and Development*, 25: 1, pp. 1–25.

Choi, Sung Jae (1996b) "The Family and Ageing in Korea: A New Concern and Challenge", *Ageing and Society*, 16: 1, pp. 1–25.

Chou, W. L. and Y. C. Shih (1995) "Hong Kong Housing Markets – Overview, Tenure Choice, and Housing Demand", *Journal of Real Estate Finance and Economics*, 10: 1, pp. 7–21.

Chow, Nelson (1982) "Development and Functions of Social Services in Hong

REFERENCES

Kong", J. Y. S. Cheng (ed.), *Hong Kong in The 1980s*, Hong Kong: Summerson Educational Research Centre.

Chow, Nelson (2000) "Ageing in Hong Kong", David R. Phillips (ed.), *Ageing in The Asia-Pacific Region*, London: Routledge, pp. 158–173.

Chu, D. K. W. (1994) "Economic Development and The Health Care System in Hong Kong", *Health Policy*, 28, pp. 211–234.

Chu, Yin-Wah (1998) "Labor and Democratization in South Korea and Taiwan", *Journal of Contemporary Asia*, 28: 2, pp. 185–202.

Chua, Beng Huat (2000) "Public Housing Residents As Clients of The State", *Housing Studies*, 15: 1, pp. 45–60.

Chung, Bong Gun (1998) *A Study of the School Leveling Policy in the Republic of Korea: Its Genesis, Implementation and Reforms, 1974–1995*, EDD Thesis, University of Hawaii.

Chung, Bong Gun (2002) "Korea's War on Private Tutoring", unpublished paper, presented at *The Second International Forum on Education Reform*, 2–5 September 2002, Bangkok, web publication: http://www.worldedreform.com/intercon2/f20.pdf.

Clark, Cal and K. C. Roy (1997) *Comparing Development Patterns in Asia*, Boulder: Lynne Rienner.

Colclough, Christopher (1996) "Education and the Market: Which Parts of the Neoliberal Solutions Are Correct?", *World Development*, 24: 4, pp. 589–610.

Collier, D. and R. E. Messick (1975) "Prerequisites Versus Diffusion: Testing Alternative Explanations of Social Security Adoption", *American Political Science Review*, 69: 4: pp. 1299–1355.

Comparative Education Policy Research Group (1998) *Towards Quality Education: A Critical Review of Education, Commission Report No. 7*, Occasional Paper Series No. 1, Hong Kong: Department of Public and Social Administration, City University of Hong Kong.

Construction and Planning Administration (1993a) *An Introduction to The Public Housing Programs*, Taipei: Construction and Planning Administration, Ministry of Interior.

Construction and Planning Administration (1993b) *Housing Development in The Taiwan Area*, Taipei: Construction and Planning Administration, Ministry of Interior.

Construction and Planning Administration (1999) *Housing Quarterly Report 1999 – 1st Quarter*, Taipei: Author.

Cummings, W. K. and A. Riddell (1994) "Alternatives For the Finance, Control, and Delivery of Basic Education", *International Journal of Educational Research*, 21, pp. 751–776.

Cuthbert, Alexander Roy (1989) "A Fistful of Dollars: Legitimation, Production and Debate in Hong Kong", University of Hong Kong (ed.), *A Fistful of Dollars: Ideological Structures and Spatial Structures in Hong Kong*, Hong Kong: University of Hong Kong, Centre of Urban Studies and Urban Planning, pp. 32ff.

Cutright, P. (1965) "Political Structure, Economic Development, and National Security Programs", *American Journal of Sociology*, 70: 5, pp. 537–550.

Dang, Thai Than *et al.* (2001) *Fiscal Implications of Ageing: Projections of Age-Related Spending*, Economics Department Working Paper No. 305, Paris: OECD.

Davies, S. N. (1997) "One Brand of Politics Rekindled", *Hong Kong Law Journal*, 7: 1, pp. 44–80.

REFERENCES

De Geyndt, Willy (1991) *Managing Health Expenditures Under National Health Insurance: The Case of Korea*, Technical Paper No. 156, Washington, DC: World Bank.

Deyo, Frederic C. (1989) *Beneath the Miracle: Labor Subordination in the New Asian Industrialism*, Berkeley: University of California Press.

Deyo, Frederic C. (1992) "The Political Economy of Social Policy Formation: East Asia's Newly Industrialized Countries", Richard P. Appelbaum and Jeffrey Henderson (eds), *States and Development in the Asian Pacific Region*, Newbury Park: Sage, pp. 267–306.

Deyo, Frederic *et al.* (1987) "Labor in the Political Economy of East Asian Industrialization", *Bulletin of Concerned Asian Scholars*, 19: 2, pp. 42–53.

DGBAS (1996) *Social Indicators in Taiwan Area of The Republic of China 1995*, Taipei: Director General of Budget, Accounting and Statistics, Republic of China.

DGBAS (1999) *Social Indicators – The Republic of China 1999*, Taipei: Director General of Budget, Accounting and Statistics, Republic of China.

DGBAS (2000) *Social Indicators in Taiwan Area of The Republic of China 1999*, Taipei: Director General of Budget, Accounting and Statistics, Republic of China.

DGBAS (2000a) *Yearbook of Statistics 2000*, Taipei: Director General of Budget, Accounting and Statistics, Republic of China.

DGBAS (2002) *Yearbook of Statistics 2002*, Taipei: Director General of Budget, Accounting and Statistics, Republic of China.

Doling, John (1999) "Housing Policies and The Little Tigers: How Do They Compare With Other Industrialised Countries?", *Housing Studies*, 14: 2, pp. 229–250.

Elola, J. (1996) "Health Care System Reforms in Western European Countries: The Relevance of Health Care Organization", *International Journal of Health Services*, 26: 2, pp. 239–251.

Eng, Soo Peck (1990) "Financing Education", paper presented at the conference on the *Fiscal System of Singapore*, Singapore, 8–10 February 1990.

Eng, Teo Siew and Lily Kong (1997) "Public Housing in Singapore: Interpreting 'Quality' in The 1990s", *Urban Studies*, 34, pp. 441–452.

ESCAP (ed.) (1998) *Asia and The Pacific Into The Twenty-First Century: Prospects for Social Development*, New York: United Nations.

Esping-Andersen, Gosta (1990) *The Three Worlds of Welfare Capitalism*, Cambridge: Polity Press.

Esping-Andersen, Gosta (1996) "Hybrid or Unique? The Japanese Welfare State Between Europe and America", *Journal of European Social Policy*, 7: 3, pp. 179–189.

Esping-Andersen, Gosta (1997) "Welfare States at The End of The Century: The Impact of Labour Market, Family and Demographic Change", OECD (ed.), *Family, Market and Community: Equity and Efficiency in Social Policy*, Paris: Organisation for Economic Cooperation and Development, pp. 63–80.

Esping-Andersen, Gosta (1999) *Social Foundations of Postindustrial Economies*, Oxford: Oxford University Press.

Evans, Robert G. (1997) "Going for The Gold: The Redistributive Agenda Behind Market-Based Health Care Reform", *Journal of Health Politics, Policy and Law*, 22: 2, pp. 427–465.

Ferrera, M. (1996) "The 'Southern Model' of Welfare in Social Europe", *Journal of European Social Policy*, 6: 1, pp. 17–37.

Flaquer, Lluís (2000) *Family Policy and Welfare State in Southern Europe*, Working

REFERENCES

Paper No. 185, The Institut de Ciències Polítiques i Socials, Universitat Autònoma de Barcelona.

Flora, Peter and Arnold J. Heidenheimer (eds) (1981) *The Development of Welfare States in Europe and America*, New Brunswick: Transaction Books.

Garrett, Geoffrey (1998) "Global Markets and National Politics: Collision Course or Virtuous Circle?", *International Organization*, 52: 4, pp. 787–824.

Garrett, Geoffrey and Peter Lange (1996) "Internationalization and Domestic Politics: An Introduction", Robert O. Keohane and Helen V. Milner (eds), *Internationalization and Domestic Politics*, Cambridge: Cambridge University Press, pp. 48–75.

Gauld, R. D. C. (1996) "Revolution Or Evolution in Health Sector Restructuring? The Experiences of New Zealand and Hong Kong", *Hong Kong Public Administration*, 5, pp. 87–104.

Gertler, Paul J. and Jeffrey S. Hammer (1997) *Strategies for Pricing Publicly Provided Health Services*, The Policy Research Working Paper No. 1762, Washington, DC: World Bank.

Gillon, Colin *et al.* (2000) *Social Security Pensions: Development and Reform*, Geneva: International Labour Office.

Goh, Keng Swee (1956) *Urban Incomes And Housing: A Report On The Social Survey Of Singapore, 1953–54*, Singapore: Department of Social Welfare.

Goodman, R. and I. Peng (1996) "The East Asian Welfare States: Peripatetic Learning, Adaptive Changes, and Nation Building", G. Esping-Andersen (ed.), *The Welfare State in Transition*, Berkeley: Sage, pp. 192–224.

Gopinathan, S. and Ho Wah Kam (2000) "Educational Change and Development in Singapore", Tony Townsend and Yin Cheong Cheng (eds), *Educational Change and Development in the Asia-Pacific Region: Challenges For the Future*, Exton, PA: Swets & Zeitlinger Publishers, pp. 163–184.

Gough, Ian (2000) "Welfare Regimes in East Asia and Europe", paper presented at *Towards The New Social Policy Agenda in East Asia*, parallel session to the Annual World Bank Conference on Development Economics, Europe 2000, Paris, 27 May 2000.

Gough, Ian and Jin Wook Kim (2000) *Tracking The Welfare Mix in Korea*, University of Bath, web publication: www.bath.ac.uk/Faculties/HumSocSci/IFIPA/GSP/wp10.pdf.

Grant, Colin and Peter Yuen (1998) *The Hong Kong Health Care System*, Sydney: School of Health Services Management, University of New South Wales.

Griffin, Charles C. (1992) *Health Care in Asia: A Comparative Study of Cost and Financing*, Washington, DC: World Bank.

Guillen, A. M. and S. Alvarez (2001) "Globalization and the Southern Welfare States", Sykes, Robert (ed.), *Globalization and European Welfare States: Challenges and Change*, Basingstoke: Palgrave, pp. 103–126.

Gupta, Sanjeev *et al.* (1999) *Does Higher Government Spending Buy Better Results in Education and Health Care?*, IMF Working Paper No. 99/21, Washington, DC: IMF.

Ha, Seong Kyu (1987) "Korea", Seong Kyu Ha (ed.), *Housing Policy and Practice in Asia*, London: Croom Helm, pp. 80–116.

Ha, Seong Kyu (1994) "Low Income Housing Policies in The Republic of Korea", *Cities*, 11, pp. 107–114.

REFERENCES

Ha, Seong-Kyu (2002) "The Seong Kyu Urban Poor, Rental Accommodations, and Housing Policy in Korea", *Cities*, 19: 3, pp. 195–203.

Haffner, Marietta E. A. and J. Oxley Michael (1999) "Housing Subsidies: Definitions and Comparisons", *Housing Studies*, 14, pp. 145–162.

Hage, J., R. Hanneman, and E. T. Gargan (1989) *State Responsiveness and State Activism*, London: Unwin Hyman.

Hahn, Jooyoun (1998) *Residential Differentiation and The Structure of Housing Provision: A Case of Seoul, 1960–1990*, PhD Thesis, University of Wisconsin, Madison.

Hammer, Jeffrey S. and Peter A. Berman (1995) "Ends and Means in Public Health Policy in Developing Countries", Peter A. Berman (ed.), *Health Sector Reform in Developing Countries: Making Health Development Sustainable*, Boston: Harvard School of Public Health, pp. 37–57.

Hanushek, Eric A. (1995) "Interpreting Recent Research On Schooling in Developing Countries", *The World Bank Research Observer*, 10: 2, pp. 227–246.

Harvard Team (1999) *Improving Hong Kong's Health Care System: Why and for Whom?*, Hong Kong: Health and Welfare Bureau.

Harvard Team (1999b), *Special Report No. 1: Estimates of Domestic Health Expenditure*, Hong Kong: Health and Welfare Bureau.

Hay, Joel W. (1992) *Health Care in Hong Kong: an Economic Policy Assessment*, Hong Kong: Chinese University Press.

Heclo, Hugh (1981) "Toward a New Welfare State?", Peter Flora and A. J. Heidenheimer (eds), *The Development of Welfare States in Europe and America*, New Brunswick, London: Transaction Books, pp. 383–406.

Heidenheimer, Adam J. (1981) "Education and Social Security Entitlements in Europe and America", Peter Flora and A. J. Heidenheimer (eds), *The Development of Welfare States in Europe and America*, New Brunswick, London: Transaction Books, pp. 269–304.

Hega, Gunther and Karl Hokenmaier (2002) "The Welfare State and Education: A Comparison of Social and Educational Policy in Advanced Industrial Societies", *German Policy Studies/Politikfeldanalyse*, 2: 1.

Heller, Peter S. (1999) "Ageing in Asia: Challenges for Fiscal Policy", *Journal of Asian Economics*, 10: 1, pp. 37–63.

Henderson, Jeffrey and Richard P. Appelbaum (1992) "Situating the State in the East Asian Development Process", Richard P. Appelbaum and Jeffrey Henderson (eds), *States and Development in the Asian Pacific Region*, Newbury Park: Sage, pp. 1–26.

Hewitt Associated and GML Consulting (1995) "Report of The Consultancy on The Mandatory Provident Fund", April 1995.

Hicks, Alexander and Lane Kenworthy (2003) "Varieties of Welfare Capitalism", *Socio-Economic Review*, 1: 1.

HKSS (2000) *Poverty Watch*, Hong Kong: Hong Kong Social Security Society, March 2000.

Ho, Lok-Sang (1996) *A Universal Fully-Funded Pension Scheme*, Hong Kong: Working Paper Series No. 96-03, Lingnan College, Faculty of Social Sciences.

Ho, Wing-Chung (1998) "Rethinking The Financing Arrangement for The Long Term Care Services to The Elderly in Hong Kong", Second Asia Regional Conference on *Social Security*, organised by The Hong Kong Council of Social Service, 24–26 January 2000.

Holliday, Ian (2000) "Productivist Welfare Capitalism: Social Policy in East Asia", *Political Studies*, 48: 4, pp. 706–723.

REFERENCES

Holzmann, R. and R. Palacios (2001) "The Case for Funded, Individual Accounts in Pension Reform", Xenia Scheil-Adlung (ed.), *Building Social Security: The Challenge of Privatization*, Geneva: ISSA, pp. 45–61.

Hong Kong (2001) *Hong Kong Annual Digest of Statistics 2000*, Hong Kong: Government Printers.

Hong Kong Census and Statistics Department (2000) *Hong Kong Annual Digest of Statistics 2000*, Hong Kong: Government Printers.

Hong Kong Census and Statistics Department (2001) *Hong Kong Social and Economic Trends*, Hong Kong: Census and Statistics Department.

Hong Kong Education Commission (2000) *Learning For Life, Learning Through Life: Reform Proposals For the Education System in Hong Kong*, Hong Kong: Education Commission.

Hong Kong Education Department (1996) *72 Education Indicators for The Hong Kong School Education System*, Hong Kong: Author, 1996.

Hong Kong Government (1997) *Homes for Hong Kong People: The Way Forward, Long Term Housing Strategy Review Consultative Document*, Hong Kong: Housing Branch.

Hong Kong Government (1998) *Homes for Hong Kong People Into The 21st Century: A White Paper On Long Term Housing Strategy in Hong Kong*, Hong Kong: Housing Bureau.

Hong Kong Government (1998a), Social Welfare Department, *Report on Review of The Comprehensive Social Security Assistance Scheme*, December 1998, web publication: www.info.gov.hk.

Hong Kong Government (1999) *The Community Chest and Funding for Social Welfare Services*, Health and Welfare Bureau, briefing notes for Legislative Council panel on welfare services meeting, 8 March 1999.

Hong Kong Government (2000) *Estimates of Revenue and Expenditure, 2000–2001*, Hong Kong: Government Printers.

Hong Kong Government, Department of Social Welfare (2003) *Social Security*, Hong Kong: Author, web publication. http://www.info.gov.hk/swd/text_eng/ser_sec/soc_secu/index.html.

Hong Kong Government, Interdepartmental Working Party (1967) *A Report by The Interdepartmental Working Party to Consider Certain Aspects of Social Security*, Hong Kong: Government Printers.

Hong Kong Housing Authority (1985) *Green Paper: Housing Subsidy to Tenants of Public Housing*, committee on housing subsidy to tenants of public housing, Hong Kong: Hong Kong Housing Authority.

Hong Kong Housing Bureau (1999) *Better Housing for All: Policy Objective for Housing Bureau*, 1999 policy address, Hong Kong: Author.

Hong Kong Human Rights Commission (1994) "A Report to The United Nations Committee on Economic, Social and Cultural Rights on Housing Rights Violations and Poverty Problem in Hong Kong", November 1994, web publication: http://is7.pacific.net.hk/~hkhrc/ice95-3.htm.

Hong Kong Social Welfare Department (2000) *Social Welfare Services in Figures 2000*, Hong Kong: Author.

Hort, Sven and Stein Kuhnle (2000) "The Coming of East and South-East Asian Welfare States", *Journal of European Social Policy*, 10: 2, pp. 162–184.

Howlett, Michael and M. Ramesh (1998) "Policy Subsystem Configurations and Policy Change: Operationalizing the Postpositivist Analysis of the Politics of the Policy Process", *Policy Studies Journal*, 26, pp. 466ff.

REFERENCES

Hsiao, William C. (1995) "Medical Savings Account: Lessons From Singapore", *Health Affairs*, 14: 2, pp. 260–266.

Hsiao, William C. (2001) "Behind The Ideology and Theory: What Is The Empirical Evidence for Medical Savings Account?", *Journal of Health Politics, Policy and Law*, 26: 4, pp. 733–737.

Hsiao, W. C. L. *et al.* (1990) "Health Care Financing and Delivery in The ROC: Current Conditions and Future Challenges", *Industry of Free China*, LXXIII: 5, pp. 13–38.

Hu, Teh-Wei and Chee-Ruey Hsieh (1999) *An Economic Analysis of Health Care Reform in Taiwan*, paper presented at the Department of Economics, National Taiwan University, 1–2 October 1999.

Hyug, Baeg Im (1992) "State, Labor and Capital in The Consolidation of Democracy", Hong Yung Lee and Dal-joong Chang (eds), *Political Authority and Economic Exchange in Korea*, Seoul: Oruem, pp. 131–162.

IMF (2000) *Government Finance Statistics 1999*, Washington, DC: Author.

International Labour Organization (1998) *The Social Impact of The Asian Financial Crisis*, Cross Departmental Analysis and Reports Team, Bangkok: ILO Regional Office.

Jacobs, Didier (2000) *Low Inequality With Low Redistribution? An Analysis of Income Distribution in Japan, South Korea and Taiwan Compared to Britain*, Casepaper 33, London: Centre for Analysis of Social Exclusion, London School of Economics.

Jao, Chih Chien (1998) "The Impact of Tax Revenue and Expenditure of Social Welfare on Income Distribution in Taiwan", paper presented at *International Conference on Economic Growth, Poverty and Income Inequality in The Asia Pacific Region*, 19–20 March 1998.

Jessop, Bob (1993) "The Schumpeterian Workfare State", *Studies in Political Economy*, 40: 7–40.

Jessop, Bob (1999) "Reflections on Globalization and its (Il)logics", Peter Dicken, Philip Kelley, Kris Olds, and Henry Yeung (eds), *Globalization and the Asia Pacific: Contested Territories*, London: Routledge, pp. 19–38.

Jones, Catherine (1993) "The Pacific Challenge: Confucian Welfare States", Catherine Jones (ed.), *New Perspectives on the Welfare State in Europe*, London: Routledge, pp. 198–217.

Jones, Gavin (1990) *Consequences of Rapid Fertility Decline for Old Age Security in Asia*, Working Papers in Demography No. 20, Canberra: Australian National University.

Jones, Gavin W. (1995) "Population and The Family in Southeast Asia", *Journal of Southeast Asian Studies*, 26: 1, pp. 184–195.

Joo, Jaehyun (1999a) "Explaining Social Policy Adoption in South Korea: The Cases of The Medical Insurance Law and The Minimum Wage Law", *Journal of Social Policy*, 28: 3, pp. 387–412.

Joo, Jaehyun (1999b) "Dynamics of Social Policy Change: A Korean Case Study from a Comparative Perspective", *Governance*, 12: 1, pp. 57–80.

Jung, Young-Tae and Dong-Myeon Shin (2002) "Social Protection in South Korea", Erfried, Adam *et al.* (eds), *Social Protection in Southeast and East Asia*, Singapore: Friedrich-Ebert-Stiftung, Office for Regional Co-operation in Southeast Asia, pp. 269–312.

Kalisch, David W. *et al.* (1998) *Social and Health Policies in OECD Countries: A Survey of Current Programmes and Recent Developments*, Paris: Directorate for Education, Employment, Labour and Social Affairs, OECD, Occasional Paper No. 33.

Kalra, Sanjay, Dubravko Mihaljek, and Christopher Duenwald (2000) *Property Prices and Speculative Bubbles – Evidence from Hong Kong SAR*, Asia and Pacific Department Series: Working Paper No. 00/2, Washington, DC: IMF.

Kang Moon-Soo (1993) "Housing Finance in The 1990s", Werner Puschra and Kwan Young Kim (eds), *Housing Policy in The 1990s: European Experiences and Alternatives for Korea*, papers and discussions from the joint KDI/FES conference, Seoul: Korea Development Institute, pp. 169–196.

KEDI (2000) *Handbook of Educational Statistics*, Seoul: Korea Education Development Institute.

Kemeny, J. (1981) *The Myth of Home-Ownership: Private Versus Public Choices in Housing Tenure*, Boston: Routledge & Kegan Paul.

Kersbergen, Kees van (1995) *Social Capitalism: A Study of Christian Democracy and The Welfare State*, London: Routledge.

Kil, Soong Hoom (1991) "Confucian State Capitalism in South Korea and Japan", paper presented at the IPSA World Congress, 1991.

Kim, Anna (1997) *State Vs. Market in Educational Open-Market Policy-Making of Korea*, PhD Thesis, University of California, Los Angeles.

Kim, Chulsoo (1996) "Determinants of the Timing of Social Policy Adoption", *Journal of Sociology and Social Welfare*, 33: 3, pp. 5–29.

Kim, Jeong-Ho and Geun-Yong Kim (1998) *A Comprehensive Overview of Housing Policies*, Seoul: Korea Research Institute of Human Settlements.

Kim, Joon-Hyung (1997) *Economic Policy-Making In Korea: Policy Change In Turbulent Times*, PhD Thesis, The George Washington University.

Kim, Kyong-Dong (1994) "Confucianism and Capitalist Development in East Asia", Leslie Sklair (ed.), *Capitalism and Development*, London: New York, Routledge.

Kim, Kyung Hwan (1993) "Housing Prices, Affordability, and Government Policy in Korea", *Journal of Real Estate Finance and Economics*, 6, pp. 55–71.

Kim, Manjae (1995) "Comparing Housing Policies in Tokyo and Seoul", *Korea Journal of Population and Development*, 24: 1, pp. 27–55.

Kim, Seong Sook (1995) "The Effectiveness of The Social Security System in Protecting The Poor: Republic of Korea", paper presented at *Expert Group Meeting on The Enhancement of Social Security for The Poor*, organised by ESCAP, Bangkok, 20–24 November 1995.

Kim, Woo-Jin (1997) *Economic Growth, Low Income and Housing in South Korea*, London: Macmillan.

Kim, Young-Hwa (2000) "Concurrent Development of Education Policy and Industrialization Strategies in Korea (1945–1995): A Historical Perspective", *Journal of Education and Work*, 13: 1, pp. 95–118.

King, Elizabeth and J. B. G. Tilak (1997) "Lessons from Cost Recovery in Education", Christopher Colclough (ed.), Marketizing Education and Health in Developing Countries: Miracle or Mirage?, Oxford: Clarendon Press, pp. 63–89.

Kitschelt, Herbert, Peter Lange, Gary Marks, and John Stephens (1999) "Convergence and Divergence in Advanced Capitalist Democracies", Herbert Kitschelt (ed.), *Continuity And Change In Contemporary Capitalism*, New York: Cambridge University Press, pp. 427–461.

Korea (1996) *Yearbook of Health and Welfare Statistics 1996*, Seoul: Ministry of Health and Welfare.

Korea (2000) *Yearbook of Health and Welfare Statistics 1999*, Seoul: Ministry of Health and Welfare.

REFERENCES

Korea National Statistical Office (1999) *Social Indicators in Korea 1999*, Daejon: Author.
Korea, NHIC (1999) *National Health Insurance Statistical Yearbook 1999*, Seoul: National Health Insurance Corporation.
Korean Government, Ministry of Finance and Economy (2000) "Policy Measures to Improve Income Distribution", web publication: http://www.mofe.go.kr/cgi-pub/.
Ku, Yeun Wen (1997) *Welfare Capitalism in Taiwan: State, Economy and Social Policy*, Basingstoke: Macmillan.
Ku, Yeun Wen (1998) "Who Will Benefit? The Planning of National Pension Insurance in Taiwan", *Public Administration and Policy*, 7: 1, pp. 33–45.
Ku, Yeun Wen (2001) "To Be Or Not to Be A Taiwanese Welfare State: Lessons From Recent Experience", Catherine Jones Finer (ed.), *Comparing The Social Policy Experience of Britain and Taiwan*, Aldershot: Ashgate, pp. 27–49.
Kuhnle, Stein (2002) "Productive Welfare in Korea: Moving Towards a European Welfare State Type?", paper presented at ECPR Workshop on *The Welfare State: Pros and Cons*, Torino, Italy, 22–27 March 2002.
Kuznets, P. (1988) "An East Asian Model of Economic Development: Japan, Taiwan, and South Korea", *Economic Development and Cultural Change*, 36: s, pp. 11–43.
Kwon, Huck Ju (1997) "Beyond European Welfare Regimes: Comparative Perspectives on East Asian Welfare Systems", *Journal of Social Policy*, 26: 4, pp. 467–484.
Kwon, Huck Ju (1998) *The Welfare State in Korea: The Politics of Legitimation*, London: Macmillan.
Kwon, Huck Ju (1999) *Income Transfers to The Elderly in East Asia: Testing Asian Values*, CASE Paper 27, London: Centre for Analysis of Social Exclusion.
Kwon, Huck Ju (2001) "Income Transfers to The Elderly in Korea and Taiwan", *International Social Policy*, 30: 1, pp. 81–93.
Kwon, Huck Ju (2002) "Welfare Reform and Future Challenges in The Republic of Korea: Beyond The Developmental Welfare State?", *International Social Security Review*, 55: 4, pp. 23–35.
Kwon, Soonman (2003) "Healthcare Financing Reform and The New Single Payer System in The Republic of Korea: Social Solidarity Or Efficiency?", *International Social Security Review*, 56: 1, pp. 75–94.
La Grange, Adrienne and Frederik Pretorius (1999) *An Innate Desire for Home Ownership Or Markets at Work: A Case Study of Hong Kong*, Hong Kong: City University of Hong Kong.
La Grange, Adrienne and F. Pretorius (2002) "Private Rental Housing in Hong Kong", *Housing Studies*, 17: 5, pp. 721–740.
Law, Wing Wah (1997) "The Taiwanisation, Democratisation, and Internationalisation of Higher Education in Taiwan", W. O. Lee and Mark Bray (eds), *Education and Political Transition: Perspectives and Dimensions in East Asia*, Hong Kong: Comparative Education Research Centre, University of Hong Kong, pp. 50–67.
Lee, Chung H. (1990) "Culture and Institutions in the Economic Development of Korea", *Korean Studies*, 14, pp. 38–49.
Lee, James (1994) "Affordability, Home Ownership and The Middle Class Housing Crisis in Hong-Kong", *Policy and Politics*, 22: 3, pp. 179–189.
Lee, James K. C. (2000) "Balancing Collectivization and Individual Responsibility:

REFERENCES

Hong Kong Social Policy under the Chinese Regime", Kwong-Leung Tang (ed.), *Social Development in Asia*, Boston: Kluwer Academic, pp. 11–22.

Lee, J. K. C. and N. M. Yip (2001) "Home-Ownership Under Economic Uncertainty: The Role of Subsidised Sale Apartments in Hong Kong", *Third World Planning Review*, 23: 1, pp. 61–78.

Lee, Jisoon (2002) *Education Policy in the Republic of Korea: Building Block Or Stumbling Block?*, Washington, DC: IBRD and World Bank.

Lee, Ching-Kwan and Tak-sing Cheung (1992) "Egalitarianism and the Allocation of Secondary School Places in Hong Kong", Gerard A. Postiglione and Julian Leung Yat Ming (eds), *Education and Society in Hong Kong: Toward One Country and Two Systems*, Armonk, NY: M. E. Sharpe, pp. 145–165.

Lee, Jong-Wha (Undated) *Economic Growth and Human Development in The Republic of Korea, 1945–1992*, Occasional Paper 24, UNDP.

Lee, Kyubang and Juhyun Yoon (Undated) *Housing in Korea*, web publication: http://www.hitel.co.kr/~b5949205/country96.htm.

Lee, R. P. L. et al. (2000) "Living Arrangments and Elderly Care: The Case of Hong Kong", William Lee and Hal Kendig (eds), *Who Should Care for The Elderly? An East–West Value Divide*, Singapore: Singapore University Press, pp. 269–296.

Lee, Sungkyun (1997) *A Comparative Study of Welfare Programs for Old Age Income Security in Korea and Taiwan*, PhD Thesis, The University of Wisconsin, Madison.

Lee, William K. M. (1999) "Gender Differences in Ageing in Singapore: Poverty and Income Maintenance", *Social Development Issues*, 21: 3, pp. 31–40.

Lee, W. K. (2001) "The Feminization of Poverty Among The Elderly Population of Hong Kong", *Asian Journal of Women's Studies*, 7: 3, pp. 31–62.

Lee, Y., W. L. Parish, and R. J. Willis (1994) "Sons, Daughters, and Intergenerational Support in Taiwan", *American Journal of Sociology*, 99: 4, pp. 1010–1041.

Leong, Yee-tak Yvonne (1995) *Housing, Planning and Social Inequality in Hong Kong*, MSc (Urban Planning) Thesis, University of Hong Kong.

Leung, Sandra Ching Wah (1993) *An Evaluation of The Housing Subsidy Policy in Hong Kong*, MPA Thesis, University of Hong Kong.

Lewin, Keith M. (1998) "Education in Emerging Asia: Patterns, Policies, and Futures Into The 21st Century", *International Journal of Educational Development*, 18: 2, pp. 81–118.

Li, William D. H. (1998) *Housing in Taiwan: Agency and Structure?*, Brookfield, VT: Ashgate.

Lim, Kim-Lian (2001) "Implications of Singapore's CPF Scheme on Consumption Choices and Retirement", *Pacific Economic Review*, 6: 3, pp. 361–382.

Lim, Kim-Meng (2002) "Singapore's Medical Savings Accounts – Beyond Rhetoric and Doctrine to 'What Works': A Response From Singapore", *Journal of Health Politics, Policy and Law*, 27: 2, pp. 302–304.

Lin, Chu-Chia Steve (1993) "The Relationship Between Rents and Prices of Owner Occupied Housing in Taiwan", *Journal of Real Estate Finance and Economics*, 6, pp. 25–54.

Lin, Kuo-Ming (1997) *From Authoritarianism to Statism: The Politics of National Health Insurance in Taiwan*, PhD Thesis in Sociology, Yale University.

Lin, Tsoyu Calvin (1996) *Housing Finance and Subsidies: Lessons From Western and Asian Countries for Taiwan*, PhD Thesis, Texas A&M University.

Ling, L. H. M. and Chih yu Shih (1998) "Confucianism with a Liberal Face: The

Meaning of Democratic Politics in Postcolonial Taiwan", *The Review of Politics*, 60: 1: pp. 55-82.
Liu, Eva and S. Y. Yue (1998) *Health Care Expenditure and Financing in Hong Kong*, Provisional Legislative Council Secretariat, 22 January 1998.
Liu, Hong (1994) *Industrial Relations In the Four Newly Industrializing Countries In East Asia*, PhD Thesis, University of Illinois at Chicago.
Liu, King-Leung (1994) *Housing Problems in Hong Kong: A Critical Analysis*, Master of Housing Management, Hong Kong: University of Hong Kong.
Lockheed, Marlaine E. and Adriaan M. Verspoor (1989) *Improving Primary Education in Developing Countries*, Washington, DC: published for the World Bank, Oxford University Press.
Lockheed, M. E. and E. Jimenez (1994) *Public and Private Schools in Developing Countries: What Are The Differences and Why Do They Persist?*, HRO Working Paper No. 43, Washington, DC: World Bank.
Low, Linda and T. C. Aw (1997) *Housing A Healthy, Educated and Wealthy Nation Through The CPF*, Singapore: Times Academic Press for The Institute of Policy Studies.
Lui, Francis T. (1998) *Retirement Protection: A Plan for Hong Kong*, Hong Kong: Hong Kong Economic Policy Studies Series, published for The Hong Kong Centre for Economic Research by Hong Kong: City University of Hong Kong Press.
Lui, Hon-Kwong (1997) *Income Inequality and Economic Development*, Hong Kong: City University of Hong Kong Press.
McCarthy, David *et al.* (2002) "Asset Rich and Cash Poor: Retirement Provision and Housing Policy in Singapore", *Journal of Pension Economics and Finance*, 1: 3, pp. 197–222.
McGinn, Noel F. (1980) *Education and Development in Korea: Studies of the Modernization of the Republic of Korea 1945–1975*, Harvard East Asian Monographs No. 90, Harvard University Press.
McLaughlin, E. (1993) "Hong Kong: A Residual Welfare Regime", Allan Cochrane and John Clarke (eds), *Comparing Welfare States: Britain in the International Context*, London: Sage, chapter 5.
McMahon, Walter W. (1999) *Education and Development: Measuring the Social Benefits*, Oxford: Oxford University Press.
Macpherson, Stewart (1993) "Social Security in Hong Kong", *Social Policy and Administration*, 27: 1, pp. 50–57.
Mahoney, James (2000) "Path Dependence in Historical Sociology", *Theory and Society*, 29: 4, pp. 507–548.
Marshall, T. H. (1963) "Citizenship and Social Class", T. H. Marshall (ed.), *Sociology at The Crossroads and Other Essays*, London: Heinemann, pp. 67–127.
Martin, John P. and Raymond Torres (2000) "Korean Labour Market and Social Safety Net Reforms", *Journal of Korean Economy*, 1: 2, pp. 287–300.
Matthias Zeylmans (Undated) "'Welfare Capitalism' and 'Social Capitalism' – Comparing The Ideals of Welfare States", web publication: http://tiss.zdv.uni-tuebingen.de/webroot/sp/spsba01_w98_1/comparison.htm. (Visited 3 June 2003.)
Meyer, Alan D. (1982) "Adapting to Environmental Jolts", *Administrative Science Quarterly*, 27, pp. 515–537.
Miles, D. (1994) *Housing, Financial Markets and The Wider Economy*, Chichester: John Wiley.

REFERENCES

Milner, Helen V. and Robert O. Keohane (1996) "Internationalization and Domestic Politics: An Introduction", Robert O. Keohane and Helen V. Milner (eds), *Internationalization and Domestic Politics*, Cambridge: Cambridge University Press, pp. 3–24.

Mingat, Alain and Jee-Peng Tan (1998) *The Mechanics of Progress in Education: Evidence From Cross-Country Data*, Policy Research Working Paper WPS 2015, Washington, DC: World Bank.

Mo, Jongryon (1996) "Political Learning and Democratic Consolidation: Korean Industrial Relations, 1987–1992", *Comparative Political Studies*, 29: 3, pp. 290–311.

Mo, Jongryon and Chung-In Moon (1998) *Democracy and the Korean Economic Crisis*, The Nautilus Institute.

Mo, Jongryon and Chung-In Moon (1999) "Democracy and the Origins of the 1997 Korean Economic Crisis", Mo, Jongryon and Chung-In Moon (eds), *Democracy and The Korean Economy*, Stanford: Hoover Institution Press, pp. 171–198.

Mok, Henry T. K. (2000) "Averting The Old Age Crisis: Problems of The Privately Managed Mandatory Provident Fund Scheme", *The Asian Journal of Public Administration*, 22: 1, pp. 33–55.

Mok, Ka-Ho (1997) *The Cost of Managerialism: The Implications for The "Macdonalisation" of Higher Education in Hong Kong*, Public Administration and Social Administration Working Paper Series No. 1997/6, Hong Kong: Department of Public and Social Administration, City University of Hong Kong.

Mok, Ka-Ho (2000) "Reflecting Globalization Effects on Local Policy: Higher Education Reform in Taiwan", *Journal of Education Policy*, 15: 6, pp. 637–660.

Morris, Paul (1996) "Asia's Four Little Tigers", *Comparative Education*, 32: 1, pp. 95–109.

MPFA (2001) *Annual Report 2000–2001*, Hong Kong: Mandatory Provident Funds Authority.

Mukhopadhaya, P. (2000) "Education Policies As Means To Tackle Income Disparity: The Singapore Case", *International Journal of Sociology and Social Policy*, 20: 11/12, pp. 59–73.

Na, Seong-Lin and Hyung-Pyo Moon (1999) *Social Impact of Current Economic Crisis in Korea*, Unspecified.

Nakajima, Mineo (1994) "Economic Development in East Asia and Confucian Ethics", *Social Compass*, 41: 1, pp. 113–119.

National Pension Corporation (1997) *National Pension Statistics Yearbook 1996*, Seoul: Author.

Nations: "The Effect of Noncash Subsidies for Health, Education and Housing", *Review of Income and Wealth*, 39, pp. 229–256.

NFMI (1997) *Outline of The Medical Insurance System in Korea*, Seoul: National Federation of Medical Insurance.

Norton, Andy *et al.* (2000) *Social Protection Concepts and Approaches: Implications for Policy and Practice in International Development*, Working Paper, Centre for Aid and Public Expenditure, Overseas Development Institute.

O'Connor, James (1988) "Convergence or Divergence? Change in Welfare State Effort in OECD Countries, 1960–1980", *European Journal of Political Research*, 16, pp. 277–299.

OECD (1999) *OECD Social Expenditure Database 1980–1996*, CD-ROM, Paris: Author.

OECD (1999a) *Review of National Policies For Education: Korea*, Paris: OECD.

REFERENCES

OECD (2000) *Reforms for an Ageing Society*, Paris: Organisation for Economic Cooperation and Development.
OECD (2000a) *OECD in Figures 2000*, Paris: OECD.
OECD (2001) *OECD in Figures 2001*, Paris: OECD.
OECD (2002) *Social Expenditure Database 1980–1998*, 3rd Edition, Paris: Organisation for Economic Cooperation and Development.
OECD (2002a) *Review of The Korean Health Care System*, Paris: OECD.
OECD (2003) *Financing Education: Investments and Returns: Analysis of the World Education Indicators 2002*, Paris: Organisation for Economic Cooperation and Development.
OECD (2003a) *OECD Economic Surveys: Korea*, Paris: Organisation for Economic Cooperation and Development.
Ogawa, Naohira and Gavin W. Jones (eds) (1993) *Human Resources in Development Along the Asia Pacific Region*, Singapore: Oxford University Press.
Orszag, Peter R. and Joseph E. Stiglitz (1999) "Rethinking Pension Reform: Ten Myths About Social Security Systems", paper presented at *New Ideas About Old Age Security*, World Bank, Washington, DC, 14–15 September, 1999.
Ou, Yongsheng (1999) "Educational Reform Advancing Towards the New Century – Taipei Experience", speech at the Hong Kong Central Policy Unit seminar on *Basic Education – Latest Developments in Shanghai, Singapore and Taipei*, 21 May 1999.
Paik, Sung Joon (1995) *Educational Finance in Korea: Its Development and General Assessment*, Seoul: Korean Educational Development Institute.
Palacios, Robert and Montserrat Pallarès-Miralles (2000) *International Patterns of Pension Provision*, World Bank, web publication: http://www.worldbank.org/pensions.
Palley, Howard A. and Chikako Usui (1995) "Social Policies for The Elderly in The Republic of Korea and Japan: A Comparative Perspective", *Social Policy and Administration*, 29: 3, pp. 241–257.
Park, Bae-Gyoon (1998) "Where Do Tigers Sleep at Night? The State's Role in Housing Policy in South Korea and Singapore", *Economic Geography*, 74, pp. 272–289.
Park, Byung Hyun (1990) The Development of Social Welfare Institutions in East Asia: Case Studies of Japan, Korea, and People's Republic of China, DSW Thesis, University of Pennsylvania.
Park, Chan-Ung (1997) *Institutional Legacies and State Power: The First State Health Insurance Movements in Great Britain, The United States, and Korea*, PhD Thesis, The University of Chicago.
Parrott, A. (2000) "The Singapore Social Security Experience: Is There a Lesson for The UK and The Rest of The World?", *Insurance Research and Practice*, 15: 2, pp. 14–27.
Patrinos, Harry Anthony (Undated) *Notes On Education and Growth: Theory and Evidence*, World Bank, web publication: http://www.worldbank.org/html/extdr/hnp/hddflash/hcwp/hrwp036.html.
Pauly, Mark V. (2001) "Savings Accounts in Singapore: What Can We Know?", *Journal of Health Politics, Policy and Law*, 26: 4, pp. 727–731.
Pauly, Mark V. and John Goodman (1995) "Tax Credits for Health Insurance and Medical Savings Accounts", *Health Affairs*, 14, pp. 126–139.
Peabody, John W. *et al.* (1995) "Health for All in The Republic of Korea: One

REFERENCES

Country's Experience With Implementing Universal Health Care", *Health Policy*, 31, pp. 29–42.

Peabody, John W. *et al.* (1999) *Policy and Health: Implications for Development in Asia*, Cambridge: Cambridge University Press.

Pei, Minxin (1998) "Democratization In The Greater China Region", *Access Asian Review*, 1: 2.

Pfaff, Martin (1990) "Differences in Health Care Spending Across Countries: Statistical Evidence", *Journal of Health Politics, Policy and Law*, 15, pp. 1–24.

Phang, Sock-Yong (2001) "Housing Policy, Wealth Formation, and The Singapore Economy", *Housing Studies*, 16: 4, pp. 443–459.

Phua, Kai Hong (1990) *Privatization and Restructuring of Health Services in Singapore*, Singapore: Institute of Policy Studies.

Post, D. (1993) "Educational Attainment and The Role of The State in Hong Kong", *Comparative Education Review*, 37, pp. 240–262.

Post, David (1996) "The Massification of Education in Hong Kong: Effects On The Equality of Opportunity, 1981–1991", *Sociological Perspectives*, 39: Spring, pp. 155–174.

Powell, Martin and Armando Barrientos (2002) *Theory and Method in the Welfare Modelling Business*, paper presented to COST A15 conference, Oslo, 5–6 April 2002.

Prescott, Nicholas and Len Nichols (1997) "International Comparison of Medical Savings Accounts", paper presented at *Financing Health Care and Old Age Security*, Organised by the Institute of Policy Studies and the World Bank, Singapore, 8 November 1997.

Priemus, Hugo (1997) "Growth and Stagnation in Social Housing: What Is 'Social' in The Social Rented Sector?", *Housing Studies*, 12: 4, pp. 549–560.

Pryor, F. L. (1968) *Public Expenditures in Communist and Capitalist Nations*, Homewood, Illinois: R. D. Irwin.

Psacharopoulos, George (1994) "Returns To Investment in Education", *World Development*, 22: 9, pp. 1325–1343.

Puiggros, Adriana (1997) "World Bank Education Policy: Market Liberalism Meets Ideological Conservatism", *International Journal of Health Services*, 27: 2, pp. 217–226.

Purcal, John T. (1995) "Economic Growth and Social Engineering in Health in Singapore", Paul Cohen and John T. Purcal (eds), *Health and Development in South East Asia*, Canberra: Australian Development Studies Network, pp. 77–102.

Quah, May Ling *et al.* (1995) "Home and Parental Influences on The Achievement of Lower Primary School Children in Singapore", *Singapore Journal of Education*, 15: 2, pp. 12–32.

Ramesh, M. (1995) "Social Security in South Korea and Singapore: Explaining The Differences", *Social Policy and Administration*, 30: 3, pp. 228–240.

Ramesh, M. (2000) "The Politics Of Social Security In Singapore", *The Pacific Review*, 13: 3, pp. 242ff.

Ramesh, M. with Mukul Asher (2000) *Welfare Capitalism in Southeast Asia: Social Security, Health, and Education Policies in Indonesia, Malaysia, The Philippines, Singapore, and Thailand*, Basingstoke: Macmillan.

Rieger, Elmar and Stephan Leibfried (2003) "Limits to Globalisation in the Age of Welfare Democracies", New York: Blackwell.

ROC, Council of Labor Affairs (2003) *Monthly Bulletin of Labor Statistics*, No. 124.

REFERENCES

ROC, Department of Health (2000) *Health and Vital Statistics*, Taipei, Taiwan: Author.

ROC, Ministry of Education (2002) *Education Statistics of The Republic of China 2001*, Taipei: Author.

ROC, Ministry of Interior (1999) *Statistical Yearbook of Interior 1999*, Taipei: Author.

ROC, Ministry of Interior (2000) *Report on The Old Age Survey, Taiwan Area, 2000*, Taipei: Author.

Rodan, Garry (ed.) (1996) *Political Oppositions in Industrialising Asia*, London: Routledge.

Rodan, Garry (1997) "Singapore in 1996: Extended Election Fever", *Asian Survey*, 37, pp. 175.

Root, Hilton L. (1996) *Small Countries, Big Lessons: Governance and The Rise of Asia*, New York: Oxford University Press.

Rozman, G. (ed.) (1991) *The East Asian Region: Confucian Heritage and Its Modern Adaptation*, Princeton: Princeton University Press.

Scheil-Adlung, Xenia (1998) "Steering The Healthcare Ship: Effects of Market Incentives to Control Costs in Selected OECD Countries", *International Social Security Review*, 51: 1, pp. 103–135.

Schieber, George J., Jean-Pierre Poullier, and Leslie M. Greenwald (1991) "Health Care Systems in Twenty-Four Countries", *Health Affairs*, Fall, pp. 22–38.

Schiffer, Jonathan R. (1991) "State Policy and Economic Growth: A Note on The Hong Kong Model", *International Journal of Urban and Regional Research*, 15: 2, pp. 180–196.

Schmitter, P. C. (1982) "Reflections on Where The Theory of Neo-Corporatism Has Gone and Where The Praxis of Neo-Corporatism May Be Going", G. Lehmbruch and P. C. Schmitter (eds), *Patterns of Corporatist Policy Making*, London: Sage, pp. 259–279.

Schneider, S. K. (1982) "The Sequential Development of Social Programs in Eighteen Welfare States", *Comparative Social Research*, 5, 195–219.

Selvaratnam, Viswanathan (1994) *Innovations in Higher Education: Singapore at The Competitive Edge*, World Bank Technical Paper No. 222, Asia Technical Department Series, Washington, DC: World Bank.

Shan, Peter Wen-Jing and Jason Chien-Chen Chang (2000) "Social Change and Educational Development in Taiwan, 1945–1999", Tony Townsend and Yin Cheong Cheng (eds), *Educational Change and Development in The Asia-Pacific Region: Challenges for The Future*, Exton, PA: Swets & Zeitlinger Publishers, pp. 185–206.

Shantakumar, C. (1995) "Ageing and Social Policy in Singapore", *Ageing International*, 22: 2, p. 49.

Sherraden, Michael *et al.* (1995) "Social Policy Based on Assets: The Impact of Singapore's Central Provident Fund", *Asian Journal of Political Science*, 3: 2, pp. 112–133.

Shin, Dong-Myeon (2000) "Economic Policy and Social Policy: Policy-Linkages in an Era of Globalisation", *International Journal of Social Welfare*, 9: 1, pp. 17–30.

Shin, Eui Hang (1999) "Social Change, Political Elections, and The Middle Class in Korea", *East Asia*, 17, pp. 2828–2860.

Shin, R. W. (1995) "The Private Provision of Capital for Public Housing Development: A Cost-Benefit Study of The Seoul Housing Project", *Public Administration and Development*, 15, pp. 53–73.

REFERENCES

Sim, Loo Lee, Lim Lan Yuan, and Tay Kah Poh (1993) "Shelter for All: Singapore's Strategy for Full Home Ownership By The Year 2000", *Habitat International*, 17, pp. 85–102.

Singapore (1993) *Affordable Health Care: A White Paper*, Singapore: Ministry of Health.

Singapore (1999) *Singapore Statistical Highlights 1999*, Singapore: Department of Statistics.

Singapore (2000) *Ministry of Health: Annual Report 2000*, Singapore: Government Printing Office.

Singapore Department of Statistics (1998) *Yearbook of Statistics, Singapore 1998*, Singapore: Author.

Singapore Department of Statistics (1999) *Income, Expenditure, Saving and Investment of The Household Sector*, Occasional Paper on Economic Statistics, Singapore: Department of Statistics.

Singapore Department of Statistics (2000) *Is Income Disparity Increasing in Singapore?*, Occasional Paper on Social Statistics, Singapore: Department of Statistics.

Singapore Department of Statistics (2001) *Yearbook of Statistics, Singapore 2000*, Singapore: Author.

Singapore Government (Various years) *The Budget for The Financial Year*, Singapore: Singapore National Printers.

Singapore Ministry of Education (2001) *Education Statistics Digest*, Singapore: Ministry of Education, Education Statistics Section.

Smart, Alan (1992) *Making Room: Squatter Clearance in Hong Kong*, Hong Kong: Center of Asian Studies, University of Hong Kong.

Smeeding, Timothy M. and Peter Saunders (1998) *How Do The Elderly in Taiwan Fare Cross-Nationally? Evidence From The Luxembourg Income Study (LIS) Project*, Working Paper No. 183, Maxwell School of Citizenship and Public Affairs, Syracuse University.

Smeeding, Timothy et al. (1993) "Poverty, Inequality, and Family Living Standards Impacts across Seven Nations: The Effect of Noncash Subsidies for Health, Education and Housing", *Review of Income and Wealth*, 39, pp. 229–256.

Smith, Peter (2002) "Developing Composite Indicators for Assessing Health System Efficiency", OECD (ed.), *Measuring Up: Improving Health System Performance in OECD Countries*, Paris: OECD.

So, Alvin Y. and Shiping Hua (1992) "Democracy as an Antisystemic Movement in Taiwan, Hong Kong, and China: A World Systems Analysis", *Sociological Perspectives*, 35, pp. 385–404.

Song, Byung Nak (1990) *The Rise of the Korean Economy*, Hong Kong: Oxford University Press.

Sorensen, C. W. (1994) "Success and Education in South Korea", *Comparative Education Review*, 38, pp. 10–35.

Starling, Jay D. (1975) "The Use of Systems Constructs in Simplifying Organized Social Complexity", T. R. La Porte (ed.), *Organized Social Complexity: Challenge to Politics and Policy*, Princeton: Princeton University Press, pp. 131–172.

Statistics Singapore (2001) *Singapore Census of Population 2000*, Advance Data Release No. 6, Households and Housing, Singapore: Department of Statistics.

Sum, Ngai-Ling (1998) "Theorizing Export-Oriented Economic Development in East Asian Newly-Industrializing Countries: A Regulationist Perspective", I. Cook (ed.), *Dynamic Asia*, Aldershot: Ashgate.

REFERENCES

Sum, Ngai-Ling (2000) *Varieties of Capitalism in Time and Space: "Embedded Exportism" and Its Governance in Hong Kong and Taiwan*, Seoul: Korea Labor Institute, web publication: http://www.kli.re.kr/news/pdf/2.16%20ngai-ling%20sum.pdf.

Sun, Way (1998) *Human Resources Policies and Labor Market Outcomes in Taiwan: The Impact of Higher Educational Planning Since the 1970s*, PhD Thesis, University of Maryland, Baltimore.

Swank, Duane (1998) "Finding The Welfare State: Global Capital and The Taxation of Business in Advanced Market Economies", *Political Studies*, 46: 4, pp. 671–691.

Synott, J. P. (1995) "The German Origins of The South Korean National Charter of Education", *Journal of East and West Studies*, 24: 1, pp. 35–48.

Tan, Lee Lee (1997) "Health Insurance for The Average Singaporeans", Tan Teck Meng and Chew Soon Beng (eds), *Affordable Health Care: Issues and Prospects*, Singapore: Prentice Hall, pp. 294–315.

Tan, Jason (1993) "The Independent Schools Scheme in Singapore and the Direct Subsidy Scheme in Hong Kong: A Comparison of Two Privatization Initiatives", Mark Bray (ed.), *The Economics and Financing of Education: Hong Kong and Comparative Perspectives*, Hong Kong: Faculty of Education, University of Hong Kong, pp. 79–95.

Tan, Jason (1997) "Education and Colonial Transition in Singapore and Hong Kong: Comparisons and Contrasts", *Comparative Education*, 33: 2, pp. 303–312.

Tan, Sook Yee (1998) *Private Ownership of Public Housing in Singapore*, Singapore: Times Academic Press.

Tang, Kwong-Leung (1997) "Noncontributory Pensions in Hong Kong: An Alternative to Social Security?", James Midgley and Michael Sherraden (eds), *Alternatives to Social Security: An International Inquiry*, Westport, CI: Auburn House, pp. 61–74.

Tang, Kwong-Leung (1998) *Colonial State and Social Policy: Social Welfare Development in Hong Kong 1842–1997*, Lanham, MD: University Press of America.

Tang, Kwong-Leung (2000) *Social Welfare Development in East Asia*, New York: St Martin's Press.

Tang, Wen-Hui Anna (1997) *Explaining Social Policy In Taiwan Since 1949: State, Politics, And Gender*, PhD Thesis, Harvard University.

Thompson, Lawrence (2001) "Operation of Pension Systems: Public Or Private?", Isabel Ortiz (ed.), *Social Protection in Asia and The Pacific*, Manila: ADB, pp. 235–256.

Thornton, William H. (1998) "Korea and East Asian Exceptionalism", *Theory, Culture and Society*, 15: 2, pp. 137–154.

Tilak, J. B. G. (1989) *Education and Its Relation To Economic Growth, Poverty, and Income Distribution: Past Evidence and Further Analysis*, World Bank Discussion Paper 46, Washington, DC: World Bank.

Tilak, Jandhyala B. G. (2001) *Building Human Capital – What Others Can Learn*, WBI Working Paper No. 22717, Washington, DC: World Bank.

Titmuss, R. (1958) *Essays on the Welfare State*, London: Allen and Unwin.

Titmuss, Richard M. (1974) *Social Policy: An Introduction*, London: George Allen and Unwin.

Tsay, Jen-Huoy (1998) *Risk Reduction, Income Redistribution, and The Financing of National Health Insurance: An Examination of The Taiwanese Case*, PhD Thesis, Columbia University.

REFERENCES

Tse, Kin-Lop (1998) *The Denationalization and Depoliticization of Education in Hong Kong, 1945–1992*, PhD Thesis, University of Wisconsin, Madison.

Tsui, Amy B. M. *et al.* (1999) "Which Agenda? Medium of Instruction Policy in Post-1997 Hong Kong", *Language Culture and Curriculum*, 12: 3, pp. 196–214.

Tsui, Steve Waicho (2002) "Reforming The Pension System in Taiwan", paper presented at international symposium on *Pension Reforms in Asian Countries*, organised by Hitosubashi University, Tokyo, 1–2 February 2002.

Tu, Wei Ming (1989) "The Confucian Dimension in The East Asian Development Model", paper presented at *Confucianism and Economic Development in East Asia*, Taipei, 29–31 May 1989.

Turner, H. A. *et al.* (1991) *Between Two Societies: Hong Kong Labour in Transition*, Hong Kong: Centre of Asian Studies, University of Hong Kong.

UNCTAD (2002) *World Investment Report 2001*, Geneva: United Nations Conference on Trade and Development.

UNDP (2002) *Human Development Indicators 2002*, Geneva: UNDP, web publication: http://hdr.undp.org/reports/global/2002/en/indicator/indicator.cfm?file=indic_283_1_1.html.

UNESCO (1993) *World Education Report 1993: Overcoming The Knowledge Gap Expanding Educational Choice Searching for Standards*, Paris: Author.

UNESCO (2001) *World Education Report 2000*, Paris: United Nations Educational, Scientific and Cultural Organization.

UNU/WIDER and UNDP/SEPED (1999) *World Income Inequality Database (WIID)*, web publication: http://www.undp.org/poverty/initiatives/wider/wiid.htm.

Uusitalo, Hannu (1984) "Comparative Research on The Determinants of The Welfare State: The State of The Art", 12, pp. 403–422.

Vasoo, S. and J. Lee (2001) "Singapore: Social Development, Housing and The Central Provident Fund", *International Journal of Social Welfare*, 10: 4, pp. 276–283.

Wad, Peter (1999) *Social Development in East Asia. Warfare, Workfare, Welfare?*, unpublished paper presented at the conference *Globalization and Social Welfare in East and Southeast Asia*, DIR, Aalborg University, March 1999.

Walford, Geoffrey (2001) "Privatization in Industrialized Countries", Henry M. Levin (ed.), *Privatizing Education: Can The Marketplace Deliver Choice, Efficiency, Equity, and Social Cohesion?*, Boulder: Westview, pp. 178–202.

Wang, George Cheng (2001) "Financing Health Care for Middle-to-Low-Income Households in Taiwan", Catherine Jones Finer (ed.), *Comparing The Social Policy Experience of Britain and Taiwan*, Aldershot: Ashgate, pp. 139–158.

Watson, Laura (1998) "Labor Relations and The Law in South Korea", *Pacific Rim Law and Policy Journal*, 7: 1, pp. 229–247.

Weil, Diana E. Cooper *et al.* (1990) *The Impact of Development Policies On Health*, Geneva: World Health Organization.

Weiss, Linda and John M. Hobson (1995) *States and Economic Development: A Comparative Historical Analysis*, Cambridge, MA: Polity Press.

Wen, Simon Chu Hsun (1988) *A Cross-National Study of Housing Development in Asian Transitional Countries: Hong Kong, Korea (South), Singapore and Taiwan*, PhD Thesis, University of Michigan.

West, Edwin G. (1995) *Education With and Without The State*, Human Capital Development Paper 61, web publication: www.worldbank.org/html/extdr/hnp/hddflash/workp/wp_00061.html.

White, Gordon and Roger Goodman (1998) "Welfare Orientalism and the Search for an East Asian Welfare Model", Roger Goodman *et al.* (eds), *The East Asian Welfare Model: Welfare Orientalism and the State*, London, New York: Routledge, pp. 3–24.
Wildeboer Schut, J. M. *et al.* (2001) *On Worlds of Welfare*, The Hague: Social and Cultural Planning Office.
Wilensky, H. L. (1975) *The Welfare State and Equality: Structural and Ideological Roots of Public Expenditures*, Berkeley: University of California Press.
Wilensky, H. and C. Lebeaux (1958) *Industrial Society and Social Welfare*, New York: Russell Sage Foundation.
Wong, Chack Kie (1997) "Attitudes of Hong Kong Chinese to State Welfare Intervention: A Study of The Relation Between Economic Growth and Welfare State Programs", *Social Development Issues*, 19, p. 55.
Wong, Chack Kie *et al.* (2002) "Neither Welfare State Nor Welfare Society: The Case of Hong Kong", *Social Policy and Society*, 1: 4, pp. 285–292.
Wong, Daniel and Park Donghyun (1997) "The Adequacy of CPF for Old Age Support", Jon D. Kendall *et al.* (eds), *East Asian Economic Issues*, Singapore: World Scientific Pub. Co.
Wong, John and Aline Wong (1989) *Confucian Values as a Social Framework for Singapore's Economic Development*, Taipei: Chung-Hua Institution for Economic Research.
Wong, Yue-Chim Richard (1998) *On Privatizing Public Housing*, Hong Kong: City University of Hong Kong Press.
Wong May-Ling, Margaret (1995) *A Critical Analysis of The Recommendations of Pressure Groups On Public Housing Policy in Hong Kong*, Master of Housing Management Thesis, Hong Kong: University of Hong Kong.
World Bank (1993) *The East Asian Miracle: Economic Growth and Public Policy*, World Bank Policy Research Report, Oxford: Oxford University Press.
World Bank (1993a) *Housing: Enabling Markets to Work*, World Bank Policy Paper, Washington, DC: World Bank.
World Bank (1994) A*verting The Old Age Crisis: Policies to Protect The Old and Promote Growth*, Oxford: Oxford University Press.
World Bank (1995) *Priorities and Strategies for Education: A World Bank Review*, Washington, DC: World Bank.
World Bank (2000) *The Korean Pension System at a Crossroads*, Report No. 20404-KO, Korea Country Management Unit, East Asia and Pacific Region.
Yang, Bong Min (1991) "Health Insurance in Korea: Opportunities and Challenges", *Health Policy and Planning*, 6: 2, pp. 119–129.
Yang, Bong Min (1997) "The Role of Health Insurance in The Growth of The Private Sector in Korea", William Newbrander (ed.), *Private Health Sector Growth in Asia: Issues and Implications*, Chichester: John Wiley and Sons, pp. 61–81.
Yang, Shen-Keng (2001) "Dilemmas of Education Reform in Taiwan: Internationalization or Localization?", paper presented at the *2001 Annual Meeting of the Comparative and International Education Society*, Washington, DC, 13–17 March 2001.
Yee, Albert H. (1995) "Higher Education in Hong Kong", Albert H. Yee (ed.), *East Asian Higher Education: Traditions and Transformations*, Oxford: Oxford University Press, pp. 36–54.
Yeo, Soek Lee (2001) *Educational Upgrading Through External Degree Program*, Occasional Paper, Singapore: Statistics Singapore.

REFERENCES

Yip, Ngai-ming and Lau, Kwok-yu (1997) "Housing", Paul Wilding *et al.* (ed.), *Social Policy in Hong Kong*, Cheltenham: Edward Elgar, pp. 39–54.

Yoo, Il Ho (1993) "Pension Policy in Korea", Lawrence B. Krause and Fun-Koo Park (eds), *Social Issues in Korea: Korean and American Perspectives*, Seoul: Korea Development Institute, pp. 483–516.

Yoo, Jae-Hyn (Undated) "The Korean 'Chonsei' Rental System: Effective Or Defective Response?", paper presented at *Symposium On Prospect On Housing Policy and Technology Development for The 21st Century*, Seoul.

Yoon, Il Seong (1994) *Housing in A Newly Industrialised Economy: The Case of South Korea*, Aldershot: Avebury.

Young, Kim (1999) "Korea – Health Care Insurance Market", *FT Asia Intelligence Wire*, 30 July 1999.

Zeigler, Harmon (1988) *Pluralism, Corporatism, and Confucianism: Political Association and Conflict Regulation in the United States, Europe, and Taiwan*, Philadelphia: Temple University Press.

Zeylmans, Matthias (Undated) "Welfare Capitalism and Social Capitalism – Comparing The Ideals of Welfare States", web publication: http://tiss.zdv.uni-tuebingen.de/webroot/sp/spsba01_w98_1/comparison.htm.

Zhang, Xin Xiang (1993) *Education as a Vehicle for Social Stratificational Change: The Case of Singapore*, Working Paper No. 118, Singapore: Department of Sociology, National University of Singapore.

INDEX

Aged 8, 10, 15, 33, 35, 38, 39, 42, 43, 45, 46, 47, 48, 49, 54, 56, 58, 59, 60, 61, 68, 71, 72, 73, 74, 75, 76, 77, 78, 79, 80, 81, 82, 93, 96, 101, 108, 116, 184, 194, 198, 199; living arrangements 73, 74–75, 76–77, 79, 81; poverty 73, 75, 76–77, 78–79, 80–82
Ageing 32, 33, 38, 82, 4, 11, 84, 89, 112, 114
Agriculture 15, 20, 21, 44, 55, 57, 58, 60, 61, 64, 68, 78, 93, 103, 111
Aims and Policy for Social Welfare in Hong Kong 39
Authoritarianism 9, 12, 164
Autonomous schools, Singapore 160, 167

Britain 3, 9, 10, 11, 24, 30, 33, 39, 42, 46, 81, 86, 88, 89, 115, 122, 139, 155, 189, 194, 196
Brocklehurst Report, Singapore 43
Budget balance 23–24
Buy or Rent Option (BRO), Hong Kong 121

Caine Report, Singapore 43
Central Provident Fund (CPF), Singapore 11, 28, 42, 43, 52, 53, 54, 59, 63, 64, 69, 71, 73, 74, 80, 83, 90, 122, 131, 135, 138, 147, 198; *see also* Income Maintenance, Defined Contribution (DC)
Chen Shui-bian 48
Chiang Kai Shek 127
Chief Executive, Hong Kong 9, 10, 88
China, People's Republic of 10, 15, 42, 46, 49, 58, 72, 118, 128, 142, 149, 155, 156, 157, 158, 164, 186, 196

Chonsei 147, 148
Civil Servants *see* Government employees
Civil Service Pension Reserve Fund (CSPRF), Taiwan 42
Commission for Promoting Education Reform, Taiwan 165
Comprehensive Social Security Assistance Scheme (CSSA), Hong Kong 39, 41, 49, 50, 59, 60, 69, 71, 72, 80, 99
Confucianism 2, 4, 5
Conservatism 5, 17, 192, 193, 194, 195
Corporatism 3, 193
Council for Economic Planning and Development (CEPD), Taiwan 48
Council for Labour Affairs, Taiwan 14, 47
Council on Education Reform, Taiwan 165
CPF Approved Housing Scheme, Singapore 122
Culture 4, 5, 95, 161, 164, 199
Current account 28, 29, 35, 67

Delivery of Medical Services in Hospitals, Hong Kong 88
Democracy 3, 9, 12, 13, 15, 36, 89, 189, 192, 194, 197
Democratic Progressive Party (DPP), Taiwan 14, 15, 197
Demography 4, 16, 18, 31, 32, 33, 38, 116, 169
Development of Medical Services in Hong Kong 87
Development of Senior Secondary and Tertiary Education, 1978, Hong Kong 156

INDEX

Direct Subsidy schools (DSS), Hong Kong 157, 166, 171
Disability 37, 43, 44, 47, 49, 51, 53, 56, 57, 71

Economic competitiveness 7, 8, 153, 158, 161, 190, 195
Economic crisis 10, 14, 45, 56, 66, 101, 119, 121, 126, 130, 143, 196
Economic development 1, 3, 6, 11, 13, 139, 140, 141, 153, 154, 162, 164, 170, 171, 173, 175, 181, 186, 190, 191, 197
Economic Planning Board (EPB), Korea 162
Economy: growth 2, 4, 5, 8, 10, 18, 19, 21, 34, 35, 39, 70, 72, 101, 153, 154, 197; Gross Fixed Capital Formation (GFCF) 136, 137, 139, 141; income distribution 21–22; 180, 182, income growth 18–19, 38; inflation 22, 101, 116, 118, 126, 127, 129, 190; sectoral distribution 19–21; unemployment 2, 4, 14, 15, 19, 38, 42, 43, 45, 46, 47, 50, 54, 55, 56, 57, 58, 62, 64, 66, 67, 69, 71, 72, 74, 76, 77, 79, 82, 92, 188, 189
Education policy: rationale 153–154; role of state and market 153–154
Education: and economic development 153–154; compulsory 156, 161, 164, 165, 169, 179, 184; costs 185; *see also* Education, Teachers' salary; enrolment 111, 156, 162, 164, 166, 167, 168, 169, 170, 171, 178, 179, 180, 181, 182, 183, 184, 185; equity 179, 180, 181, 182, 184, 186; expenditures 172–178; financing arrangements 171–174; higher 10, 17, 53, 95, 96, 154, 157, 159, 161, 162, 163, 164, 165, 166, 167, 168, 169, 170, 172, 173, 174, 175, 176, 177, 178, 179, 180, 181, 182, 183, 184, 186, 187, 191, 195; illiteracy 184; language of instruction 155, 158, 159, 186; pre-school 158, 165, 166, 167, 170, 175, 176, 178, 180, 181, 183, 186; primary 154, 155, 156, 158, 161, 162, 163, 165, 166, 167, 169, 172, 173, 175, 176, 177, 178, 179, 180, 181, 182, 183, 185; private 47, 55, 154, 156, 157, 158, 160, 163, 166, 168, 169, 171, 172, 174, 181; public 154, 156, 160, 163, 168, 169, 174, 175; pupils' achievements 185; qualifications 178, 179, 181, 182, 184; secondary 9, 156, 157, 158, 159, 161, 162, 163, 165, 166, 167, 169, 170, 171, 172, 173, 174, 175, 176, 177, 178, 179, 180, 181, 182, 183, 186, 187, 191, 197, 198; social and economic benefits of 153–154
streaming in schools, Singapore 159, 161, 180; structure of national systems 158, 161–162, 163–164, 165–166; teachers' salary 177–178; tuition fees 154, 157, 160, 164, 167, 168, 171, 172, 173, 174, 175, 177; vocational 156, 159, 161, 162, 164, 165, 168, 169, 170, 173, 174, 177, 181, 182, 196
Edusave, Singapore 160
Elections 9, 11, 12, 13, 15, 128
Employees: informal 21, 35, 44, 47, 193; public 4, 9, 12, 42, 45, 47, 49, 51, 53, 54, 55, 56, 57, 59, 61, 62, 63, 64, 65, 66, 69, 72, 75, 76, 77, 78, 80, 83, 86, 94, 99, 100, 103, 107, 128, 134, 137, 188, 195, 196, 197; private 44, 47, 49, 51, 53, 54, 56, 57, 61, 69, 77, 92, 102, 103, 110, 128, 134
Employment Insurance, Korea *see* Income maintenance, unemployment benefits
English-speaking "family of nations" 194
Equity 17, 21, 22, 35, 41, 42, 83, 85, 89, 107, 108, 111, 139, 140, 141, 163, 179; *see also* Inequality
Esping-Andersen, Gosta 4, 16, 17, 192, 199
Europe 6, 7, 11, 86, 98, 122, 194,

Family 22, 68, 80, 192, 193, 194, 195, 196, 198
Farmers Insurance (FI), Taiwan 47, 57, 67, 69
Foreign direct investment (FDI) 11, 18, 29–31, 35

Germany 7, 59, 91, 92, 189, 192, 194
Gifted Education Programme, Singapore 160
Globalization 18, 21, 153, 158, 191
Gough, Ian 1, 5

225

INDEX

Government Employees Insurance (GEI), Taiwan 47, 56, 57, 61, 66, 67, 69, 77, 80, 93

Government Employees Pension (GEP), Korea 44, 54

Government Employees Retirement and Compensation Fund (GERCF), Taiwan 47, 57, 67, 68, 77

Government: public expenditure 3, 4, 5, 10, 12, 15, 17, 23, 24, 25, 27, 29, 31, 33, 35, 42, 62, 64, 66, 70, 71, 78, 99, 100, 101, 103, 109, 114, 115, 118, 136, 138, 139, 142, 153, 156, 164, 172, 173, 174, 175, 176, 177, 185, 187, 191, 194; public expenditure, social policies 25–29; revenue 13, 23, 25, 35, 63, 89, 163, 173, non-tax 24–25, tax 11, 24, 74; subsidy 37, 47, 58, 67, 69, 78, 89, 90, 91, 95, 96, 99, 100, 101, 102, 103, 104, 106, 107, 108, 109, 117, 119, 120, 121, 123, 125, 128, 129, 131, 134, 135, 136, 137, 138, 139, 145, 154, 156, 157, 160, 163, 165, 168, 172, 180, 189, 190; tax benefits 11, 43, 45, 53, 56, 63, 71, 74, 125, 127, 132, 135, 142, 190; *see also* subsidy

Harvard Report, Hong Kong *see* "*Improving Hong Kong's Health Care System: Why and For Whom?*"

Health Care Reform Committee, Korea 92

Health care 15, 39, 47, 50, 58, 68, 84, 85, 86, 87, 88, 89, 90, 91, 92, 94, 96, 97, 98, 100, 101, 103, 104, 108, 110, 112, 172; expenditure 99–105, co-payment 90, 94, 103, 104, 105, 106, 110, 111, 115, 189, out-of-pocket 17, 90, 100, 101, 102, 103, 104, 105, 108, 109, 173, 189; financing arrangements 104–107; hospital occupancy 90, 94, 96, 97; hospitals, private 94, 95, 96, 97, 98, 108, 110, 115; hospitals, public 85, 86, 88, 89, 90, 91, 94, 95, 96, 97, 99, 100, 104, 108, 109, 115; in-patient 8, 10, 17, 43, 52, 90, 189, 191, 194, 195, 198, 86, 87, 88, 89, 90, 91, 93, 94, 95, 96, 97, 99, 102, 104, 106, 107, 108, 109, 111, 112, 114, 115; out-patient 90, 93, 94, 95, 96, 97, 99, 100, 102, 103, 104, 105, 107, 108, 109, 111, 112, 189; physicians 93, 95, 97, 98, 104, 111; subsidy 96, 99–100, 102, 103; utilization 107–112

Health-care policy: adequacy 107, 108, 109, 111; efficiency 108, 109–110, 111; equity 107–108, 109, 110, 111; rationale 84; role of state and market 84–86

Health for All The Way Forward, Hong Kong 88

Health Insurance *see* Health Care Financing arrangements

Health Insurance Review Agency, Korea 92

Health Protection Account (HSP), Hong Kong 89, 104, 108

Health Review Committee, Singapore 90

Health Status 107, 112–113

Heavy and Chemical Industrialization Plan, Korea 125

Holliday, Ian 5, 6

Home Ownership Scheme (HOS), Hong Kong 119, 121, 122, 129, 137, 145

Home Ownership Scheme, Singapore 122

Home Starter Loan Scheme (HSLS), Hong Kong 121, 129

Hong Kong Housing Society 118

Hong Kong Settler's Housing Corporation 118

Hospital Authority (HA), Hong Kong 88, 94, 99, 107

Hospital Security Plan (HSP), Hong Kong 89

Household size 33–34

Housing Authority, Hong Kong 119, 129, 137, 143, 145

Housing Bond, Korea 124, 125, 126, 132, 139, 148

Housing Construction Ten-Year Plan (1972–1981), Korea 124

Housing Development Board (HDB), Singapore 122, 123, 130, 131, 137, 138, 141, 145, 146

Housing policy: adequacy 143, 145, 147, 148–149, 150; efficiency, 148, 149; equity 145, 149; programmes 118–121, 122–123, 124–126, 127–128, 129–131, 132–133, 134; rationale 116–117; role of state and market 117

INDEX

Housing: affordability 7, 116–117, 119, 127, 128, 130, 144–145, 146–148, 150–151, 152, 190, 193; conditions 143, 146, 147, 149; expenditure 136–138, 139, 140–141, 142–143; finance 43, 117, 119, 120, 121, 122, 124, 125, 127, 128, 131, 134, 135, 136, 137, 138, 139, 140, 141, 142, 144, 152, 190; financing arrangement 119–121, 122, 125–126, 127, 136–138, 139–142; investment 136, 137, 139, 140, 141; land 22, 24, 117, 118, 119, 121, 123, 125, 126, 129, 130, 132, 136, 137, 138, 141, 142, 144, 151, 190, 195; ownership 12, 117, 119, 120, 121, 122, 123, 124, 125, 127, 128, 129, 130, 131, 133, 136, 138, 143, 145, 146, 147, 148, 149, 150, 151, 152, 166, 190, 194, 198; price 73, 119, 120, 121, 123, 130, 139, 143–144, 147, 149, 150, 151, 152, 195; public 7, 9, 10, 11, 15, 70, 119, 120, 121, 122, 123, 124, 127, 128, 129, 130, 131, 133, 134, 135, 136, 138, 140, 141, 142, 143, 144, 145, 146, 147, 151, 152, 180, 190, 194; rent 118, 122, 126, 129, 131, 133, 138, 143, 144, 147, 148, 149, 150, 151; rental 117, 119, 120, 121, 125, 126, 128, 129, 130, 131, 132, 133, 136, 137, 138, 141, 143, 144, 145, 147, 148, 149, 152, 190, 198; stock 130, 131, 133, 134, 135–136; tax benefits 127, 128
Housing Subscription Savings, Korea 133
Hsiao, William 88
Human Development Index (HDI) 2, 3, 20

Improving Hong Kong's Health Care System: Why and For Whom? 88
Income distribution *see* Economy, income distribution
Income maintenance: benefits, replacement rate 12, 32, 72, 73, 74, 75, 76, 77, 79, 193; Defined Benefits (DB) 20, 36–37, 42, 44–45, 46–47, 48, 50, 51–52, 53, 54–55, 62, 63, 64–65; Defined Contribution (DC) 36–38, 40–41, 42–43, 46, 48–49, 50, 51, 52–53, 57–58, 59, 62, 63–64, 83, 90, 105, 108, 198; definition 36; Employer-Liability 47–48, 49, 54, 55, 56, 57, 65, 66, 67, 68, 71, 77; informal 73, 74–75, 76–77, 78–79, 80–82; pension 4, 10, 12, 13, 14, 15, 37, 42, 44, 45, 46, 48, 49, 51, 53, 54, 56, 57, 58, 59, 62, 63, 64, 65, 66, 69, 71, 75, 78, 80, 81, 83, 188, 194, 195, 196, 197, 198; provident fund 36, 40, 41, 42, 43, 58, 59, 71, 79, 82, 83, 122, 188, 189, 190, 191; *see also* Income Maintenance, Defined Contribution; public assistance 8, 14, 36, 37, 38, 39, 41, 43, 45, 47, 49, 50, 52, 53, 54, 56, 58, 60, 61, 63, 66, 68, 69, 71, 72, 74, 76, 78, 80, 82, 83, 91, 92, 95, 99, 103, 188, 191, 194, 195, 196; social insurance 12, 36, 37, 39, 40, 43, 45, 46, 48, 54, 55, 56, 58, 59, 60, 61, 65, 66, 67, 69, 70, 78, 79, 82, 83, 90, 93, 94, 101, 102, 103, 104, 106, 112, 114, 115, 188, 189, 191, 193, 195, 196; *see also* Income Maintenance, Defined Benefits; unemployment benefits 15, 43, 45, 47, 54, 55, 56, 57, 64, 65, 66, 69, 76, 77, 82, 188
Income maintenance policy: adequacy 72, 73, 74, 75–76, 77, 78, 79; coverage 71–72, 73, 75–76, 77, 78, 79; equity 72, 74, 75–76, 77, 78, 80; rationale 38
Income tax rates 24
Independent schools, Singapore 160, 167, 172
Individual Retirement Account (IRA) *see* Income maintenance, Defined Contribution (DC)
Industrial Policy 169
Industrialization 6, 7, 10, 38, 84, 170, 187, 197
Inequality 3, 21, 22, 61, 72, 74, 78, 80, 85, 107, 110, 111, 117, 145, 149, 179, 180, 181, 186, 187, 191; *see also* equity
Infant Mortality Rate 112–113
Informal employment *see* Employees, informal
Insurance for Teachers and Staff of Private Schools (ITASPS), Taiwan 57, 67
International Labour Organization (ILO) 43, 55, 60
International Monetary Fund (IMF) 44, 70, 126, 142, 176
Internationalization and Social Policy 13–14, 15, 28–31

227

INDEX

Japan 3, 6, 7, 22, 31, 33, 42, 59, 81, 91, 92, 93, 115, 139, 162, 164, 181, 189, 194
Jessop, Bob 7
Jones, Catherine 4, 5, 33

Kemeny, J. 152
Korea Housing Administration (KHA) 124
Korea Housing Bank (KHB) 124, 125, 126, 132, 133, 139, 140, 148
Korea Land Corporation (KOLAND) 125
Korea Land Development Corporation (KLDC) 125
Korea National Housing Corporation (KNHC) 14, 15, 20, 46, 47, 124, 132, 133, 164, 197

Labour Insurance (LI), Taiwan 47, 49, 56, 57, 61, 67, 69, 77, 80, 93
Labour Retirement Fund (LRF), Taiwan 47, 49, 57, 68, 69, 77
Labour force *see* Employees
Labour unrest *see* Trade unions
Land Acquisition Act, Singapore 130
Legislative Council (Legco), Hong Kong 9, 40, 41, 42
Liberalism 3, 17, 192, 193, 194, 195, 196, 199
Life Expectancy 112–113
Lifelong Investment in Health, Hong Kong 89
Livelihood Protection scheme, Korea 45, 56, 76
Long Service Payment, Hong Kong 51
Long term Housing Strategy 1987, Hong Kong 119, 144
Long Term Housing Strategy 1998, Hong Kong 121, 144

Malaysia 38, 40, 43
Mandatory Provident Fund (MPF) 40, 41, 42, 49, 50, 51, 59, 62, 69, 72, 83, 188
Manpower Development Plans (MDP), Taiwan 164
Manufacturing 20, 30, 34
Martial Law 14, 15, 164, 197
McFadzean Commission, Singapore 42
Medicaid, Korea 92, 109, 110
Medical *see* Health care

Medical Development Advisory Committee, Hong Kong 87
Medifund, Singapore 91, 100, 109
Medisage, Hong Kong 89
Medisave, Singapore 52, 53, 89, 90, 100, 101, 104, 105, 109, 114, 115
Medishield, Singapore 89, 90, 100, 101, 104, 105, 108, 109, 114
Mediterranean welfare states 194
Medium Term Plan for Developing and Improving Infant Education, 1993 (Taiwan) 165
Middle class 120, 122, 123, 145, 148, 152
Military 12, 44, 47, 53, 54, 57, 59, 63, 64, 65, 66, 67, 69, 75, 76, 78, 80, 83, 128, 134, 162, 188, 193, 197
Military Servicemen's Insurance (MI), Taiwan 47, 57, 61, 67
Multinational Corporations (MNCs) 7, 72

National Development Plan, Taiwan 127
National Health Insurance (NHI) 47, 57, 66, 68, 91, 92, 93, 96, 97, 103, 104, 106, 111, 115
National Health Insurance Corporation (NHIC), Korea 92
National Health Plan, Singapore 90
National Health Service (NHS), UK 88
National Housing Fund (NHF), Korea 125, 126, 132, 139, 140
National Pension Plan (NPP), Taiwan 48, 80
National Pension Savings Insurance, Taiwan 48
National Pension Scheme (NPS), Korea 44, 45, 54, 55, 61, 64, 65, 69, 75, 76, 80
Newly Industrializing Economies (NIEs): historical context 8–16; political conditions, NIEs 10–15; similarities and differences 2–3
Northeast Asia 3, 4, 11, 21, 31, 35, 98, 115, 187, 189, 191

Occupational Retirement Schemes Ordinance (ORSO), Hong Kong 40, 49, 50, 51, 59, 62, 69, 72, 79
Old Age Pension Scheme (OPS), Hong Kong 41

INDEX

Organization for Economic Cooperation and Development (OECD) 4, 5, 6, 9, 12, 13, 18, 19, 20, 21, 23, 24, 25, 30, 31, 32, 33, 34, 36, 37, 44, 64, 70, 75, 76, 79, 82, 93, 96, 98, 101, 105, 106, 112, 113, 147, 148, 153, 154, 155, 163, 168, 171, 175, 176, 177, 178, 181, 183, 184, 186, 187, 188, 193, 194, 199

Park Chung Hee 12, 162
Patten, Chris 40
Paul Wilding 5
People's Action Party (PAP), Singapore 11, 43, 89, 122, 196
Perspective on Education in Hong Kong, 1992 (Llewellyn Report) 156
Policy regime 191, 194–197
Population 22, 31, 32, 33, 34, 75, 81, 82, 150, 153, 184
Poverty 2, 6, 8, 10, 21, 22–23, 35, 36, 39, 42, 45, 46, 47, 53, 56, 58, 59, 60, 61, 62, 64, 71, 72, 73, 75, 76, 78, 80, 81, 82, 83, 84, 85, 92, 93, 104, 110, 111, 116, 117, 118, 143, 152, 154, 161, 163, 189, 195
Presidential Commission for Education Reform, Korea 163
Primary Education and Pre-Primary Services, 1981, Hong Kong 156
Private Sector Participation Scheme (PSPS), Hong Kong 119, 121, 129, 137
Privatization 11, 45, 85, 90, 163
Productive Welfare, Korea 46
Productivist welfare capitalism 6
Provident fund *see* Income maintenance, Defined Contribution.
Public Assistance Scheme (PAS), Hong Kong 39
Public Housing Committee of the Executive Yuan, Taiwan 127
Public Housing Construction and Planning Committee, Taiwan 127
Public opinion 5, 9, 11, 41, 110

Research Group for Education Reform, Taiwan 164
Resettlement Department, Hong Kong 118
Rieger, Elmar and Stephan Leibfried 5
Rudimentary Conservative welfare states 194

Sale of Apartments to Sitting Tenants, Hong Kong 120
Sandwich Class Housing Scheme, Hong Kong 120
Savings and Employee Retirement Plan Scheme (SAVER), Singapore 53
Scott, W. D. 88
Secondary Education in Hong Kong Over the Next Decade, 1974, Hong Kong 156
Shek Kip Mei, Hong Kong 39, 118
Social democratic 192
Social development 1, 2, 3, 6, 15
Social insurance *see* Income Maintenance, Defined Benefits
Social policy 1, 3, 4, 5, 6, 7, 8, 9, 10, 11, 12, 13, 14, 15, 16, 17, 18, 21, 25, 27, 28, 31, 32, 35, 153, 39, 47, 188, 190, 191, 192, 193, 194, 195, 196, 197, 198, 199; and families, NIEs 5–6; in the NIEs, existing studies 4–7; in the NIEs, significance 1–2; explanations 3–8
Social protection 1, 36, 45, 46, 73, 82, 193; *see also* Income Maintenance
Social security 1, 4, 5, 8, 10, 11, 13, 15, 17, 29, 32, 33, 34, 35, 36, 37, 39, 41, 42, 43, 44, 46, 63, 66, 70, 71, 79, 80, 81, 116, 190, 194; *see also* Income Maintenance
Social Security Allowance Scheme (SSAS), Hong Kong 39, 42, 49
Social services 11, 39, 46, 63, 66, 68, 78, 194
Social welfare 1, 4, 5, 6, 11, 13, 39, 46, 63, 66, 93, 133, 190, 194
Social Welfare into the 1990s and Beyond Hong Kong 40
Social Welfare Office (SWO), Hong Kong 39
Southern Europe 17, 192, 194
Southern European "family of nations" 194
Stewart, F. 155
Supplementary Retirement Scheme (SRS), Singapore 44, 59
Surviving Spouse and Children's Pensions Scheme, Hong Kong 62

Tang Kwong-Leung 5
Task Force on Land Supply and Property Prices, Hong Kong 121
Ten Year Housing Plan (1973–§983), Hong Kong 119

229

INDEX

Tenant Purchase Scheme (TPS), Hong Kong 120, 129, 137
Tiananmen Square incident 10
Towards Better Health, Hong Kong 88
Trade unions 11, 13, 15, 45, 193
Trade, international 30–31
Tung Chee Hwa 10, 41, 157
Two Million Housing Construction Plan, Korea 126

United Nations Development Programme (UNDP) 20, 21
United Nations Educational, Scientific and Cultural Organization (UNESCO) 153, 170, 176, 183, 185
United States of America (USA) 22, 23, 24, 33, 41, 42, 43, 44, 46, 48, 49, 50, 51, 52, 53, 54, 56, 57, 58, 60, 62, 63, 64, 65, 66, 67, 68, 71, 73, 75, 76, 80, 81, 91, 92, 94, 95, 96, 97, 99, 100, 101, 102, 103, 105, 107, 109, 110, 119, 120, 121, 122, 123, 126, 127, 128, 129, 130, 131, 132, 133, 136, 137, 139, 143, 145, 160, 162, 164, 165, 171, 172, 173, 190, 195, 198, 199

Urbanization 6, 34, 38, 116, 117
User charges 10, 24, 85, 99, 104, 114, 115, 189, 198

Welfare societies 5
Welfare society, Korea 46
Welfare state 5, 6, 7, 9, 11, 12, 13, 16, 17, 40, 41, 44, 75, 82, 188, 190, 194, 196, 197, 198, 199
Welfare Vision 2010, Korea 46
Wilensky, Harold 6, 192
Women 22, 33, 38, 72, 73, 77, 78, 113, 153, 181, 182, 183, 184
Working Group on Retirement Protection, Hong Kong 40
Working Party on the Future of the Elderly, Hong Kong 40
World Bank 3, 21, 36, 44, 48, 55, 56, 65, 76, 85, 98, 105, 106, 112, 116, 117, 150, 153, 154, 176
World Health Organization (WHO) 106